Transformative Relationships

Transformative Relationships

The Control–Mastery Theory of Psychotherapy

GEORGE SILBERSCHATZ
EDITOR

Routledge
Taylor & Francis Group
NEW YORK AND HOVE

Cover design: Sarah Figueroa

Published in 2005 by
Routledge
Taylor & Francis Group
270 Madison Avenue
New York, New York 10016
www.routledgementalhealth.com

Published in Great Britain by
Routledge
Taylor & Francis Group
27 Church Road
Hove, East Sussex
BN3 2FA U.K.
www.routledgementalhealth.co.uk

Copyright © 2005 by Taylor & Francis Books, Inc.

Routledge is an imprint of the Taylor & Francis Group.

Printed in the United States of America on acid-free paper.

All rights reserved. No part of this book may be reprinted or reproduced or utilized in any form or by any electronic, mechanical, or other means, now known or hereafter invented, including photocopying and recording, or in any information storage or retrieval system, without permission in writing from the publishers.

10 9 8 7 6 5 4 3 2 1

Library of Congress Cataloging-in-Publication Data

Transformative relationships : the control-mastery theory of psychotherapy / edited by George Silberschatz.—1st ed.
      p. cm.
  Includes bibliographical references and index.
  ISBN 0-415-95027-9 (hb : alk. paper)
 1. Psychoanalysis. 2. Psychotherapy. I. Silberschatz, George, 1950–
II. Title.
  RC506.T724 2005
  616.89'14—dc22

2004017071

To my teachers,
students, and patients
with gratitude for all
that you have taught me.

TABLE OF CONTENTS

Contributors	ix
Acknowledgments	xi
Introduction	xiii

Part I Theory		1
Chapter 1.	The Control-Mastery Theory GEORGE SILBERSCHATZ	3
Chapter 2.	How Previously Inaccessible Experiences Become Conscious GEORGE SILBERSCHATZ	25
Chapter 3.	Safety JOSEPH WEISS	31
Chapter 4.	The Role of Unconscious Guilt in Psychopathology and in Psychotherapy MARSHALL BUSH	43
Part II Therapy		67
Chapter 5.	The Assessment of Pathogenic Beliefs JOHN T. CURTIS AND GEORGE SILBERSCHATZ	69
Chapter 6.	Clinical Use of the Plan Formulation in Long-Term Psychotherapy POLLY BLOOMBERG-FRETTER	93

Chapter 7.	Treatment by Attitudes HAROLD SAMPSON	111
Chapter 8.	A Long-Term Therapy Case Illustrating Treatment by Attitude KATHRYN PRYOR	121
Chapter 9.	How Patients Coach Their Therapists in Psychotherapy JOHN BUGAS AND GEORGE SILBERSCHATZ	153

Part III Research and Integration — 169

Chapter 10.	A Developmental Basis for Control-Mastery Theory ROBERT SHILKRET AND SARA A. SILBERSCHATZ	171
Chapter 11.	An Overview of Research on Control-Mastery Theory GEORGE SILBERSCHATZ	189
Chapter 12.	The Control-Mastery Theory: An Integrated Cognitive–Psychodynamic–Relational Theory GEORGE SILBERSCHATZ	219
Index		237

CONTRIBUTORS

Polly Bloomberg-Fretter, Ed.D., is a clinical psychologist in private practice in Berkeley, California. As a 25-year veteran of the San Francisco Psychotherapy Research Group, she is a psychotherapy researcher as well as a clinician and participates in a variety of clinical and research studies of psychotherapy.

John Bugas, Ph.D., has been a member of the San Francisco Psychotherapy Research Group for over 18 years. He currently has a private practice in Sacramento, California.

Marshall Bush, Ph.D., is Clinical Director of the San Francisco Psychotherapy Research Group and a teaching and training analyst at the San Francisco Psychoanalytic Institute. He has a private practice in San Francisco.

John T. Curtis, Ph.D., is a clinical professor in psychiatry at the University of California, San Francisco, School of Medicine; a member of the San Francisco Psychotherapy Research Group; and has a private practice in San Francisco.

Kathryn Pryor, Ph.D., is a psychotherapist in private practice in Menlo Park, California. She has been an active member of the San Francisco Psychotherapy Research Group for over 10 years.

Harold Sampson, Ph.D., is a member of the San Francisco Psychoanalytic Institute; president of the San Francisco Psychotherapy Research Group; Emeritus Clinical Professor in Psychiatry at the University of California, San Francisco, School of Medicine; and has a private practice in San Francisco. He is coauthor of *The Psychoanalytic*

Process and has published numerous articles on psychopathology and psychotherapy.

Robert Shilkret, Ph.D., is the Norma Cutts Dafoe Professor of Psychology at Mount Holyoke College and visiting professor at the Smith College School for Social Work. His research includes the influence of family history variables on college adjustment and many of his studies examine the role of guilt, considered from a control-mastery perspective.

George Silberschatz, Ph.D., is a clinical professor in psychiatry at the University of California, San Francisco, School of Medicine and a member of the San Francisco Psychotherapy Research Group. He was codirector of the National Institute of Mental Health-funded psychotherapy research project at Mount Zion Hospital and has published extensively in the areas of psychotherapy and psychotherapy research. He maintains a private practice in San Francisco.

Sara A. Silberschatz, B.A., recently graduated from New York University with a degree in psychology.

Joseph Weiss, M.D., was chairman of the San Francisco Psychotherapy Research Group and training and supervising analyst at the San Francisco Psychoanalytic Institute. He published two books and numerous articles on his theory of how psychopathology develops and how psychotherapy works. He died in November 2004, just prior to the publication of this book.

ACKNOWLEDGMENTS

My 30-year professional relationship with Harold Sampson, Joseph Weiss, and the San Francisco Psychotherapy Research Group (formerly known as the Mount Zion Psychotherapy Research Group) was the impetus for the publication of this book. It has been a privilege to be part of such a lively, stimulating, and intellectually exciting group of clinicians and researchers. So much of my clinical, theoretical, and research thinking has been influenced by this long, productive collaboration that it is practically impossible to separate out my original or distinctive contributions. In presenting and teaching these theoretical and clinical concepts, I have often been told, "this is such an innovative, powerful theory of therapy, it should be more accessible." This book is part of my effort to make the work available to a wider audience.

    A number of people read and critiqued various chapters. Their thoughtful comments and suggestions improved both the substance and clarity of the book. With appreciation and gratitude, it is a pleasure to acknowledge the contributions of Polly Bloomberg-Fretter, Suzaane Brumer, Marshall Bush, Marcia Caval, Melanie Clark, Sandra Cohen, Alan Dreyfus, Lewis Engel, Ken Frankel, Heather Folsom, Steve Foreman, John Gibbins, Helene Goldberg, Susan Packer, Arlene Rothschild, Cynthia Shilkret, Robert Shilkret, Sara A. Silberschatz, Molly Sullivan, Linda Tetzlaff, Richard Tuite, and Steve Weintraub. I am especially grateful to my daughter, Sara A. Silberschatz, who read and edited every chapter, spent many hours discussing my ideas and how to present them more clearly, and who took primary responsibility for bringing it all together in the end. My wife, Diana Owyang, lent loving support, encouragement, and her eagle eye throughout the process. Finally, I wish to thank the editorial and production staff at Brunner-Routledge for their hard work, diligence, and professionalism.

I also wish to acknowledge various copyright holders who allowed copyrighted material to be published in this volume. Portions of chapter 2 are adapted from Silberschatz and Sampson (1991) and are reprinted with the permission of the Guilford Press. Sections of chapter 4 are taken from Bush (1989) and are used with the permission of the Guilford Press. The case presented in chapter 6 was published by Fretter (1995); the material is used by permission of John Wiley & Sons. The case of Mrs. W in chapter 7 was originally published by Sampson (1990) and is used by permission of the William A. White Institute. Chapter 9 was originally published by Bugas and Silberschatz (2000) and is reprinted by permission of the Division of Psychotherapy, American Psychological Association. The test sequence from the case of Diane along with Figures 2 and 3 in chapter 11 were originally published by Silberschatz and Curtis (1993) and are used by permission of the American Psychological Association. Figure 5 in chapter 11 was originally published by Jones et al. (1993) and is reproduced by permission of the American Psychological Association. Figure 6 in chapter 11 was originally published by Horowitz et al. (1978) and is reproduced by permission of the American Psychological Association.

INTRODUCTION

George Silberschatz

In 1952, Joseph Weiss published a short, one-page paper called "Crying at the Happy Ending" (Weiss, 1952) in which he sought to explain why a person often cries at the happy ending of a sad movie rather than at the saddest point of the film. Weiss proposed that during the saddest parts of the film the moviegoer is in danger of feeling overwhelmed by sadness and consequently suppresses it. At the happy ending, when the viewer no longer has reason to feel sad, she unconsciously decides that it is safe to experience her emotions and lifts her defenses against the warded-off sad feelings.

Subsequently, Weiss turned his attention to the question of how patients in psychotherapy make progress. He systematically studied detailed process notes of psychotherapy sessions and identified clearly discernable instances of therapeutic progress, such as the emergence of new affects, memories, or behaviors. He then studied the clinical material to determine what immediately preceded these progressive instances (Weiss, 1967, 1971; Sampson, Weiss, Mlodnosky, & Hause, 1972). Similar to his explanation of "crying at the happy ending," Weiss found that patients make progress when they feel they can do so safely; that is, the patient makes an unconscious decision to experience previously warded-off emotions or thoughts when he or she feels it is safe to do so. Moreover, he found that patients make frequent appraisals of their interpersonal world—including relationships with their therapists—to assess conditions of danger versus safety.

The "Crying at the Happy Ending" paper marked the beginning of a powerful new theory that Weiss, in collaboration with Harold Sampson and the Mount Zion Psychotherapy Research Group (now called the San Francisco Psychotherapy Research Group), would continue developing over the next 50 years and that came to be known as the control-mastery theory (Sampson, 1976). The name of the theory stems from two of its basic premises: (1) people exercise considerable *control* over their conscious and unconscious mental life (thoughts, feelings, defenses, wishes) and their control is regulated by unconscious appraisals of safety and danger, and (2) people are highly motivated to *master* psychological conflicts and psychic trauma.

The control-mastery theory is not a school of therapy or new set of techniques. It is a theory of how the mind works, how psychopathology develops, and how psychotherapy works. It provides a powerful set of concepts that can help a clinician understand a particular patient's problems and goals for therapy. It also provides a broad sense of how the therapist can help a particular patient achieve his or her goals. Moreover, the main concepts of the control-mastery theory have been subjected to rigorous scientific research and have been empirically supported (Silberschatz, Curtis, Sampson, & Weiss, 1991; Silberschatz & Curtis, 1993; Silberschatz, Fretter, & Curtis, 1986; Weiss, Sampson, & The Mount Zion Psychotherapy Research Group, 1986; for an overview of this research, see chapter 11).

From its inception, the control-mastery theory has been anchored in a commitment to empiricism. When Weiss began to study process notes of therapy sessions, he relied on an empirical approach as his primary investigative tool. He investigated how patients change in psychotherapy by identifying instances of significant therapeutic progress, and then he systematically examined what the therapist had done immediately preceding such instances. Similarly, when Weiss and Sampson began their collaboration in 1967 they did so with "the crucial conviction that therapeutic processes—although case-specific, subtle, and always dependent on subjective experiences within and between the participants—are ordinarily understandable and lawful" (Sampson, 1995, p. 4). This conviction about the inherent lawfulness of therapeutic processes stimulated an extensive body of research on control-mastery theory (see chapter 11).

One distinctive aspect of the control-mastery theory's development is that the clinical thinking strongly influenced the research, and the scientific or empirical attitude underlying the research has shaped the theory and approach to clinical work. My 25-year involvement in control-mastery theory as a researcher, psychotherapist, teacher, and clinical supervisor has taught me that a considerable overlap exists between good research and clinical thinking. Both require (1) that ideas or hypotheses be stated clearly and logically, (2) a method of evaluating hypotheses and critically assessing evidence, and (3) a receptivity to new ideas or new findings.

The aim of this book is to present the control-mastery theory as concisely and as clearly as possible and to illustrate its clinical applications. None of the chapters aim to be comprehensive in their literature reviews or in placing control-mastery ideas in the context of other work (the interested reader is referred to www.transformativerelationships.com, which provides a comprehensive bibliography of the publications pertaining to the theory). The book's title reflects my belief that relationships are inherently transformative and that the psychotherapeutic relationship is one particular type of interpersonal relationship in which transformation is a primary goal. The control-mastery theory provides a lucid, coherent, and powerful theory of the transformative process. This book is intended for a professional audience of practicing therapists as well as therapists in training. Members of all mental health disciplines—psychology, psychiatry, social work, and counseling, as well as graduate students at various levels of training—are likely to find this book useful in their work.

Part I of *Transformative Relationships* is devoted to theory. Chapter 1 describes the control-mastery theory of psychopathology and the theory of therapy, chapter 2 focuses on how previously inaccessible experiences become conscious, chapter 3 discusses the role of safety in emotional regulation, and chapter 4 addresses the role of unconscious guilt in psychopathology and in psychotherapy.

Clinical applications of the theory are covered in Part II. Chapter 5 discusses an empirically supported clinical method for assessing a patient's pathogenic beliefs. Chapter 6 describes an intensive psychotherapy of a depressed patient treated by a control-mastery therapist. Chapter 7 presents "treatment by attitude," how the therapist's attitudes toward the patient may help the patient disconfirm pathogenic beliefs, and chapter 8 presents a long-term therapy case illustrating treatment by attitude. Chapter 9 describes the concept of patients coaching their therapists and shows the various ways that patients may coach their therapists in order to achieve their therapeutic goals.

Part III covers research and integration. Chapter 10 discusses some of the developmental assumptions of control-mastery theory and provides an overview of relevant research from developmental psychology that supports them. Chapter 11 provides an overview of research on the theory and chapter 12 presents the control-mastery theory as an integrative, cognitive–psychodynamic–relational theory.

Throughout the book, the word "patient" is routinely used and I would like to comment briefly on its usage. None of the contributors to this book nor I adhere to a medical model of psychotherapy in which "the doctor treats the patient." All of us view psychotherapy as a collaborative relationship requiring active involvement, participation, and emotional investment by both participants. We use "patient" in the original sense of the word—a sufferer, one who endures suffering (from the Latin, *pati*, to endure, *Oxford English Dictionary*). In order to avoid the narrow medical connotation of "patient," I had considered simply substituting "client" for "patient" throughout the book, but that term does not quite capture our understanding of therapy either. When I think about the people I work with in therapy, I do not think of them as patients or clients. A more accurate description would be "a person I'm working with in therapy" or "a person who is working with me in therapy." I could not come up with a term that captures such a description, but this is what we intend when we use the term "patient."

REFERENCES

Sampson, H. (1976). A critique of certain traditional concepts in the psychoanalytic theory of therapy. *Bulletin of the Menninger Clinic, 40,* 255–262.

Sampson, H. (1995, April 26). Psychoanalysis: The second century. Invited address, American Psychological Association, Division 39, Los Angeles, California.

Sampson, H., Weiss, J., Mlodnosky, L., & Hause, E. (1972). Defense analysis and the emergence of warded-off mental contents: An empirical study. *Archives of General Psychiatry, 26,* 524–532.

Silberschatz, G., & Curtis, J. T. (1993). Measuring the therapist's impact on the patient's therapeutic progress. *Journal of Consulting and Clinical Psychology, 61,* 403–411.

Silberschatz, G., Curtis, J. T., Sampson, H., & Weiss, J. (1991). Mount Zion Hospital and Medical Center: Research on the process of change in psychotherapy. In L. E. Beutler & M. Crago (Eds.), *Psychotherapy research: An international review of programmatic studies* (pp. 56–64). Washington, DC: American Psychological Association.

Silberschatz, G., Fretter, P. B., & Curtis, J. T. (1986). How do interpretations influence the process of psychotherapy? *Journal of Consulting and Clinical Psychology, 54,* 646–652.

Weiss, J. (1952). Crying at the happy ending. *Psychoanalytic Review, 39,* 338.

Weiss, J. (1967). The integration of defenses. *International Journal of Psychoanalysis, 48,* 520–524.

Weiss, J. (1971). The emergence of new themes: A contribution to the psychoanalytic theory of therapy. *International Journal of Psychoanalysis, 52,* 459–467.

Weiss, J, Sampson, H., and the Mount Zion Psychotherapy Research Group. (Eds.). (1986). *The psychoanalytic process: Theory, clinical observation, and empirical research.* New York: Guilford.

Part I
Theory

1
THE CONTROL-MASTERY THEORY

George Silberschatz

My purpose in this chapter is to provide an overview of the control-mastery theory. All of the theory's concepts will be described and illustrated with brief examples so that a reader who is new to this approach can develop a sufficient familiarity with it to follow its application and understand its clinical implications, which are described in the subsequent chapters of this volume. In the interest of conciseness and clarity, I will not focus on the evolution of the control-mastery theory or how it relates to other theories. The interested reader is referred to Silberschatz, Curtis, Sampson, & Weiss (1991), Weiss, Sampson, and the Mount Zion Psychotherapy Research Group (1986), Weiss (1993), and to chapters 10 and 12 of this volume.

I will first describe how control-mastery theory explains the development of psychopathology, i.e., the concept of pathogenic beliefs. Then I will discuss the patient's "plan" for therapy, which is based on the idea that patients are motivated in an organized way to master their conflicts and solve their problems. A discussion of how patients and therapists work together to disconfirm pathogenic beliefs then follows. The last section is a brief discussion of how the control-mastery theory relates to several prominent clinical concepts such as the therapeutic alliance, transference, resistance, psychotherapeutic technique, and the corrective emotional experience.

HOW PSYCHOPATHOLOGY DEVELOPS

Control-mastery theory begins with an assumption that is prevalent in modern biology, ethology, and the behavioral sciences: the adaptive imperative. All animals, according to this imperative, are motivated—indeed, they are predisposed ("hardwired") by evolution—to adapt to their environment. For humans (and most mammals), survival and adaptation require maintaining a stable connection or attachment to parents, family members, or other caregivers (Bowlby, 1969, 1973, 1980, 1988, 1989). A key to adaptation in humans is the formation of a reliable conception of reality, an internal map of the physical and interpersonal world. This map-making process begins early in infancy (for further discussion, see chapter 10), and one of the primary ways we develop our map of reality is by forming and testing hypotheses about how the world works (Gopnik, Meltzoff, & Kuhl, 1999; Stern, 1985, 2002; Weiss, 1993). In other words, in order to adapt to our environment we develop *beliefs* about our family, our relationships, our world, and ourselves. This process of developing and testing beliefs begins shortly after birth and continues throughout life.

Another fundamental assumption of control-mastery theory is that human behavior is regulated by perceptions of safety and danger (see chapters 2 and 3). These perceptions are an integral part of the map-making process. In order to develop a reliable and useful conception of reality, the individual must frequently assess his internal and external world to determine which experiences are safe and which are dangerous. Traumatic emotional experiences are, for example, experiences of danger. Indeed, according to this model, trauma is defined as any situation that overwhelms a person with anxiety or fear, or that leads a person to believe an important goal must be renounced in order to avoid the danger of hurting loved ones or the danger of being hurt by them.

The control-mastery theory of psychopathology builds on these fundamental assumptions. Weiss (1986, 1993) posited that psychopathology stems from *pathogenic beliefs* (maps) that typically stem from traumatic childhood experiences. These beliefs, which are usually unconscious, are extremely frightening and constricting because they suggest that the pursuit of an important goal is fraught with danger. For example, a single, middle-aged man who lived with his elderly mother was traumatized early in life by his mother's chronic unhappiness and frequent bouts of severe depression. When he was a young boy, he noticed his mother became very sad when he left for school, and he concluded that his leaving caused her depression. He quickly developed a severe school phobia that consequently restricted him to staying at home with his mother. What initially appeared as a fear of school was in fact based on the pathogenic belief that if he separated from his mother (i.e., left her alone while he was in school) she would become sad or depressed. By the age of 10 or 11, the patient showed signs of depression that persisted into his adulthood and that ultimately led him to seek psychotherapy.

The brief example described here illustrates several important aspects of pathogenic beliefs. The patient formed his belief as part of an effort to adapt to his environment (growing up with a depressed mother) and in an effort to preserve a stable relationship with his mother. The belief was strongly influenced by his perception of danger. Leaving his mother to go to school or play with friends was dangerous because she would become depressed. He also developed a distorted view about his ability to affect his mother's emotional states. By staying at home with her, he felt he could cheer her up and prevent her depressive feelings. His occasional success at staving off mother's depression led him to feel excessively responsible for her moods. Thus, when she was sad or depressed (a very frequent occurrence), he came to believe that it was *his fault* and that he should have been able to do something to prevent her unhappiness. The patient's depression stemmed from self-punitive feelings (he punished himself because he was unable to "cure" his mother) and represented a powerful, unconscious identification with his depressed mother. By unconsciously identifying with her, he punished himself for failing to "cure" her. Thus, what began as an adaptive effort to form a map of reality soon became maladaptive—indeed, pathogenic—because it forced him to renounce crucial developmental goals (e.g., appropriate separation and individuation, attending school, developing friendships), led to exaggerated feelings of responsibility and self-blame, and ultimately resulted in severe psychopathology.

Clinicians from various theoretical perspectives frequently have an intuitive understanding of the pathogenic belief concept. A patient who has difficulty expressing anger, for instance, is frequently ruled by a pathogenic belief that angry feelings would wound or destroy a loved one. A person who suffers from work inhibitions and who sabotages his or her own success often has the unconscious pathogenic belief that success would be injurious to a loved one. Individuals who experience physical or emotional abuse in childhood often develop a pathogenic belief readily familiar to most therapists, regardless of their theoretical orientation. The abuse victim typically believes that he or she was "bad" and deserved the treatment he or she received at the hand of his or her abuser (Suffridge, 1991). Like all pathogenic beliefs, this belief begins as an effort at adaptation (Rappoport, 1996; Weiss, 1993). In order to survive, the abused child needs his parents, even if they are hurting him. Consequently, he would prefer to see himself as bad or flawed rather than see his parents as being flawed. Fairbairn (1943/1952) articulated this same idea far more poetically when he said that, for a child, it is safer to be a "sinner in a world ruled by God than to live in a world ruled by the Devil. A sinner in a world ruled by God may be bad; but there is always a certain sense of security to be derived from the fact that the world around is good ... " (pp. 66–67). However, this irrationally self-blaming belief ultimately leads to psychopathology because a person who believes (consciously or unconsciously) that he or she is flawed and deserves to be mistreated frequently becomes involved in abusive or destructive relationships and suffers from depression, severe anxiety, self-destructive behavior patterns, and/or personality disorders.

A person's response to trauma—and his or her propensity to develop pathogenic beliefs in response to it—is influenced by a variety of factors, such as personality and temperamental variables, the specific nature of the trauma, and the familial or social context in which the trauma occurs. Thus, siblings who grow up together with the same parents may respond quite differently to similar traumatic experiences. Pathogenic beliefs can develop as a result of *shock trauma*—discrete catastrophic events such as the severe illness or death of a parent, family member, or loved one—or *stress trauma*, recurrent and persistent traumatic experiences from which the child cannot escape and that force the child to renounce crucial developmental goals.

Let us look more closely at how pathogenic beliefs develop. The child experiences a traumatic event (shock trauma) and is overwhelmed by fear, anxiety, or other disruptive emotions. She is strongly motivated to prevent its recurrence. As part of this effort, she develops a theory to help her determine what she did to cause the event and what she could have done to prevent it. In this theorizing process, she is vulnerable to irrational self-blame and guilt (see chapter 4), because children lack the cognitive ability, experience, and knowledge to understand that their behavior, thoughts, or wishes are entirely unrelated to the traumatic event (see chapter 10).

Consider, for example, a 5-year-old boy whose parents had recently adopted a 2-year-old daughter. The boy bitterly resented the intrusion of a new sister and was particularly upset that his mother, with whom he had been very close, seemed to be spending an inordinate amount of time with the new intruder. The boy openly expressed his anger and displeasure, frequently yelling at his mother to "take her [sister] back where she came from." Several months after the adoption, the mother and adopted daughter were in a serious car accident, resulting in a 2-week hospital stay for the mother and a 6-week hospitalization for the little girl. The boy and his father had a very difficult time coping with this traumatic event. The boy became sullen, withdrawn, phobic, and depressed, while his father started drinking heavily, ultimately losing his job and eventually his marriage. This trauma was a catastrophic event in this young boy's life, and he developed the pathogenic belief that his anger and his wish to get rid of the new sibling caused the accident and the demise of his family. He simply lacked the knowledge and cognitive resources to understand he was not the cause of this family catastrophe. Like most traumatized children, he blamed himself for what occurred and punished himself by his withdrawal from life.

This example illustrates the formation of pathogenic beliefs that stem from false inferences or incorrect theories regarding cause and effect. Indeed, shock traumas typically lead to pathogenic beliefs because of such faulty reasoning. However, children also frequently develop unconscious pathogenic beliefs on the basis of *accurate* inferences about traumatic experiences. A child whose parents consistently neglected or mistreated him (stress trauma) develops pathogenic beliefs because of the way that he truly *was* mistreated. Sampson (1992) pointed out that in such instances the child's real experiences produce pathogenic beliefs about morality. Children assume that the ways they have been treated in the past (reality) are the ways they deserve to be treated (morality) now and in the future.

Sampson (1992) also described a study by Beres (1958) of young children who were placed in foster homes. These children inferred that their parents had rejected them and had done so because the child was bad; in other words, the child developed the pathogenic belief that he or she deserved to be rejected. Moreover, the belief that they deserved to be rejected (i.e., a pathogenic belief about morality) "regulated their subsequent relationships. They believed not only that they *would* be rejected, but that they *should* be rejected" (Sampson, 1992, p. 518).

Pathogenic beliefs are not dry, intellectualized, abstract thoughts; they are powerful, emotion-laden, painful belief structures that cause severe emotional distress. The child who was emotionally mistreated and subsequently developed the pathogenic belief that he deserved the mistreatment suffers from an emotionally crippling and destructive belief system that includes both an affective and cognitive component (Silberschatz & Sampson, 1991). Pathogenic beliefs are typically unconscious. Patients are frequently unaware of the cognitive aspects of the belief, but they experience the overwhelming anxiety, fear, depression, guilt, self-loathing, and self-destructive impulses, or various other disruptive, constricting emotions that stem from their pathogenic beliefs.

In view of how painful and destructive pathogenic beliefs are, why do they persist? Why would a person maintain beliefs about him- or herself that lead to intense suffering and dysfunction? According to the control-mastery theory, people are highly motivated to relinquish or disconfirm pathogenic beliefs, but they are impeded from doing so by their perceptions of danger. Pathogenic beliefs develop as part of an effort to cope with danger, and they are held in place by a person's ongoing perception of danger (for further discussion of this point, see chapters 2 and 3). Thus, the person holding pathogenic beliefs has a high degree of emotional conviction about them and believes them to be true. He is most likely afraid to test them. In addition, pathogenic beliefs are typically unconscious and therefore not under a person's conscious or volitional control. Finally, pathogenic beliefs are deeply entrenched and have a great deal of momentum or weight behind them. Consequently, considerable evidence and multiple disconfirmatory experiences are required to disconfirm them. In this respect, pathogenic beliefs are no different from other theories or attitudes that a person holds. We typically do not change our theories or fundamental attitudes with a single piece of new information or evidence, even when the evidence is compelling. Most people require repeated instances of new evidence before they can relinquish or alter a cherished theory or worldview.

THE PATIENT'S PLAN

Control-mastery theory assumes that people who seek psychotherapy are motivated to disconfirm or relinquish pathogenic beliefs in order to proceed with normal developmental goals. This primary motivation toward mastering conflict and solving problems is embedded in the concept of the *patient's plan*. Control-mastery theory posits that patients come to therapy in order to get better and that they have an unconscious plan or strategy for doing so; the plan is to disconfirm pathogenic beliefs. Just as pathogenic beliefs are uniquely formed in the patient's early relational history, the patient's plan for disconfirming these beliefs in the therapeutic relationship is highly individualized and case-specific. For instance, depressed patients suffer from a variety of pathogenic beliefs and consequently they will have varying plans for disconfirming them. What patients share in common, according to this model, is their motivation—their plan—to disconfirm pathogenic beliefs. Saying that a patient has a "plan" to disconfirm pathogenic beliefs is not to say that it is easy or straightforward to do so. As noted previously, altering any theory, belief, or attitude is difficult and requires considerable work; the plan concept simply states that the patient is powerfully motivated to do this work.

Before further discussing the clinical aspects of the patient's plan for therapy, I would like to discuss the concept of plans more broadly. Miller, Galanter, and Pribram (1960) defined a plan as an internal process that controls the order in which a sequence of operations should be performed. They drew an analogy between a plan and a computer program. The program dictates the order for executing certain instructions and specifies that certain instructions are to be implemented in the event of certain contingencies. Plans organize behavior and play an important role in evaluating and filtering information.

For instance, a college student who plans to apply to graduate school in physics will pay careful attention to the reactions of her science professors in order to assess which one she might approach for a letter of recommendation. The accolades and enthusiastic encouragement she receives from her music professor are less likely to carry the same weight or importance as the comments of her physics professor. Her plan organizes her behavior; it tells her what she must do, how to prioritize her activities, and how to evaluate information and reactions from people around her.

A person's plans may be conscious as well as unconscious (Weiss, 1993). Recent research in cognitive and experimental psychology provides strong support for the concept of unconscious cognition and planning (e.g., Bargh, Gollwitzer, Lee-Chia, Barndollar, & Troetschel, 2001; Fitzsimons & Bargh, 2003; Lewicki, Hill, & Czyzewska, 1992; Lewicki, Hill, & Czyzewska, 1994; Steele & Morawski, 2002; Westen, 1999; see also Caspar, 1995; Grawe, 2004). Just as a person's conscious plan organizes behavior, Weiss (1993) suggested that a patient's unconscious plan serves as an organizer of behavior in therapy (Curtis & Silberschatz, 1997; Silberschatz & Curtis, 1986; Silberschatz, Curtis, & Nathans, 1989). For example, Jill, a very compassionate, altruistic middle-aged woman, sought therapy because her elderly, demented mother overwhelmed her emotionally. Jill suffered from the pathogenic belief that taking care of herself and her needs meant that she was selfish, irresponsible, and cruel. Her unconscious plan for therapy was to overcome this pathogenic belief so she could find a suitable nursing home for her mother. Jill's plan shaped how she understood and assimilated the therapist's attitude, questions, or interpretations and her plan strongly influenced how she would proceed in therapy. For instance, could she criticize her mother without the therapist taking her mother's side? If she put her needs above others, would the therapist accuse her of being selfish?

Another patient, Myra, sought psychotherapy for anxiety, depression, difficulty concentrating, and insomnia. She was in a long-term relationship with an alcoholic, chronically unemployed, needy man. Myra's unconscious plan for therapy was to extricate herself from this unsatisfying, dysfunctional relationship. She was impeded from leaving him by a powerful pathogenic belief that leaving would devastate him and forever ruin his life. This pathogenic belief originated in Myra's childhood and her dysfunctional relationship with her needy, alcoholic mother.

To summarize, strong evidence supports the fact that people make and carry out plans unconsciously as well as consciously. In psychotherapy, as in everyday life, a person's plans organize behavior and influence how the person is likely to filter and process information.

HOW PSYCHOTHERAPY WORKS

Control-mastery theory integrates how psychopathology develops and how psychotherapy works. Psychopathology stems from pathogenic beliefs originating from traumatic experiences. In psychotherapy, patients and therapists work together to *disconfirm the patient's pathogenic beliefs* (Silberschatz, 1986; Silberschatz & Curtis, 1986; Weiss, 1986, 1993), and they can do so in three primary ways. Patients may (a) use the therapeutic relationship per se to disconfirm beliefs, (b) use the knowledge or insight conveyed by the therapist's interpretations to disconfirm beliefs, and (c) test the pathogenic belief directly with the therapist. These three ways of working are by no means mutually exclusive; indeed, in most psychotherapies patients rely on a combination of all three.

The therapeutic relationship, in and of itself, can be a powerful vehicle for disconfirming pathogenic beliefs (Sampson, 1991, 1992; Weiss, 1993; see also chapters 7 and 8). Consider, for example, a patient who had been severely mistreated by her aloof, distant father and by her rejecting, sadistic mother. Early in childhood, she developed the pathogenic belief that she deserved to be mistreated and emotionally neglected, and sadly most of her relationships were consistent with this pathogenic belief. The patient sought psychotherapy at a teaching clinic where she was randomly assigned to a therapist, who by nature happened to be warm, empathic, kind, respectful, and emotionally attentive. These personal qualities of the therapist and the relationship that resulted from them helped the patient disconfirm her pathogenic belief that she was unworthy of kindness and affection (for further discussion and illustration, see chapter 7).

A second way therapists can help patients in psychotherapy is by providing relevant knowledge or insights that will disconfirm pathogenic beliefs. According to the control-mastery theory, a therapist's interpretations are only useful to the extent that they disconfirm the patient's specific pathogenic beliefs (Bush & Gassner, 1986; Fretter, 1984; Silberschatz & Curtis, 1986; Silberschatz, Fretter, & Curtis, 1986; Silberschatz et al., 1989; Weiss, 1992, 1993). If a particular patient is working in therapy to become more comfortable expressing loving feelings, then only those interpretations that disconfirm pathogenic beliefs connected to that particular conflict will be helpful. Interpretations focusing on work inhibitions or career difficulties are unlikely to be effective at that point in the therapy, because they do not address the specific pathogenic belief(s) the patient would like to relinquish.

An excellent example of an interpretation that helped disconfirm a pathogenic belief can be found in the case of Myra (Silberschatz et al., 1989), a woman who wanted to end her dysfunctional relationship with an older, alcoholic man but was impeded from doing so because she believed she would devastate him if she left. During the course of the therapy, she did end the relationship; he acted devastated and made her feel guilty. In this particular session, Myra reported her former partner had recently told her he could not imagine spending his life with anyone but her, and she then went on to say she was not interested in dating either. The therapist then made the following interpretation: "It's hard to know how interested you are in other men until you've gotten away from him [the ex-partner], and that's been hard for you to carry through. There is a parallel between the emotional tie with [the ex-partner], who has difficulty establishing relationships, and the emotional tie your mother has to you. Your deep feelings of obligation and guilt toward them make it hard to find something more rewarding for yourself." This interpretation was very useful to Myra because it conveyed an insight that was helpful in disconfirming her pathogenic belief. It helped her understand the connection between her excessive feelings of responsibility toward her ex-partner and the feelings of responsibility she developed in childhood toward her mother. The interpretation also helped her recognize that her lack of interest in dating stemmed from irrational feelings of guilt.

Patients may also disconfirm pathogenic beliefs by *testing* them directly in the therapeutic relationship. A test is a trial action, initiated by the patient, that is intended to provide information about and assess the validity of a pathogenic belief (Silberschatz & Curtis, 1986, 1993; Weiss, 1986, 1993). Testing sequences vary considerably from case to case; in some instances, tests are discrete episodes and in others testing is a lengthy process that continues over many sessions. Patients initiate tests in order to disconfirm pathogenic beliefs and usually are not aware they are testing the therapist.

For example, a patient was traumatized during childhood by his domineering, rigid father who was unable to tolerate his son's independence, occasional willfulness, and his developmentally appropriate autonomous strivings. The patient developed the pathogenic belief that his being independent or strong would be hurtful to other men, and consequently he developed a self-demeaning, subservient attitude toward men, particularly toward male authority figures such as teachers, supervisors, and his male therapist. The patient tested this pathogenic belief in his relationship with the therapist by shifting from his typical subservient style to experimenting with more independent, willful behavior such as being a few minutes late to sessions, disagreeing with the therapist's comments, and developing his own insights. Although he was unconscious of the testing process, the patient was attempting to determine whether the therapist could comfortably tolerate these new behaviors in a way his father could not. When the therapist did not become defensive or act critically toward the patient, he *passed the test*; that is, the therapist disconfirmed the patient's pathogenic idea that his autonomy would be detrimental to or threaten the therapeutic relationship. The therapist *failed the test* when he responded in ways that the patient experienced as being bothered by or critical of his independent strivings.

Control-mastery theory delineates two distinct testing strategies: *transference tests* and *passive-into-active tests* (Silberschatz & Curtis, 1986, 1993; Weiss, 1986, 1993). In a transference test, the patient attempts to assess whether the therapist will traumatize her in the same ways as she was previously traumatized in her family of origin. The previous example of the subservient patient experimenting with acting willfully and independently clearly illustrates a transference test. The patient was testing to see if the therapist would be intolerant of autonomy in the same ways his father had been intolerant. Had the patient been traumatized by a father who was overly competitive and unable to acknowledge his son's achievement, the types of tests posed in therapy would be very different.

A talented artist came to therapy because he felt depressed, frustrated by his lack of success, and he suffered from low self-esteem. Both of his parents were extremely successful and preoccupied with their professional lives, and throughout his childhood and adolescence they had practically no time or energy for him. Although his teachers and his nanny were impressed by his artistic ability and strongly encouraged him to pursue art, his parents were "too busy" to notice and he rarely showed them his artwork. During his senior year of college, one of his paintings won a prestigious award, and he decided to give the painting to his parents as an anniversary gift. After several months, his parents finally hung the painting in a rarely used guest bedroom of their ski cabin.

Early in therapy, the therapist asked the patient about his art and expressed interest in seeing some of the work. The patient seemed pleased by the therapist's interest, but he consistently "forgot" to bring slides or samples of his work to the sessions. The therapist adamantly pursued this topic for several weeks and finally the patient came to a session carrying two large portfolios. The patient sheepishly and somewhat apologetically explained he had an appointment with an art dealer after the session and did not want to leave the portfolios in his car, but he showed no inclination to share it with the therapist. When the therapist again expressed his interest in seeing the artwork, the patient enthusiastically took out all the paintings and drawings, displaying them around the office. This case provides a dramatic example of a sequence of transference tests; the patient was repeatedly testing to see if the therapist would traumatize him by ignoring or disregarding his artistic talent in the way his parents had traumatized him.

Different types of transference tests require different types of responses. Although a warm, caring, respectful, unconditionally accepting therapeutic stance is likely to pass many tests, certain kinds of tests require a more challenging, confrontational approach. For example, a patient who came to therapy to address career and marital conflicts mentioned in passing that he had had problems with alcohol. The therapist tried to explore his drinking, but the patient consistently tried to minimize the extent of it. When pressed by his therapist, the patient described a serious and long-standing pattern of heavy drinking, but he continued to downplay it as a problem. The therapist confronted him with his denial and told the patient he was an alcoholic. He also told the patient that if the therapy was to be of any value, he would need to stop drinking. The patient appeared deeply offended by being diagnosed as an alcoholic; he accused the therapist of being overly critical, uncaring, condescending, and incompetent. The therapist weathered this onslaught, taking an exploratory stance but also maintaining a firm attitude regarding his diagnosis. The patient subsequently revealed new historical information that confirmed a long history of drug and alcohol abuse.

At the end of the therapy, the patient noted that he stayed in therapy largely because of the therapist's attitude toward his drinking. He reported that he had been able to fool previous therapists into overlooking or underestimating his alcohol and drug abuse. Even though he was angry when his therapist called him an alcoholic, he also felt he could trust him because of the therapist's firm, unwavering stance. The patient derived considerable benefit from this therapy primarily because he no longer felt in danger of being able to fool or overwhelm his therapist (this case example comes from Curtis & Silberschatz, 1986).

In a passive-into-active test, the patient tries to traumatize the therapist, as the patient had been traumatized earlier in life, in order to see if the therapist can deal with trauma in a more effective manner than the patient could (Foreman, 1996; Sampson, 1991, 1992; Silberschatz & Curtis, 1986, 1993; Weiss, 1986, 1993). These kinds of tests may be characterized as "doing unto others what was done unto you." A patient who was emotionally abused throughout her childhood by her sadistic, alcoholic stepmother tested her therapist for long periods of time by passive-into-active testing. For instance, she ruthlessly denigrated the therapist as she had been denigrated by her stepmother, telling the therapist he was worthless and disgusting. The therapist passed these tests by disconfirming in several ways the patient's pathogenic belief that she deserved the abuse meted out by her stepmother. Sometimes he explored the patient's feelings and behavior, at other times he interpreted her behavior, and occasionally he confronted the patient with the inappropriateness of her behavior, always in a way that communicated he was not harmed by her denigration. According to control-mastery theory, the patient's primary motive in testing the therapist is adaptive. The patient is attempting to disconfirm powerful, and often crippling, pathogenic beliefs.

The following case example illustrates how a patient frequently tests the therapist through passive-into-active testing and transference testing. Mr. M. (Silberschatz & Curtis, 1986; Silberschatz & Sampson, 1991), a 25-year-old single man who had completed a year of graduate school, came to therapy because he felt depressed, dissatisfied, and hopelessly stuck in a menial job. He was lonely, directionless, and periodically suicidal. Mr. M.'s father was described as an extremely passive, joyless man who had remained in a low-level job throughout his career and had serious health problems for which he never sought medical treatment. For instance, the father suffered from chronic emphysema, yet he refused to stop smoking. Similarly, the father refused for years to consult a dentist, and when he finally did so his condition was so poor that all of his teeth had to be removed. The patient characterized his mother as a kind, though very weak and submissive woman, who complied with her husband's drab, hopeless lifestyle.

Mr. M.'s primary pathogenic belief was that he was responsible for the unhappiness of both parents and, most manifestly, for the unhappiness of his father. Because he felt irrationally responsible for his father, the patient felt deeply frustrated by his inability to do anything useful for him. Throughout his life, the patient's own initiative had been squelched in various ways: by an unconscious identification with his passive parents, by the deeply discouraging failure of any action he took to actually change his parents' situation, and by his unconscious belief that both parents were hurt by any initiative, independence, or happiness the patient displayed. He unconsciously resisted any move toward independence and happiness because he believed such moves would threaten his connection (attachment bond) to his parents. The patient worked to disconfirm his pathogenic beliefs by testing them in relation to the therapist, particularly by a lengthy process of passive-into-active testing. For instance, he gave the therapist responsibility for his suffering and unhappiness just as he had felt responsible for his parents' suffering and unhappiness. The patient also tested whether the therapist would feel helpless and discouraged by the patient's doubts, criticisms, and lack of responsiveness as he himself had been discouraged by his parents' behavior.

These tests, which took place repeatedly over many sessions, were an integral part of the therapeutic process. The therapist did not feel irrationally responsible for the patient's misery, and as a result the patient gradually disconfirmed the pathogenic belief that he was responsible for his parents' misery. How did this process work? The patient inflicted onto the therapist a version of the trauma that had been inflicted on him growing up (passive into active). In doing so, Mr. M. was unconsciously testing a pathogenic belief that grew out of his traumatic family experience: He believed he was responsible for his parents' unhappiness and he felt discouraged by his inability to change them. The therapist experienced the trauma that the patient inflicted on him, developed some mastery over the trauma, and the patient, through identifying with the therapist's capacity, began to master the trauma as well.

In addition to passive-into-active tests, Mr. M. also posed a variety of transference tests during his treatment. He frequently tested to see if his initiative, enthusiasm, or independence would hurt the therapist (in the ways that he perceived his parents to have been hurt). For example, he obliquely alluded to wanting to complete his graduate education and pursue a professional career as part of a test to see if the therapist would be supportive. In another instance, he casually mentioned he was interested in taking up backcountry hiking and rock climbing. The therapist passed these tests by being openly supportive and encouraging the patient's initiative. However, it is important to emphasize that these tests could have been passed in a myriad number of ways. The therapist could have made a transference interpretation or focused on the very tentative and guarded manner in which Mr. M. presented his ideas. He could have used a more experiential approach by focusing on the patient's emerging feelings, or he could have relied on various behavioral or cognitive therapy strategies to help Mr. M. effectively develop and pursue his goals. The control-mastery theory does not dictate or prescribe a single strategy or technique for passing tests. It posits that the therapist's primary focus should be on helping the patient disconfirm pathogenic beliefs and that the optimal manner for doing so will vary as a function of the particular patient–therapist dyad.

One important clinical implication of the testing concept is that the meaning of a therapist's interventions will vary depending on what specific pathogenic beliefs the patient is testing. In other words, the concept of testing is highly case-specific. Identical patient behaviors or tests often have very different meanings and frequently require different responses from the therapist (Silberschatz, Curtis, Fretter, & Kelly, 1988). A therapist's response is effective only to the extent that it disconfirms the patient's particular pathogenic beliefs (Silberschatz et al., 1986; Silberschatz & Curtis, 1993; Weiss, 1993).

For instance, Myra (referred to previously) brought up termination with the therapist as part of a test to see if he would feel disturbed by her leaving or try to make her feel guilty as her boyfriend had done. The therapist discussed her thoughts about terminating in a pleasant and agreeable manner, which Myra experienced as a strong disconfirmation of her pathogenic belief (i.e., his response passed her test). By contrast, a patient who had been neglected and emotionally mistreated during childhood brought up terminating therapy as a test to see if the therapist would neglect her and fail to protect her as her parents had (see the case of Roberta in chapter 3). When the therapist adamantly told her she should not terminate her treatment, she was very reassured, felt safer in the relationship, and brought up significant new material to work on. Had this therapist adopted the same agreeable manner as Myra's therapist, this patient would have experienced the therapist's response as neglectful and hence as a confirmation of her pathogenic belief (i.e., such a response would have failed her test).

RELATION OF CONTROL-MASTERY THEORY TO VARIOUS CLINICAL CONCEPTS

This section will briefly discuss how the control-mastery theory relates to several important clinical concepts in psychotherapy: the therapeutic alliance, transference, psychotherapeutic technique, resistance, and the corrective emotional experience. Because one or more chapters could easily be devoted to each of these topics, my aim in this discussion is not to be comprehensive. I simply want to provide a broad outline of how these central clinical topics are understood from the perspective of the control-mastery theory.

Therapeutic Alliance

A therapeutic alliance represents a strong, collaborative relationship between the patient and therapist. Both the clinical and the research literature in psychotherapy have consistently suggested that the therapeutic alliance is an essential ingredient in successful therapy (Horvath, 2001) and indeed in all helping relationships (Luborsky, 1976). However, the literature is less clear about the factors that contribute to this critically important therapeutic ingredient. In his review of the literature, Horvath (2001) pointed out that therapists who are able to maintain an open, flexible, collaborative stance (as opposed to a rigid, controlling one) are more likely to build positive alliances. According to the control-mastery theory, the single most salient factor leading to a positive therapeutic alliance is the therapist's ability to help the patient disconfirm conscious and unconscious pathogenic beliefs. This can be accomplished by the therapist either passing tests, providing information or knowledge (insights) that will help the patient with specific pathogenic beliefs, and/or by creating a relationship that is conducive to the disconfirmation of the patient's pathogenic beliefs.

Resistance

Most patient behaviors described as resistance or efforts to avoid change can be understood as the patient testing the therapist. While testing, patients may *appear* to be resisting therapeutic work. Mr. M.'s discouraging attitude toward the therapist and his lack of responsiveness certainly look like resistance in the most traditional sense. But, in fact, Mr. M. was testing the therapist and productively working to overcome a fundamental pathogenic belief. As Sampson (1992) pointed out, testing is not a defensive repetition of the past "or simply an unconscious resistance or an unconscious effort to perpetuate the past in the present in order to avoid change. Rather, it is an unconscious attempt to learn something about [the therapist] that may enable patients to disconfirm a pathogenic belief that is causing them much misery and interfering with their progress toward valued goals" (p. 524).

Patient behavior that is typically seen as resistance may also be viewed as the expression of fundamental pathogenic beliefs. For example, Rita (Curtis & Silberschatz, 1986), a 60-year-old successful executive sought therapy because she was unable to have fun. She worked far too many hours, frequently going to her job on weekends or even in the middle of the night. When she had time off, she felt lost and would call one of her grown children to see if she could babysit or perform some household chore for them. Rita grew up in a dysfunctional, impoverished family. Her mother was an extremely self-sacrificing, masochistic woman who acted as if her main purpose in life was to serve others, especially her relentlessly critical, abusive husband. The patient reported that her mother looked 60 when still in her 30s and had died in her 40s, apparently worn down by the effects of poverty, an abusive husband, and the need to care for 10 children (both her own and those of relatives).

In the early hours of therapy, the patient responded to the therapist's questions in a very circumspect, perfunctory manner. There were long and frequent silences, few spontaneous associations, and she took no initiative in presenting or discussing issues. When the therapist inquired about her thoughts or feelings during the silences, she would reply, for example, that she had been thinking about the therapist's shoes, and then say no more. Rather than seeing this pattern as resistance, the therapist interpreted the patient's silence as a reflection of her unconscious pathogenic belief that a woman's role in life was to selflessly and masochistically serve others. He pointed out that Rita had difficulty thinking about her own needs in part because of an unconscious identification with her mother and in part because she felt uncomfortable about getting more out of life than her mother had.

Following this interpretation, the patient began associating more and exploring issues in a more involved way. She also confirmed the interpretation by recalling how her mother, upon returning home from the hospital after having a foot amputated, hopped around on one leg, waiting on her healthy but indolent husband (Curtis & Silberschatz, 1986, pp. 18–19).

Transference

The concept of transference plays a central role in all psychodynamic and insight-oriented therapies. Transference refers to thoughts, feelings, or wishes originating in important early relationships (usually with parents, siblings, family members, or other important figures in a child's life) that are subsequently transferred or projected onto current relationships. In his classic paper, Freud (1912/1958) defined transference as a set of (usually unconscious) anticipations or a "stereotype plate" that is constantly repeated in various relationships throughout life. In clinical writings, the term transference is used in a shorthand manner to refer to early feelings and thoughts that are transferred to the therapy relationship, and particular emphasis is placed on the mutative effects of transference interpretation, i.e., interpretations that address the patient–therapist relationship explicitly. Transference is a central concept in the control-mastery theory. As Fretter, Bucci, Broitman, Silberschatz, & Curtis (1994) pointed out, pathogenic beliefs are "conscious and unconscious 'anticipatory ideas' that derive from traumatic childhood experiences and are constantly repeated in new relationships throughout a person's life" (p. 67). Moreover, the concepts of the patient's plan and testing are firmly based on the theory of transference. However, the control-mastery theory does not privilege or give special weight to transference interpretations involving the therapist. The disconfirmation of pathogenic beliefs—whether in love relationships, friendships, work relationships, or the therapeutic relationship—is viewed as the mutative component of psychotherapy (Fretter et al. ; Silberschatz et al., 1986).

Psychotherapeutic Technique

During the past decade, the field of psychotherapy has witnessed a strong and growing interest in developing practice guidelines based on empirically supported treatments (Chambless & Hollon, 1998; Goldfried & Wolfe, 1996; Levant, 2003; Norcross, 2001; Persons & Silberschatz, 1998). At the heart of this rapidly growing trend is the idea that certain therapeutic approaches or techniques are best suited to groups of patients with particular psychiatric (Diagnostic and Statistical Manual of Mental Disorders [DSM]) diagnoses. In contrast to this trend, the control-mastery theory is highly case specific; a technique that is helpful to one patient may not be appropriate or helpful to another patient, even when the patients share the identical diagnosis (Persons & Silberschatz, 1998, pp. 128–130).

The control-mastery theory posits that a primary determinant of effective and successful treatment is the therapist's ability to correctly discern the patient's early traumas and the pathogenic beliefs that emerged from those traumatic experiences. Armed with a clear understanding of a patient's pathogenic beliefs, the therapist may use a wide array of techniques to help the patient disconfirm those beliefs. The techniques employed in any given treatment will be determined in part by the therapist's background, training, and personality, as well as by the patient's particular problems, needs, and preferences. How effective the therapy is will be determined not by the technique that is used but by the extent to which the therapist disconfirms the patient's pathogenic beliefs.

Corrective Emotional Experiences

Alexander and French (1946) first articulated the concept of a corrective emotional experience, arguing that it is essential for therapists to adopt a role that is in direct contradistinction to the patient's transference expectations. In all forms of psychotherapy, they wrote, "the basic therapeutic principle is the same: to reexpose the patient, under more favorable circumstances, to emotional situations which he could not handle in the past. The patient, in order to be helped, must undergo a corrective emotional experience suitable to repair the traumatic influence of previous experiences" (p. 66). They conclude that "only the actual experience of a new solution in the transference situation or in his everyday life gives the patient the conviction that a new solution *is possible* and induces him to give up the old neurotic patterns" (p. 338). They point out that the therapist is in a unique position "to provide the patient with precisely that type of corrective experience which he needs for recovery. It is a secondary question what technique is employed to bring it about" (p. 338).

The control-mastery theory also emphasizes the importance of corrective emotional experiences in psychotherapy. Indeed, any interaction in which a therapist disconfirms the patient's pathogenic beliefs may be viewed as a corrective emotional experience. The control-mastery concepts of trauma and pathogenic beliefs provide a precise, case-specific definition of the kinds of experiences that are likely to be "corrective" (i.e., helpful) to any given patient (for further discussion, see chapter 7).

SUMMARY

This chapter has described the control-mastery theory of how psychopathology develops and how psychotherapy works. It discussed the concepts that are central to the theory—pathogenic beliefs, the patient's plan, and how patients test pathogenic beliefs—and illustrated them with clinical examples. Finally, the chapter briefly discussed how the theory relates to the concepts of therapeutic alliance, resistance, transference, psychotherapeutic technique, and corrective emotional experiences.

REFERENCES

Alexander, F., & French, T. M. (1946). *Psychoanalytic therapy: Principles and applications.* New York: Ronald Press.

Bargh, J. A., Gollwitzer, P. M., Lee-Chai, A., Barndollar, K., & Troetschel, R. (2001). The automated will: Nonconscious activation and pursuit of behavioral goals. *Journal of Personality & Social Psychology, 81,* 1014–1027.

Beres, D. (1958). Certain aspects of superego functioning. *Psychoanalytic Study of the Child, 13,* 324–351.

Bowlby, J. (1969). *Attachment and loss. Volume 1: Attachment.* New York: Basic Books.

Bowlby, J. (1973). *Attachment and loss. Volume 2: Separation: Anxiety and anger.* New York: Basic Books.

Bowlby, J. (1980). *Attachment and loss. Volume 3. Loss: Sadness and depression.* New York: Basic Books.

Bowlby, J. (1988). *A secure base: Parent–child attachment and healthy human development.* London: Routledge.

Bowlby, J. (1989). The role of attachment in personality development and psychopathology. In S. I. Greenspan & G. H. Pollock (Eds.), *The course of life, Vol. 1: Infancy* (pp. 229–270). Madison, CT: International Universities Press.

Bush, M., & Gassner, S. (1986). The immediate effect of the analyst's termination interventions on the patient's resistance to termination. In J. Weiss, H. Sampson, & the Mount Zion Psychotherapy Research Group (Eds.), *The psychoanalytic process: Theory, clinical observation, and empirical research* (pp. 299–322). New York: Guilford.

Caspar, F. (1995). *Plan analysis.* Bern: Hogrefe & Huber.

Chambless, D. L., & Hollon, S. D. (1998). Defining empirically supported therapies. *Journal of Consulting and Clinical Psychology, 64,* 497–504.

Curtis, J. T., & Silberschatz, G. (1986). Clinical implications of research on brief dynamic psychotherapy: I. Formulating the patient's problems and goals. *Psychoanalytic Psychology, 3,* 13–25.

Curtis, J. T., & Silberschatz, G. (1997). Plan formulation method. In T. D. Eells (Ed.), *Handbook of psychotherapy case formulation* (pp. 116–136). New York: Guilford.

Fairbairn, W. R. D. (1952). The repression and the return of bad objects (with special reference to the "war neuroses"). *Psychoanalytic Studies of the Personality* (pp. 59–81). London: Tavistock. (Original work published in 1943.)

Fitzsimons, G. M., & Bargh, J. A. (2003). Thinking of you: Nonconscious pursuit of interpersonal goals associated with relationship partners. *Journal of Personality & Social Psychology, 84,* 148–163.

Foreman, S. A. (1996). The significance of turning passive into active in control mastery theory. *Journal of Psychotherapy Practice and Research, 5,* 106–121.

Fretter, P. B. (1984). The immediate effects of transference interpretations on patients' progress in brief, psychodynamic psychotherapy. (Doctoral dissertation, University of San Francisco, 1984). *Dissertation Abstracts International, 46*(6). (University Microfilms No. 85-12, 112).

Fretter, P. B., Bucci, W., Broitman, J., Silberschatz, G., & Curtis, J. T. (1994). How the patient's plan relates to the concept of transference. *Psychotherapy Research, 4,* 58–72.

Freud, S. (1958). The dynamics of the transference. In J. Strachey (Ed.), *The standard edition of the complete psychological works of Sigmund Freud* (Vol. 12, pp. 97–108). London: Hogarth Press. (Original work published 1912.)

Goldfried, M. R., & Wolfe, B. (1996). Psychotherapy practice and research: Repairing a strained alliance. *American Psychologist, 51,* 1007–1016.

Gopnik, A., Meltzoff, A. N., & Kuhl, P. K. (1999). *The scientist in the crib: Minds, brains, and how children learn.* New York: Morrow.

Grawe, K. (2004). *Psychological therapy.* Bern: Hogrefe & Huber.

Horvath, A. O. (2001). The alliance. *Psychotherapy, 38,* 365–372.

Levant, R. F. (2003). The empirically-validated treatments movement: A practitioner perspective. *Psychotherapy Bulletin, 38,* 36–39.

Lewicki, P., Hill, T., & Czyzewska, M. (1992). Nonconscious acquisition of information. *American Psychologist, 47,* 796–801.

Lewicki, P., Hill, T., & Czyzewska, M. (1994). Nonconscious indirect inferences in encoding. *Journal of Experimental Psychology: General, 123,* 257–263.

Luborsky, L. (1976). Helping alliances in psychotherapy. In J. L. Cleghorn (Ed.), *Successful psychotherapy* (pp. 92–116). New York: Brunner/Mazel.

Miller, G. A., Galanter, E., & Pribram, K. H. (1960). *Plans and the structure of behavior.* New York: Henry Holt & Co.

Norcross, J. C. (2001). Purposes, processes, and products of the task force on empirically supported therapy relationships. *Psychotherapy: Theory, Research, Practice, Training, 38,* 345–356.

Persons, J. B., & Silberschatz, G. (1998). Are results of randomized controlled trials useful to psychotherapists? *Journal of Consulting and Clinical Psychology, 66,* 126–135.

Rappoport, A. (1996). Freeing oneself from pathogenic adaptations: A contribution to control-mastery theory. *Psychotherapy Bulletin, 31,* 27–33.

Sampson, H. (1991). Experience and insight in the resolution of transferences. *Contemporary Psychoanalysis, 27,* 200–207.

Sampson, H. (1992). The role of "real" experience in psychopathology and treatment. *Psychoanalytic Dialogues, 2,* 509–528.

Silberschatz, G. (1986). Testing pathogenic beliefs. In J. Weiss, H. Sampson, & The Mount Zion Psychotherapy Research Group (Eds.), *The psychoanalytic process: Theory, clinical observation, and empirical research* (pp. 256–266). New York: Guilford Press.

Silberschatz, G., & Curtis, J. T. (1986). Clinical implications of research on brief dynamic psychotherapy: II. How the therapist helps or hinders therapeutic progress. *Psychoanalytic Psychology, 3,* 27–37.

Silberschatz, G., & Curtis, J. T. (1993). Measuring the therapist's impact on the patient's therapeutic progress. *Journal of Consulting and Clinical Psychology, 61,* 403–411.

Silberschatz, G., Curtis, J. T., Fretter, P. B., & Kelly, T. J. (1988). Testing hypotheses of psychotherapeutic change processes. In H. Dahl, H. Kachele, & H. Thoma (Eds.), *Psychoanalytic process research strategies* (pp. 129–145). Springer–Verlag: Berlin.

Silberschatz, G., Curtis, J. T., & Nathans, S. (1989). Using the patient's plan to assess progress in psychotherapy. *Psychotherapy: Theory, Research, Practice, Training, 26,* 40–46.

Silberschatz, G., Curtis, J. T., Sampson, H., & Weiss, J. (1991). Mount Zion Hospital and Medical Center: Research on the process of change in psychotherapy. In L. E. Beutler & M. Crago (Eds.), *Psychotherapy research: An international review of programmatic studies* (pp. 56–64). Washington, DC: American Psychological Association.

Silberschatz, G., Fretter, P. B., & Curtis, J. T. (1986). How do interpretations influence the process of psychotherapy? *Journal of Consulting and Clinical Psychology, 54,* 646–652.

Silberschatz, G., & Sampson, H. (1991). Affects in psychopathology and psychotherapy. In J. D. Safran & L. S. Greenberg (Eds.), *Emotion, psychotherapy, and change.* New York: Guilford Press.

Steele, R. S., & Morawski, J. G. (2002). Implicit cognition and the social unconscious. *Theory & Psychology, 12,* 37–54.

Stern, D. N. (1985). *The interpersonal world of the infant.* New York: Basic Books.

Stern, D. N. (2002). *The first relationship: Infant and mother.* Cambridge, MA: Harvard University Press.

Suffridge, D. R. (1991). Survivors of child maltreatment: Diagnostic formulation and therapeutic process. *Psychotherapy, 28,* 67–75.

Weiss, J. (1986). Theory and clinical observations. In J. Weiss, H. Sampson, & The Mount Zion Psychotherapy Research Group (Eds.), *The psychoanalytic process: Theory, clinical observation, and empirical research* (pp. 3–138). New York: Guilford.

Weiss, J. (1992). The role of interpretation. *Psychoanalytic Inquiry, 12,* 296–313.

Weiss, J. (1993). *How psychotherapy works.* New York: Guilford Press.

Weiss, J., Sampson, H., & The Mount Zion Psychotherapy Research Group. (Eds.). (1986). *The psychoanalytic process: Theory, clinical observation, and empirical research.* New York: Guilford.

Westen, D. (1999). The scientific status of unconscious processes: Is Freud really dead? *Journal of the American Psychoanalytic Association* (Special Issue: Between the millennia: Freud and psychoanalysis), *47,* 1061–1106.

2
HOW PREVIOUSLY INACCESSIBLE EXPERIENCES BECOME CONSCIOUS

George Silberschatz

A fundamental question for psychodynamic and all uncovering therapies is, how do previously warded-off thoughts, feelings, or memories become conscious? The control-mastery theory emphasizes that a person exerts considerable control over his or her conscious and unconscious mental life, and that perceptions of danger and safety (derived from conscious and unconscious beliefs about reality) play a central role in explaining human motivation and behavior (Weiss, 1971, 1986, 1993). The theory postulates that a patient may unconsciously decide to bring previously warded-off feelings or thoughts into his or her awareness and that the decision is based on the patient's appraisal of whether he or she feels it can be done safely.

Weiss (1971) identified three processes in psychotherapy that may influence a person's perception of safety or danger: *external circumstances*, *degree of control over defenses*, and *the therapeutic relationship*. The phenomenon of "crying at the happy ending" (Weiss, 1952; see also chapter 3) is an example of how an external change may make it safe for a person to experience previously warded-off affects. A person watching a movie of a love story may experience little emotion while the lovers quarrel but is moved to tears at the happy ending when they are reunited. According to Weiss's explanation (1986), the moviegoer identifies unconsciously with one of the lovers. When the lovers are separated, the viewer is in danger of feeling extremely sad and consequently intensifies her defenses against sadness. When the lovers reunite, the moviegoer no longer has reason to feel sad. She unconsciously decides it is safe to experience sadness (because it is now less of a threat) and lifts her defenses against the previously warded-off sadness. Patients in psychotherapy similarly make unconscious decisions to experience previously warded-off feelings, thoughts, or experiences when they feel it is safe to do so (Weiss, 1971, 1986; for empirical research supporting this view, see Curtis, Ransohoff, Sampson, Brumer, & Bronstein, 1986; Gassner, Sampson, Brumer, & Weiss, 1986; Horowitz, Sampson, Siegelman, Weiss, & Goodfriend, 1978; Horowitz, Sampson, Siegelman, Wolfson, & Weiss, 1975).

As a clinical example of how an external event may make it safe for a person to bring forth previously repressed painful feelings and memories, we will examine a patient who came to therapy shortly after divorcing her alcoholic, physically abusive husband. During the first two years of therapy, the patient was unable to talk about her traumatic marriage. However, after several months of dating and subsequently becoming engaged to a kind, loving man, she was able to begin describing some of the traumatic, horrifying experiences of abuse at the hands of her first husband. The patient's ability to bring forth previously warded-off painful feelings and memories parallels the moviegoer's crying at the happy ending. The patient repressed her traumatic marital experiences because she was in danger of feeling overwhelmed by feelings of grief and the irrational idea that somehow she had caused her husband's abusive behavior. Her engagement to a man who was consistently loving and kind led her to feel that she could tolerate and safely face her repressed grief without feeling devastated and overwhelmed. Thus, a change in the patient's external circumstances—becoming engaged to a kind, respectful man—made it safe for her to experience and face previously inaccessible feelings and memories.

A second factor that may increase a person's sense of safety and facilitate the emergence of warded-off affects is a change in internal regulatory mechanisms, an example of which may be seen in Weiss's (1967) discussion of the integration of defenses. A person who has little control over a defense is likely to feel endangered by the affects, ideas, or memories the defense is warding off. If a person is able to develop control over his defenses (e.g., through successful therapeutic work), then he or she can use the defense to regulate the emergence of unconscious contents:

The patient's capacity to regulate the warded-off mental content makes it safe for him to experience it, because he can control the experience, turning away from it at will if it becomes too painful or threatening. In this way, the patient can dose the new experience (warded-off content), and can reassess the danger associated with it. (Sampson, Weiss, Mlodnosky, & Hause, 1972, p. 525)

Horowitz, Sampson, Siegelman, Weiss, and Goodfriend (1978) studied how developing greater control over defenses makes it safer to experience previously warded-off feelings. They investigated the relationship between the patient's ability to distance him- or herself from others (referred to as Type D behaviors and feelings) and his or her ability to express loving feelings and be close to others (Type C feelings). A particular patient sought treatment because of a chronic inability to feel close to her husband and enjoy sexual relations with him. Horowitz et al. suggested that the patient's difficulty feeling close to others was related to her inability to distance herself from others. They reasoned that if the patient lacked the capacity to distance herself, then intimacy could be experienced as dangerous because she would not be able to disengage from closeness when she wanted to and would thus run the risk of feeling stuck or entrapped. Once the patient gained the capacity to distance herself, she would have more confidence in her ability to regulate intimacy, and consequently feelings of closeness would not be as threatening. Indeed, the investigators found that progress in Type C feelings followed progress in expressing Type D feelings. As the patient became more comfortable disagreeing with others and expressing critical feelings, she progressively felt less vulnerable. As a result, she could allow herself to experience feelings of closeness, affection, and intimacy.[1]

The third factor influencing a patient's feeling of safety is the therapeutic relationship. Just as a change in external circumstances or in the degree of control over defenses can make it safe for a person to experience previously warded-off thoughts, feelings, or experiences, so too may a change in a patient's relationship with the therapist. An important part of a patient's effort to solve problems and conflicts in therapy is bringing disavowed and warded-off feelings into consciousness. In order to do so, the patient must work to overcome the internal danger he or she would face if the patient were to experience the warded-off feelings. He or she does this by attempting to create a relationship with the therapist that would protect him or her from this danger. The patient tests the therapist to assure him- or herself that were the warded-off feelings or experiences brought to consciousness, the therapist "could be relied upon to respond in a way that would afford protection against the danger" (Sampson, 1976, p. 257).

For example, the patient referred to previously who was unable to feel close to her husband (she had to become more comfortable feeling distant before she could feel close) tested the therapist by tentatively disagreeing with him and expressing critical feelings toward him. The patient's father had been unable to tolerate any criticism and would react to such feelings by either becoming enraged or by withdrawing and sulking. When the therapist responded to these tests by encouraging the patient to say more about her critical feelings or by pointing out her tentativeness or discomfort in criticizing him, the patient felt reassured (an increased sense of safety) and frequently brought up previously warded-off memories and affects (Silberschatz, 1978, 1986). Indeed, several research studies have shown a high correlation between the therapist passing tests and the patient's subsequent productivity (e.g., Silberschatz & Curtis, 1993; see chapter 11).

The concept of pathogenic beliefs helps explain why these three factors (external changes, defensive control, and the therapeutic relationship) all may lead to increased safety and greater accessibility to previously warded-off experiences. A person's assessment of safety and danger is strongly influenced by his or her unconscious pathogenic beliefs. Thus, any experience or interaction that helps to disconfirm a pathogenic belief will increase a person's sense of safety and thereby allow him or her to lift defenses against warded-off feelings, ideas, and memories.

In the phenomenon of "crying at the happy ending," a change in external events may help a person disconfirm a pathogenic belief. The patient who had divorced her alcoholic, abusive husband suffered from the pathogenic belief that her husband's abusive behavior was her fault. Like so many other victims of abuse, she believed that if only she had been a "better," more tolerant, and more understanding wife, her husband would not have abused her. The patient developed the unconscious pathogenic belief that she deserved the treatment she received. Her involvement and marriage to a decent, kind, loving man helped her disconfirm the belief that she deserved to be mistreated. Once this belief was disconfirmed, she could recall the traumatic memories of abuse and for the first time experience them not as punishment but as a tragic and undeserved period of grief, horror, and victimization.

Similarly, a positive change in the therapeutic relationship often reflects a change in pathogenic beliefs. Patients in psychotherapy work to disconfirm pathogenic beliefs by testing them in relation to the therapist. As the patient disconfirms the pathogenic beliefs, he or she becomes less frightened of the dangers they foretell. Consequently, the patient may decide (unconsciously) that he or she can safely experience certain previously warded-off feelings or memories and that it is safe to bring them to consciousness.

To summarize, control-mastery theory postulates that a patient may unconsciously decide to bring previously warded-off experiences, feelings, or thoughts into awareness, and that the decision is based on the patient's appraisal of whether he or she feels it can be done safely. A person's unconscious pathogenic beliefs play a determining role in his or her assessment of safety and danger. Thus, any experience or interaction that helps to disconfirm a pathogenic belief will increase a person's sense of safety and thereby allow him or her to lift defenses against warded-off feelings, ideas, and memories.

ENDNOTE

1. Using a different theoretical framework—the assimilation of problematic experiences—(Stiles 1999, 2001; Stiles, Elliott, Llewelyn, Firth-Cozens, Margison, Shapiro, et al., 1990; Stiles, Morrison, Haw, Harper, Shapiro, & Firth-Cozens, 1991; see also Knobloch, Endres, Stiles, & Silberschatz, 2001) identified processes that are very similar to Weiss's concept of the integration of defenses.

REFERENCES

Curtis, J. T., Ransohoff, P., Sampson, F., Brumer, S., & Bronstein, A. A. (1986). Expressing warded-off contents in behavior. In J. Weiss, H. Sampson, & The Mount Zion Psychotherapy Research Group (Eds.), *The psychoanalytic process: Theory, clinical observation, and empirical research* (pp. 171–186). New York: Guilford Press.

Gassner, S., Sampson, H., Brumer, S., & Weiss, J. (1986). The emergence of warded-off contents. In J. Weiss, H. Sampson, & The Mount Zion Psychotherapy Research Group (Eds.), *The psychoanalytic process: Theory, clinical observation, and empirical research* (pp. 187–205). New York: Guilford Press.

Horowitz, L. M., Sampson, H., Siegelman, E. Y., Weiss, J., & Goodfriend, S. (1978). Cohesive and dispersal behaviors: Two classes of concomitant change in psychotherapy. *Journal of Consulting and Clinical Psychology, 46*, 556–564.

Horowitz, L. M., Sampson, H., Siegelman, E. Y., Wolfson, A., & Weiss, J. (1975). On the identification of warded-off mental contents: An empirical and methodological contribution. *Journal of Abnormal Psychology, 84*, 545–558.

Knobloch, L. M., Endres, L. M., Stiles, W. B., & Silberschatz, G. (2001). Convergence and divergence of themes in successful psychotherapy: An assimilation analysis. *Psychotherapy, 38*, 31–39.

Sampson, H. (1976). A critique of certain traditional concepts in the psychoanalytic theory of therapy. *Bulletin of the Menninger Clinic, 40,* 255–262.

Sampson, H., Weiss, J., Mlodnosky, L., & Hause, E. (1972). Defense analysis and the emergence of warded-off mental contents: An empirical study. *Archives of General Psychiatry, 26,* 524–532.

Silberschatz, G. (1978). Effects of the analyst's neutrality on the patient's feelings and behavior in the psychoanalytic situation. *Dissertation Abstracts International, 39,* 3007B. (University Microfilms No. 78–24, 277).

Silberschatz, G. (1986). Testing pathogenic beliefs. In J. Weiss, H. Sampson, & The Mount Zion Psychotherapy Research Group (Eds.), *The psychoanalytic process: Theory, clinical observation, and empirical research* (pp. 256–266). New York: Guilford Press.

Silberschatz, G., & Curtis, J. T. (1993). Measuring the therapist's impact on the patient's therapeutic progress. *Journal of Consulting and Clinical Psychology, 61,* 403–411.

Stiles, W. B. (1999). Signs and voices in psychotherapy. *Psychotherapy Research, 9,* 1–21.

Stiles, W. B. (2001). Assimilation of problematic experiences. *Psychotherapy: Theory, Research, Practice, Training, 38,* 462–465.

Stiles, W. B., Elliott, R., Llewelyn, S. P., Firth-Cozens, J. A., Margison, F. R., Shapiro, D. A., et al. (1990). Assimilation of problematic experiences by clients in psychotherapy. *Psychotherapy: Theory, Research, Practice, Training, 27,* 411–420.

Stiles, W. B., Morrison, L. A., Haw, S. K., Harper, H., Shapiro, D. A., & Firth–Cozens, J. A. (1991). Longitudinal study of assimilation in exploratory psychotherapy. *Psychotherapy, 28,* 195–206.

Weiss, J. (1952). Crying at the happy ending. *Psychoanalytic Review, 39,* 338.

Weiss, J. (1967). The integration of defenses. *International Journal of Psychoanalysis, 48,* 520–524.

Weiss, J. (1971). The emergence of new themes: A contribution to the psychoanalytic theory of therapy. *International Journal of Psychoanalysis, 52,* 459–467.

Weiss, J. (1986). Theory and clinical observations. In J. Weiss, H. Sampson, & The Mount Zion Psychotherapy Research Group (Eds.), *The psychoanalytic process: Theory, clinical observation, and empirical research* (pp. 3–138). New York: Guilford.

Weiss, J. (1993). *How psychotherapy works.* New York: Guilford Press.

3

SAFETY

Joseph Weiss

One of our most powerful motives and one frequently overlooked by theoreticians is the quest for a sense of safety. Our pursuit of a sense of safety is rooted in biology and is to a considerable extent unconscious. We seek this sense through our relations with others. A child seeks it through relations with parents, and patients through relations with their therapists. Moreover, a sense of safety is a precondition for optimal functioning. A child's sense of safety with parents facilitates the child's becoming adventurous and pursuing developmental goals. Patients' sense of safety with their therapists facilitates their overcoming the pathogenic beliefs underlying their psychopathology and pursuing the goals previously inhibited by these beliefs (Weiss, 1993; Weiss, Sampson, and The Mount Zion Psychotherapy Research Group, 1986). The patient's sense of safety with the therapist is crucial for the success of the therapy.

We also seek a sense of safety in fantasized relations. We arouse ourselves sexually by fantasizing a sexual relationship with a partner with whom we feel safe. In addition, a desperate, endangered person will give him- or herself a temporary sense of relief by dreaming of being in a safe relationship.

THE THERAPIST SHOULD HELP THE PATIENT FEEL SAFE

The observation that the success of therapy is based around the patient's sense of safety gives rise to an important technical prescription. The therapist's task of helping the patient feel safe takes precedence over other technical ideas, including the idea that the therapist should offer insight by interpretation (Weiss et al., 1986; Weiss, 1993). The idea that the therapist should help the patient feel safe is consistent with the observation, discussed later, that patients (and people in everyday life) unconsciously regulate their access to their own warded-off mental contents and that they do so by the criteria of safety and danger. They keep mental contents unconscious as long as they unconsciously assume that their making them conscious would endanger them, and they bring these contents forth once they unconsciously decide that they can safely experience them. They regulate their unconscious inhibitions by the same criteria. They maintain their inhibitions while they unconsciously assume that removing them would endanger them. They remove them and seek the goals previously inhibited by them once they unconsciously decide they can safely do so.[1]

The following sections illustrate these concepts clinically and indicate their centrality to psychotherapeutic technique. However, because these concepts run counter to the intuitions of most therapists, we shall begin by discussing how I first became convinced of their validity.

Weeping for Joy

The concept that when people feel safe they may bring forth previously repressed mental contents was first suggested to me by the everyday observation that a person may weep for joy (Weiss, 1952). This was a useful observation to study. My attempts to explain it suggested not only the concept of safety described previously but also several other concepts relevant to our theory of therapy. These concepts are that a person has a powerful unconscious wish to solve problems and also strong unconscious cognitive capacities and controls that make it possible for the person to do so (Lewicki, 1986; Lewicki & Hill, 1989).

The example of weeping for joy that first intrigued me was that of the moviegoer watching a romance. The moviegoer does not weep while the lovers are quarreling but does weep when, at the end of the film, they are happily reunited (Weiss, 1952). I explained this by assuming that the moviegoer is sad during the lovers' quarrel but is pained by the sadness then and so suppresses it. At the film's happy ending, when the lovers resolve the quarrel, the moviegoer is no longer endangered by the sadness and so expresses it by weeping.

This explanation has the merit of connecting weeping for joy and weeping for sadness. In both instances, the weeping is for sadness.

However, in the instance of weeping for joy, the sadness is suppressed until at the joyful resolution the moviegoer can safely express it.

Louise: A Clinical Illustration

Nonetheless, the example of the moviegoer is not entirely satisfactory. For although it assumes that the moviegoer, while weeping, is expressing sadness, the moviegoer in most instances does not feel sad. He or she simply feels happy. However, this example did alert me to the observation that a person at a moment of happiness may also bring forth previously repressed sad memories of traumatic experiences. A good example[2] (which I have reported elsewhere but repeat here because it so well illustrates my point) was told to me by a colleague, Louise, with whom I had discussed my explanation of weeping for joy. Louise had lost a 2-year-old son many years before. She was overwhelmed by sadness then and repressed it along with memories of her son so thoroughly that on one occasion she failed to recognize her son from a photo in the family photo album.

Many years later, in a second marriage, Louise gave birth to another son and was overjoyed when he was brought to her in the maternity ward. She immediately began to weep, remembering her first son. She remembered how much she had loved him and how sad she had felt when he died. Though predominantly happy, she was also aware of being sad.

Louise was surprised at her sudden weeping and at the eruption of the memories of her first son into her consciousness. She was talking with the floor nurse when her second son was brought to her, and her sudden weeping interrupted their conversation. My explanation of Louise's sudden weeping was modeled after my explanation of the moviegoer's weeping. I assumed Louise was overwhelmed with sadness at the loss of her first son and had repressed her sadness. The birth of her second son greatly compensated for the loss of the first and made this loss bearable, so it became safe for her to experience her sadness at his death.

This explanation of Louise's experience raises several important questions. It does not account for Louise bringing forth the previously repressed memories just as soon as she unconsciously realized she could safely do so. Just because somebody can safely do something doesn't account for their doing it at all, much less for their doing it as soon as possible.

I explained Louise's bringing forth the sad memories immediately by suggesting that she had a powerful unconscious wish to master the trauma of her son's death. To fully master a trauma, one must make it conscious. Louise was so highly motivated to master this trauma that she made it conscious as soon as she could safely do so. According to Louise, she did attain a sense of mastery. She became comfortably able to remember a period of her life that she previously had great difficulty thinking about. She compared her new capacity to think about this period to that of a person who had been afraid to enter certain rooms in her house. The person then became able to do so and was subsequently able to roam about her house at will.

Another question raised by Louise's experience concerns what went on in her mind between her seeing her baby and her beginning to weep. Whatever did go on was not conscious. Louise did not decide consciously to search her mind for the memories of her first son. Indeed, as reported, Louise was surprised by the sudden eruption of these memories into her consciousness.

Nor was her reaction an automatic response to the sight of her baby. Louise brought the sad memories of her first son to consciousness only after she unconsciously realized that having a new baby boy made it safe for her to remember the death of her first son. This required unconscious thought, assessment, and decision making. Louise must have realized unconsciously that having a baby was precisely the event that would make it safe for her to remember, and she acted on this realization. The idea that her decision to remember was unconscious is indicated by Louise's conscious surprise at the sudden emergence of her sad memories.

PSYCHOTHERAPY

The following case studies illustrate how the patient's sense of safety determines their unconscious decisions to bring forth previously inaccessible memories and emotions. In some cases, the patient's sense of safety allows them to make progress without explicitly discussing the repressed material. I also highlight the techniques and stance employed by the therapist to help the patient feel safe and secure in therapy.

The Case of Roberta

My explanation of a person weeping for joy also applies to certain patients weeping when a change in their relationship with the therapist helps them feel more secure. This can be illustrated by the therapy of Roberta, a lawyer in her early thirties, who came to therapy complaining of feeling depressed, unattractive, and lonely. From her childhood experiences with her parents, she had acquired the belief that she would and should be rejected. She experienced her parents as joyless, taciturn, and burdened by having to take care of her. She assumed that the care they gave her was motivated not by love, but by duty.

In her therapy, Roberta was diffident and awkward. She apparently did not expect me to be interested in her. I tried to help her feel more comfortable and deserving by showing an accepting attitude, by accommodating her occasional requests for schedule changes, by showing interest in what she was saying, and by discussing her fear of rejection with her. Roberta made modest progress. She began to get along better with her supervisor and became friendlier with her colleagues. She also began to date.

After four years of treatment, Roberta surprised me by announcing one day she had gotten all that she wanted from therapy. She planned to stop and suggested a termination date a few months later. I implicitly opposed Roberta's stopping. I indicated that she had made only modest progress and could go much further. I suggested that perhaps by stopping she was protecting herself from the possibility that I would reject her. I also told her that as a consequence of her experience with her parents she felt undeserving. Perhaps she assumed that she did not deserve therapy. Roberta was genuinely interested in my comments and seemed a little relieved by them, but was undeterred in her plan to stop at the date she had set.

When we came close to her deadline, I finally told her, "I want you to continue." Roberta seemed relieved and reluctantly agreed to come a few more weeks. Shortly afterwards she began to weep uncontrollably and brought forth a very sad memory of her mother's rejection of her. On one occasion when she was 6 years old, a labor riot broke out in her neighborhood. Instead of trying to protect her, her mother sent her out to buy groceries. Roberta assumed her mother wanted her to be killed.

Several weeks later, Roberta acknowledged that to her surprise she was relieved that I had urged her to continue and that she agreed not to stop. Apparently, she felt that, unlike her parents, I did not feel burdened by her. She assumed I cared about her. Her feeling more secure with me enabled her to safely face the sad, traumatic memories of maternal rejection.

I had still more to learn from Roberta's therapy. Having acquired considerable respect for a person's unconscious capacity to think and to make and carry out decisions, I hypothesized that Roberta had unconsciously threatened to stop in order to test me, and that by testing me she was unconsciously working to feel safe with me. She unconsciously craved evidence that I cared about her and that I realized she had much more to gain from her therapy. She feared that although I said the right things I did so mostly out of a sense of duty.

Roberta's threatening to stop was an excellent way, perhaps the only way she could find out if I was committed to helping her. Because she stated she was satisfied by her treatment and seemed eager to terminate, I could have let her go with a clear conscience. She assumed that if I were burdened by her I would do just that. By testing me in this way, Roberta was taking a big risk, but it was one she had to take. She unconsciously knew she could not safely face her fear of rejection and her profound sadness without some convincing assurance of my concern and reliability.

Many months after Roberta agreed to continue, I obtained some confirmation of my hypothesis that she had threatened to stop in order to test me. She reported that on one occasion in grammar school she had tested ("tested" was Roberta's word) her only friend by telling her she was breaking their date to go to the Saturday film matinee. Roberta was relieved when her friend became upset and urged her to keep the date. I suggested that she had tested me in the same way, and she replied, "I've been thinking about that. It does seem the same."

My examples so far are all concerned with people bringing forth repressed, unconscious sadness. Of course, people, including patients, bring forth a variety of previously warded-off content, and not just sadness, when they unconsciously decide they can safely do so. Moreover, the therapist may help the patient feel safe enough to move forward by using a variety of different means, including the therapist's attitude, passing the patient's tests, and giving helpful comments and interpretations. However, in some therapies, the patient may be so averse to interpretation that the therapist cannot help the patient in that way. Because such cases are of considerable theoretical interest, I shall present several examples of them below.

Samir

This example concerns a 26-year-old computer salesman, Samir, who specializes in large installations for factories and big businesses. I learned from the referring physician that he had come to this country from India with his parents and older siblings when he was 10. Being quite bright, he had obtained scholarships at a highly rated college and graduate school.

During the first session, Samir, who had talked to my secretary about her computer, told me how for a relatively modest sum I could upgrade my computer system. He then began telling me about a party he had been to the night before. I became acutely aware that he was not discussing why he had come to see me, and I made some attempt to turn his attention to this topic. Samir ignored this and continued talking about a variety of things unrelated to his problems. During the next session, he was friendly and eager to talk, again about a variety of topics unrelated to his problems, and again he rebuffed my attempts to focus on why he was coming.

I began to wonder if Samir had felt nagged and intruded upon by his parents and, if so, whether he was testing me, hoping I would not nag him. I decided I would simply listen or chat with him about any topic he introduced. Moreover, except for a few unsuccessful attempts to help him by interpretation, I continued this policy throughout the four and a half years of Samir's therapy.

I very soon became confident about this policy, because after Samir had seen me for only a few sessions the family physician who had referred him called me. He reported that since Samir had begun treatment he had greatly improved and was no longer depressed. He was working well, beginning to install a new large computer system, and trying to find new customers. Samir continued to improve throughout the treatment. He became a good worker, made an excellent income, and became progressively more able to enjoy himself.

During the entire therapy, I learned very little about Samir's childhood and development. However, he did tell me on several occasions (quite matter-of-factly) that his mother had been depressed, critical, and intrusive. In addition, he implied that he enjoyed the sessions and felt supported by our relationship.

He did not talk about himself in psychological terms, but he provided the evidence that he felt discouraged by his mother being critical and intrusive, he had not felt safe working because he expected his mother to criticize his efforts, and he felt unsupported by her. Samir also did not like my interpretations because he assimilated them with his mother's intrusive criticism. In other words, he experienced my interpretations as pulling rank and putting him down unnecessarily. By the same token, he experienced my merely chatting with him and listening to him as supportive, noncritical, and nonintrusive. He experienced my behavior as expressing confidence that he could figure things out on his own and felt encouraged by it. Feeling supported by me, he could safely get down to work.

Albert

In this example, I helped an adolescent patient, Albert, feel safe by another unusual technique. Albert was lonely and depressed. He had considerable difficulty relating to his fellow high school students and teachers. With me, he had difficulty talking during the first few sessions. During the fifth session, he confided he had a strong interest in math and was eager to learn more about it. Remembering a little of my college math, I offered to teach him calculus. Albert brightened up and soon became an eager student. We spent many of his sessions doing math together. I bought him an elementary calculus textbook, and he worked from it at home each week. Albert made a strong connection to me. He idealized me and felt proud of our relationship. He also felt proud of the knowledge he was acquiring. His increased sense of self-worth made it safe for him to become friendlier with fellow students and teachers. He made progress in overcoming the belief he was an outsider.

Albert's therapy lasted only 8 months, and after he stopped I lost track of him. However, a few years later I learned that he had obtained a scholarship to MIT, where he was majoring in math and physics.

Gordon

Another patient, Gordon, came to me after a failed psychoanalysis. One of his complaints, that he had difficulty taking initiative, would have surprised his colleagues because he had made a number of important and interesting accomplishments. However, his accomplishments made him feel tense and anxious. Gordon, the only child of a busy working mother and a depressed father, had felt extremely dominated by his father. As Gordon experienced it, his father, who had not satisfied his own ambitions, was quite ambitious for Gordon and developed a program for him, intending to bring him fame and financial success. If Gordon demurred, his father would become very upset. Gordon, afraid of hurting his father, suppressed any inclination to deviate from his father's plans. He felt it was dangerous to think for himself. Indeed, he became so compliant that he did not know what he wanted to do.

In the failed analysis, Gordon had experienced the analyst as he had experienced his father. He made a strong effort to follow the analyst's injunction to lie on the couch and free-associate, and, as he told me, he free-associated very well indeed. However, he felt that he was free-associating for the analyst and not for himself. Needless to say, he made no progress in his struggle to feel comfortable taking initiative.

Early in the treatment with me, Gordon told me he wanted to make his therapy his and not mine. He suggested that he pay a month in advance and feel completely free to come or not come, according to his inclination. Also, he suggested that rather than free-associate, he would tell me his goals and take the lead in working toward them. My task would be to help him in this effort.

Gordon was pleased that I readily accepted his suggestion and he benefited from the new arrangements. He began to feel he could safely take charge of his treatment and permit himself to think about what he wanted. In addition, he began to take more initiative, both in his professional and personal life.

Considerable research has shown that when a patient feels safe he or she becomes bolder and more insightful (this is reported in chapter 11 as well). As the research demonstrates, a patient may be helped to feel safe when the therapist passes the patient's tests or offers him or her interpretations that disconfirm pathogenic beliefs.

SEXUAL FANTASIES MAKE IT SAFE FOR THE FANTASIZER TO BECOME AROUSED

As stated earlier, a person may rely on a fantasized relationship to acquire a sense of safety. A person may become sexually aroused by fantasizing about someone with whom he may safely become aroused (Weiss, 1998; Bader, 2001). In other words, just what kind of fantasy people find arousing depends on the particular dangers inherent for them in a real or fantasized sexual encounter. They produce fantasies designed to deny or in some way minimize these dangers, thereby making it safe for them to become sexually aroused. Consider, for example, a man who felt deeply rejected by his mother and who generalized from his maternal relationship by expecting rejection from any woman with whom he was intimate. This man aroused himself with the fantasy that a number of attractive women were fascinated by him and sexually drawn to him.

For another example, a woman who had a strict Catholic upbringing unconsciously had complied with her parents, whom she assumed disapproved of her sexuality. As an adult, she frequently aroused herself by fantasizing that the Pope was urging her to have sex.

My next example concerns a woman who in childhood worried excessively about her parents whom she feared she could easily upset. As an adult, she worried that in a sexual encounter with a man she would overwhelm him. She aroused herself with the fantasy that a man was forcing her to have sex with him. (For numerous and varied examples of the many ways people use sexual fantasies to acquire a sense of safety, see Bader 2001.)

The previous examples illustrate the special power of fantasy to create conditions of safety. In each example, a person depends on fantasy to attain arousal. Thus, the man who feared rejection could easily arouse himself by the fantasy of being fascinating to women. However, he could not arouse himself by rational thoughts in which he could tell himself that many women consider him attractive, and that he is endowed with physical and personal qualities that women admire. The man's fantasy of being fascinating to women, unlike his conscious thoughts about his attractiveness, helped him deny his unconscious fear of rejection because he experienced the fantasy as though it was reality.

Sexual fantasies are created unconsciously (but may be elaborated consciously). Thus, in many instances, people do not understand consciously why they find their particular sexual fantasies so compelling. I believe this is because the dangers that the fantasies are designed to deny are not fully conscious. People who feel endangered in an intimate relationship repress their anxieties about intimate relationships so as not to be prevented by the anxieties from developing such relationships. Because they are only dimly aware of the unconscious dangers, they do not understand the significance of the fantasies designed to deny these dangers.

For example, the man who aroused himself by imagining himself as fascinating to women was not fully conscious that he deeply feared rejection from women. He had to repress his fear of rejection, lest he feel impeded in his efforts to develop and maintain relations with women. Therefore, he did not have conscious awareness of why in order to become aroused he relied so heavily on his fantasies of being especially attractive to women.

In my experience, patients who use masochistic fantasies to arouse themselves are almost invariably baffled by their reliance on such fantasies. This was the case for two patients whose fantasies I discussed in a recent report (Weiss, 1998). One aroused himself with bondage fantasies, the other with beating fantasies. Both patients were baffled by their fantasies because they were not conscious of the dangers they denied by means of these fantasies. They both felt endangered in an intimate relationship with a woman by an intense fear of emotionally harming the woman. They each suffered from a painful sense of responsibility for their partners whom they considered fragile and helpless. Both patients acquired the pathogenic beliefs underlying these dangers in their early childhood relations with their mothers whom they experienced as fragile and burdened by having to take care of them. Both patients repressed their intense worry about their mothers (and later about other women with whom they were intimate) in order to free themselves from their mothers and become more independent. Both patients found great relief, and indeed a sense of safety, from the fantasy that a strong, cheerful woman was overpowering them. They did not have to worry about the powerful woman of their fantasies. Indeed, they were relieved by their fantasies of a painful sense of responsibility for the woman.

DREAMS

As with sexual fantasies, people may provide themselves with a sense of safety through dreams (Weiss, 1993). Desperate, endangered, or guilt-ridden individuals may find reassurance by dreaming they are in a safe relationship or in a safe situation. Thus, certain dreams, like sexual fantasies, are much more reassuring than conscious thought, even though they may be highly implausible. For example, prisoners in Vietnamese prison camps who were severely mistreated by their captors found great relief in dreaming they were safely home and happy, and the sense of relief persisted for months (Balson, 1975). In these dreams, they defied their captors and reassured themselves that one day they would be home and happy. However, they could not reassure themselves by the rational thought that one day the war would be over and they would be able to go home.

Another example concerns a man who accidentally killed his wife when a gun he was cleaning misfired. He felt intense, unbearable remorse for many months. However, he felt considerable relief from a dream in which, as the man explains, "My gun misfired and the bullet seriously wounded my wife. She staggered over and fell on my lap and said, 'I forgive you.'" The patient felt such relief from this dream that he kept it in his mind for months. Before having the dream, he told himself repeatedly he was certain his wife would forgive him if she could. However, by this conscious thought he was unable to give himself the relief that he gave himself by his dreams (author's professional experience).

That dreams have a greater power than conscious verbal thought to offer reassurance is not surprising. Dreams, with their adaptive function, have played a part in the lives of mammals for several hundred million years, whereas conscious verbal thought is no more one hundred thousand years old.

FINAL REMARKS

A sense of safety is crucial for our development and functioning, and we are highly motivated unconsciously and sometimes consciously to attain it through our relations with others. The child works to attain it in relation to his or her parents, and the patient in relation to the therapist. The patient's sense of safety with the therapist is crucial to the success of the treatment. The single most important thing a therapist can do is help the patient feel safe.

A person may rely on a fantasized relationship to attain a sense of safety. Thus, a person may fantasize a sexual encounter with a partner whose behavior helps the person feel it is safe to become sexually aroused. In addition, a desperate, endangered person may give him- or herself profound relief by dreaming of being in a safe relationship or a safe situation.

ENDNOTES

1. It was Freud (1926, 1940) who first discussed concepts about unconscious regulation by the criteria of safety and danger. However, he did so only briefly and in abstract theoretical terms. He did not indicate their relevance for therapy.
2. This example and the following example on Roberta are reported in an article, "The Development of a Research Program," to appear in *Psychoanalytic Inquiry*.

REFERENCES

Bader, M. J. (2001). *Arousal: The secret logic of sexual fantasies*. New York: St. Martin's Press.

Balson, P. (1975). *Dreams and fantasies as adaptive mechanisms in prisoners of war in Vietnam*. Unpublished manuscript written in consultation with M. Horowitz and E. Erickson, San Francisco Psychoanalytic Institute.

Freud, S. (1959/1926). Inhibitions, symptom, and anxiety. In J. Strachey (Ed. and Trans.), *The standard edition of the complete psychological works of Sigmund Freud* (Vol. 20, pp. 77–175). London: Hogarth Press. (Original work published 1926).

Freud, S. (1964/1940). An outline of psychoanalysis. In J. Strachey (Ed. and Trans.), *The standard edition of the complete psychological works of Sigmund Freud* (Vol. 23, pp. 141–207). London: Hogarth Press. (Original work published 1940).

Lewicki, P. (1986). *Non-conscious social information processing*. San Diego, CA: Academic Press.

Lewicki, P., & Hill, T. (1989). On the studies of unconscious processes in human cognition: Comments on Reber. *Journal of Experimental Psychology: General, 118,* 239–241.

Weiss, J. (1952). Crying at the Happy Ending. *Psychoanalytic Review, 39,* 338.

Weiss, J. (1993). *How psychotherapy works*. New York: Guilford Press.

Weiss, J. (1998). Beating fantasies and bondage fantasies. *The Psychoanalytic Quarterly, 67,* 626–644.

Weiss, J., Sampson, H., & The Mount Zion Psychotherapy Research Group. (Eds.). (1986). *The psychoanalytic process: Theory, clinical observation, and empirical research*. New York: Guilford.

4

THE ROLE OF UNCONSCIOUS GUILT IN PSYCHOPATHOLOGY AND IN PSYCHOTHERAPY

Marshall Bush

This chapter presents an interrelated set of ideas about the role of unconscious guilt as a root cause of psychopathology and a key factor in understanding the therapeutic process. Special attention will be given to (a) the relation of unconscious guilt to irrational unconscious beliefs about how one has harmed significant others and deserves to be punished, (b) the patient's own unconscious efforts to master problems with guilt in psychotherapy, and (c) the ways in which the therapist can best assist the patient in those efforts. Because unconscious guilt manifests itself in such disguised, unexpected, and diverse forms, its significance as a determinant of psychopathology and its role in the therapeutic process is often misunderstood, underestimated, or overlooked. Control-mastery theory posits that unconscious guilt develops out of the child's attachments to family members, that it is an extremely powerful force in human development and behavior, that it plays a prominent role in most forms of psychopathology, and that it is capable of producing tormenting and far-reaching inhibitions, symptoms, affects, and maladaptive character traits (Weiss, 1986, 1993).

DEVELOPMENTS IN ACADEMIC PSYCHOLOGY

Before going on to present Weiss's theory of unconscious guilt, I want to refer briefly to an emerging literature in academic psychology on the salutary functions of guilt. At the same time Weiss was developing his views about the origins and pathogenic consequences of irrational guilt, Hoffman (1982) was developing a related approach to understanding the origins and beneficial functions of conscious guilt. Hoffman's (1982, 1998, 2000, 2001) and Zahn-Waxler's (Zahn-Waxler, Radke-Yarrow, & King, 1979; Zahn-Waxler & Kochanska, 1990; Zahn-Waxler, Kochanska, Krupnick, & McKnew, 1990; Zahn-Waxler & Robinson, 1995) pioneering studies ushered in a renewed academic interest in guilt as an adaptive interpersonal emotion (Barrett, 1995, 1998; Baumeister, Stillwell, & Heatherton, 1994, 1995; Bohart & Stipek, 2001; Bybee, Merisca, & Velasco, 1998; Bybee & Quiles, 1998; Donenberg & Weisz, 1998; Estrada-Hollenbeck & Heatherton, 1998; Exline & Lobel, 1999; Ferguson & Stegge, 1995, 1998; Fischer & Tangney, 1995; Jones, Kugler, & Adams, 1995; Lindsay-Hartz, De Rivera, & Mascolo, 1995; Mascolo & Fischer, 1995; Tangney, 1998, 2001; Tangney, Burggraf, & Wagner, 1995; Zahn-Waxler & Robinson, 1995). These authors consider conscious guilt to be an exemplar of a pro-social emotion because (a) it is rooted in empathic distress for another's suffering and feelings of responsibility for having caused that suffering, and (b) it inhibits aggression and promotes reparative behaviors that restore communal bonds. Bybee and Quiles (1998) offered the following assessment of the adaptive virtues of guilt:

> Guilt is good: It permits individuals to live and function freely in the absence of a police state, it encourages individuals to foment close communal relationships and to behave altruistically, and it gives rise to motivated and goal-directed behavior. By providing punishment from within, punishment from without becomes less necessary. When guilt is absent, aggression, acting out, and even sociopathy may ensue. (p. 287)

Although conscious feelings of guilt may indeed inhibit aggression, one important limitation of this literature is that it does not recognize the role unconscious guilt can play in contributing to aggression and antisocial behavior. For instance, some children who are inappropriately aggressive and lacking in empathy may consciously appear to be devoid of guilt while unconsciously being dominated by guilt-based loyalties to abusive parents. People are usually unaware of how they defend themselves against their guilt or when they are suffering from its consequences.

The relationship between conscious and unconscious guilt is a largely unexplored topic. Harder (1995) observed that attempts to measure shame and guilt assume a high degree of correspondence between conscious and unconscious affects, although "there is no independent way to verify this belief" (p. 375). It is reasonable to assume that individuals who suffer from elevated levels of conscious guilt also suffer from a high degree of unconscious guilt. However, the reverse may not be true. Certain people with high levels of unconscious guilt may develop strong defenses to protect themselves from experiencing it consciously. Therefore, one cannot safely infer from a low score on a "conscious" guilt scale that someone either lacks guilt or does not suffer from its effects.

When guilt becomes overly intense, it may threaten to derail a child's normal development. If it cannot be alleviated through taking some reparative action, it is typically repressed or defended against in some other way. Some commonly recognized defenses for dealing with both conscious and unconscious guilt involve denying responsibility for having caused harm; blaming, derogating, or avoiding the victim; engaging in self-destructive actions; developing an exaggerated sense of entitlement; or taking care of others in a self-sacrificing way (Baumeister et al., 1994; Bybee et al., 1998; Exline & Lobel, 1999; Hoffman, 1982, 2001). Unrelieved guilt is not only intensely distressing but it is also dangerous because it produces a need to incur punishment and makes one vulnerable to being exploited by others.

Individuals suffering from intense guilt who are unable to or are prevented from making amends may resort to desperate measures in their efforts at restitution. Unconscious efforts at restitution are often based on magical ideas according to which the suffering of another person can be redressed by submitting to the injured person's wishes or by taking an analogous form of suffering upon oneself. In extreme instances, people may be driven to suicide or to such exaggerated degrees of submissiveness and compliance that they sacrifice their individuality and basic sense of self.

A CLINICALLY USEFUL MODEL OF UNCONSCIOUS GUILT

This chapter presents the control-mastery model of guilt, describes the origins of unconscious guilt, and presents a detailed clinical example illustrating my ideas. The conceptualization of guilt that I shall present is based on the most clinically helpful approach to treating patients, according to control-mastery theory. Guilt is a complex and distressing emotion that has multiple determinants and exists in a variety of forms. It can be chronic or transitory, as well as conscious or unconscious. It overlaps with and often contributes to the experience of shame, even though guilt and shame have observably different behavioral correlates. Because shame is such a painful affect, it is often unconsciously evoked as a punishment in order to relieve guilt. Feelings of guilt and shame may also serve the purpose of preserving one's unconscious attachments to blaming or shaming (or guilt- or shame-ridden) parents. According to Weiss (1993), shame "is almost always held in place either by guilt or by the wish to maintain ties to parents" (p. 44).

Control-mastery theory, like several other research-based developmental theories (Ferguson & Stegge, 1998; Hoffman, 2000; Mascolo & Fischer, 1995; Zahn-Waxler & Kochanska, 1990), sees guilt as emanating from the child's feelings of empathy and concern for family members. Freud (1930/1961) understood the formation and functioning of guilt (i.e., the superego) in terms of an internalized fear of parental punishment that becomes infused with the child's own aggression. However, we believe that the most debilitating types of guilt stem from children's irrational feelings of responsibility for the well-being and misfortunes of their parents and siblings. Unconscious guilt, according to the control-mastery theory, arises from unconscious irrational beliefs about how one has harmed or been disloyal to someone for whom one feels a strong bond of affection and sense of responsibility, such as a parent, sibling, or child. Such beliefs may be formed outside of a conscious awareness in early childhood or may be conscious initially but subsequently repressed.

Freud recognized the importance of the guilt that comes from feeling one has harmed another person, and especially a primary love object, such as a parent or other family member. However, he considered this type of guilt to be secondarily derived from the child's more basic fear of punishment or loss of love. According to the control-mastery theory, what often *appears* to be a fear of punishment may represent an unconscious attempt to restore a weak and vulnerable parent. When children comply with and internalize their parents' prohibitions and values, they may unconsciously be motivated less by a fear of punishment or loss of love than by a fear of their power to hurt their parents and lose them as attachment figures.

Although fear of punishment may create anxiety, it does not necessarily lead to unconscious guilt, and it is not the most significant motive in superego formation. The threat of punishment or actual punishment is much more likely to create unconscious guilt when children take the punishment as an indication that they have hurt a parent and jeopardized their relationship with him or her. Although many patients begin therapy with fearful memories of a punitive parent, these memories may screen deeply repressed guilt-laden memories of that same parent seeming very pathetic, vulnerable, or impaired.

As childhood family relationships become internalized, the attachment figures people unconsciously try to protect are representations rather than the actual people in the child's life. Children may permanently adhere to their parents' values and internalize their parents' condemnations, no matter how objectionable and injurious they find them to be, because the idea of rejecting those values and judgments creates intolerable feelings of guilt, disloyalty, aloneness, or insecurity. Because attachment figures provide the child with a basic feeling of security (Bowlby, 1988), the prospect of losing one's unconscious emotional bonds to important attachment figures increases one's sense of vulnerability and loneliness. Fear of hurting one's parents or losing them as internal attachment figures remains a powerful motive for complying with parental values and identifying with parental traits throughout the life cycle. Children may develop highly antisocial character traits out of a strong sense of unconscious loyalty to psychopathic parents.

A mutually reinforcing relationship exists between unconscious guilt and the degree of responsibility one feels for other people's welfare. Children who feel highly responsible for the well-being of other family members tend to develop unconscious guilt about the misfortunes and problems of their parents and siblings. Conversely, the more guilt a child has developed in relation to other family members, the more that child will tend to feel responsible for and obligated to those individuals. We therefore expect that the intensity of one's unconscious guilt will be positively related to how excessively responsible one feels for other people's welfare, how overly powerful one feels in terms of being able to cause other people's happiness or unhappiness, and how much blame one has assumed for contributing to the problems and suffering of other family members.

Searles (1958, 1975) based his explanation of the etiology of psychosis and other severe psychopathologies on the principle that prepsychotic children sacrifice their individuality in an effort to restore their damaged mothers. Although Searles does not necessarily assume that the child feels responsible for having caused the mother's suffering and impairments, he believes that the child feels deeply responsible for curing the mother and consequently suffers from "unconscious, lifelong guilt at having failed in his therapeutic effort, begun very early in life, to enable his ego-fragmented mother to become a whole and fulfilled mother to him"(1975, p. 99). He also notes that the child believes that separating from his mother would be very damaging to him and therefore "he cannot bear to grow out of the relationship and leave her there, tragically crippled ... "(1958, p. 575). In other words, the idea of separating from the mother makes the child feel intolerably guilty not because the child wishes to hurt her, but because the child loves her, feels sorry for her, and does not want to hurt her. According to Searles, these children identify with their mothers' deficiencies in an effort to rescue her by taking her difficulties and suffering themselves.

THE ORIGINS OF UNCONSCIOUS GUILT[1]

Our view of how guilt originates is based on Freud's (1926/1961) theory of signal anxiety. According to Freud, the primary function of anxiety is to remove an individual from an unconsciously perceived situation of danger. A child develops beliefs about situations of danger from previously experienced traumatic situations that are unconsciously remembered. On the basis of those beliefs, children institute defenses and develop symptoms and inhibitions in order to remove themselves from situations of danger and thereby prevent the recurrence of previously experienced traumas. Just as anxiety is a primary reaction to being traumatized, guilt may be considered a primary reaction to believing that one has traumatized a significant other. Following the analogy with the signal theory of anxiety, "signal guilt" (see also Baumeister, 1998; Hoffman, 1982, 1998; 2000; Zahn-Waxler & Kochanska, 1990) would be an anticipatory warning reaction to a perception that one is in danger of hurting someone else, and it would serve the function of initiating corrective action or defensive activity to avoid that danger. Thus, people tend to develop conscious feelings of guilt and anxiety when they are worried about their power to hurt significant others if they pursue a contemplated course of action. It is not a person's wishes that cause guilt reactions but the potentially harmful consequences for someone else should those wishes be pursued.

Irrational guilt stems from the fact that children (as well as adults) often make false causal connections between their own behavior and the harmful things that happen to themselves and others. Children are prone to developing distorted ideas about how their behavior has hurt or may hurt others for a variety of reasons. Young children tend to be egocentric, omnipotent, and magical in their thinking. Because of the child's limited understanding of accurate causal relationships and the immature nature of childhood cognition, children are inclined to blame themselves for their parents' and siblings' problems, misfortunes, and unhappiness (Donenberg & Weisz, 1998; Hoffman, 1982; Zahn-Waxler & Robinson, 1995). They may respond to parental suffering by assuming they have done something to injure the parent or that they have failed in their responsibility to make their parents happy. This tendency will be further intensified if parents falsely blame children for things that they did not cause or hold a child responsible for their (parent's) state of mind.

Children tend to blame themselves for any mistreatment they experience at the hands of their parents for a very important reason. Children need to love, trust, and depend on their parents, and to feel loved and protected by them. It is therefore very difficult for them to attribute malevolent motives to their parents (Berliner, 1940, 1947). Young children also rely on their parents to help them interpret inner and outer reality. When they are mistreated or falsely accused of harboring destructive intentions, they will tend to accept their parents' interpretations and believe they must have done something bad to deserve their mistreatment. Children do not realize that parents may irrationally condemn, punish, reject, abuse, or neglect them because of the parent's own psychopathology. Moreover, their efforts to protest against parental mistreatment are often met with such hurt or angry responses that they become even further convinced of their own wrongdoing.

Children develop their own theories about how their behavior has been or may be hurtful to their parents and siblings from a variety of sources. They observe what seems to hurt their parents and siblings in their interactions with each other and with people outside the family. Children pay close attention to those things their parents or siblings do that hurt them, and they take special notice of how their parents and siblings react to different kinds of behavior on their part. In developing their beliefs about how they affect others, children are guided not only by what their parents say but even more importantly by what they do. For example, if a parent becomes withdrawn, assaultive, or rejecting whenever the child gets close to someone else, the child may infer that developing other relationships is very hurtful to that parent, despite the fact that the parent may reproach the child for being too clingy or not having friends.

Because of their intense need and desire to maintain good relations with their parents, children will condemn as bad any behavior or motive that they believe might harm another family member. In this manner, children often develop guilt about not only morally reprehensible impulses but also about healthy developmental strivings, such as strivings towards autonomy, responsibility, mutuality, intimacy, success, sexual satisfaction, or happiness. Modell (1965, 1971), Asch (1976), Weiss (1986, 1993), and Friedman (1985) have all written about the phenomenon of separation guilt and its role in psychopathology. Sprince (1971) discussed the psychoanalytic treatment of a severely regressed adolescent boy who suffered from intense guilt and anxiety about his strivings towards independence and masculinity. She found that the patient's pathology "hinged upon his unconscious conviction that his mother's health and sanity depended upon his remaining a sick and helpless failure" (p. 455). It took several years of therapeutic work to uncover the patient's unconscious belief that his mother could not bear to watch him develop physically and mentally while she was aging and daily losing these very qualities. He also believed she might commit suicide if he did not constantly demonstrate he was tied to her apron strings. Loewald (1979) similarly described the guilt children may experience in attempting to separate from their parents:

> In an important sense, by evolving our own autonomy ... we are killing our parents. We are usurping their power, their competence, their responsibility for us .... In short, we destroy them in regard to some of their qualities hitherto most vital to us. Parents resist as well as promote such destruction no less ambivalently than children carry it out. (p. 758)

No sharp dividing line exists between rational and irrational guilt. One easily blends into the other. The psychologically stronger and more fortunate one's parents and siblings are, the less justification will a child have to make for experiencing what Hoffman (2000) has referred to as "development guilt" (i.e., guilt over growing up).

THE ROLE OF TRAUMA IN THE ORIGINS OF UNCONSCIOUS GUILT

Because of children's propensity for assuming responsibility for anything bad that happens to them or to other family members, the traumatic aspects of early childhood are an especially potent source of unconscious guilt. In this discussion, I use the term "trauma" broadly to include any experience that is detrimental to normal development or is injurious to the individual (Greenacre, 1967, p. 277). In the absence of mitigating factors, those individuals who have had the most traumatic life histories will also tend to have the most severe problems with unconscious guilt and more serious emotional disturbances.

Beres (1958) studied the reaction of children to being separated from their parents and placed in a residential facility. His work provides an important clinical illustration of how children may develop guilt as a result of traumatic experiences:

> Our observations indicate the extraordinary readiness of the child to interpret the experience of separation as an expression of hostility on the part of the parent, and to assume that this action was justified by the child's wrongdoing. The child identifies with the hostile rejecting parent, an example of identification with the aggressor, accepts the fantasy of a crime that deserves punishment, and assumes the guilt which such an act requires. (p. 348)

Traumas that befall oneself, especially those stemming from parental mistreatment and neglect, tend to produce very deepseated unconscious convictions that one is unworthy and deserving of punishment. This type of belief is illustrated by Berliner's (1940) description of masochistic personalities: "There is a deep conviction in the masochist that he is not supposed to be loved and to be happy but that he has to meet the desires of those who hate him, to whom his existence or his happiness is unwanted"(p. 327). Steele (1984) found that individuals who were abused and neglected as children grew up believing that they did not deserve to experience pleasure or to have happy lives. As adults, they could not enjoy themselves, their spouses, or their children.

Traumatic experiences that befall other family members can become a crippling source of unconscious guilt because children often assume that they deserve the same fate or that their preferential treatment (by fate or their parents) contributed to the suffering of the victim. This type of "survivor guilt" has been discussed by Neiderland (1961, 1981), Modell, (1965, 1971), Weiss (1986), and Friedman (1985). Modell (1971) observed that survivor guilt is often based on an unconscious belief that the good things in life come in a fixed quantity and that whatever success and happiness a person experiences diminishes the amount available to other family members:

> There is, I believe, in mental life something that might be termed an unconscious bookkeeping system, i.e., a system that takes account of the distribution of the available "good" within a given nuclear family so that the current fate of other family members will determine how much "good" one possesses. If fate has dealt harshly with other members of the family, the survivor may experience guilt, as he has obtained more than his share of the "good." (p. 340)

O'Connor (2000) described the evolutionary basis for survivor guilt in terms of its survival value for *Homo sapiens*. She noted that survivor guilt presumes an innate capacity to make social comparisons and to evaluate inequity in social exchanges (an evolutionary perspective on Modell's unconscious bookkeeping system). Separation and survivor guilt have also become the subject of empirical research and theorizing in academic psychology (Baumeister et al., 1994; Exline & Lobel, 1999; Hoffman, 1982, 1998, 2000; Lindsay-Hartz et al., 1995; O'Connor, Berry, Weiss, Bush, & Sampson, 1997; O'Connor, Berry, & Weiss, 1999; Zahn-Waxler & Kochanska, 1990).

Survivor guilt may lead to a variety of masochistic behaviors that primarily serve the function of redressing the imbalance perceived to exist between one's own fate and that of less fortunate family members. Weiss (1986) proposed that most inhibitions and symptoms represent either compliances or identifications with other family members towards whom one unconsciously feels guilty and attached. Pathological compliances are typically self-tormenting or self-destructive behaviors that are unconsciously intended to placate the other person, whereas pathological identifications are imitations of pathological behavior patterns exhibited by the person. For example, a very cultured person may develop slovenly personal habits out of an unconscious identification with an alcoholic father and be unusually passive in his love relationships as a compliance to a domineering mother. Symptoms may also represent mixtures of compliance and identification. One unconscious purpose of these compliances and identifications is to reduce guilt through a visibly self-sacrificial restoration of loyalty to an injured parent or sibling.

Although my focus here has been on the pathological consequences of childhood trauma, it should be noted that massive trauma can have the same pathogenic effects at any point in the life cycle, as shown by Neiderland's (1961, 1981) study of concentration camp survivors. In the following clinical illustration, the patient's primary traumas occurred during both his childhood and his late adolescent years.

CLINICAL ILLUSTRATION: MR. S.

The following case is intended to illustrate the role of guilt-based identifications and compliances in the psychopathology of a young man who suffered from intense separation and survivor guilt.

Mr. S. sought treatment because he was doing very poorly in graduate school. He felt profoundly discouraged, humiliated, undeserving, and paralyzed. He was a handsome and athletic young man who had dropped out of one professional training program and was about to flunk out of another. His manner was flat and lifeless. He did things in a mechanical and joyless way and led a very constricted and solitary life, even though his history suggested he had good social skills and a prior capacity to develop and maintain close relationships. Mr. S. claimed he had no motivation to study and that his attitude toward his future was one of futility and pessimism. He was unable to compete with other students and was devoid of any ambition to do well or be successful. He expected to die at an early age and was in fact neglecting some serious health problems.

He believed that if he were to let himself get very engrossed in studying he would lose touch with reality. He reported that his mind was not working well and that he had trouble thinking. Despite his marked dissatisfaction with his life, the patient displayed no motivation to work on any problems in therapy. In his sessions, he was usually listless, taciturn, and generally unresponsive to therapeutic interventions.

The family history suggested, and later material subsequently confirmed, that Mr. S. was suffering from severe unconscious separation guilt and survivor guilt, both of which had begun during his childhood but were massively intensified during his adolescence when a series of traumatic events befell other family members. At the outset of the therapy, the patient had absolutely no awareness he was suffering from intense unconscious guilt. He connected his conscious guilt feelings to the fact that he was doing poorly in school and therefore did not deserve to be there.

Mr. S. was the middle and only male child of a family with three children. His father, who died of mysterious causes 6 years before the patient began therapy, had been a very driving, prominent, and successful professional in the community. His mother, while well educated and intelligent, had built her life entirely around her role as a wife.

Mr. S. described her as dutiful, efficient, overcontrolled, unemotional, unaffectionate, and psychologically opaque in the sense that he could never tell how she felt about anything. She tended to be secretive and did not share personal things with him. His father, by contrast, had a strong and outgoing personality. He was moralistic, opinionated, and domineering. He took an active interest in his only son and made time to do special things with him but not with the patient's sisters. Mr. S. felt his sisters and mother were envious of the time his father spent with him. Unconsciously, Mr. S. believed that he took his father's love and attention away from his sisters, towards whom his father was intolerant and critical.

When the patient was 8 years old, his father had an unsuccessful operation for a dangerous medical illness that left him in acute and chronic pain. The father kept not only his pain secret from the children and the rest of the community, but also the fact that he had become severely addicted to a narcotic used to control the pain. His father remained addicted for the next 10 years while his mother became totally absorbed in taking care of his father and keeping his secrets.

Beginning in Mr. S.'s early adolescence, his father developed another increasingly debilitating, painful, and progressive illness. The once powerful, vigorous, proud, and confident man gradually became more and more depressed over a period of several years and eventually died of a suspected suicide. During this same period, while his father was slowly deteriorating, both his sisters had psychotic breaks and were unable able to complete college or pursue professional training. His younger sister recovered, but his older sister did not. At the time of his father's death, the patient was abroad on a special study program during his senior year of college. The father's real illness had been kept hidden from the children and the rest of the community so that the patient did not understand the realistic basis for his father's increasing withdrawal, anguish, and despair. Consequently, he assumed it was somehow related to his absence.

Mr. S. felt very guilty for being gone during the father's last months. It was the first time the patient had lived away from home. He was relieved to be removed from the grim family atmosphere, although he also felt he was being disloyal to his family by not sharing in their suffering. When Mr. S. was in his final year of high school, he expressed an interest in applying to Harvard upon the suggestion of a teacher. His father opposed his going away to college on the grounds that he could not afford to do the same for his sisters, even though neither of them were interested in going away to college. The patient had opportunities to get scholarships because of his excellent academic record but did not pursue them out of an unconscious compliance with what he perceived to be his father's unspoken wishes. Mr. S. unconsciously concluded that his father could not bear the separation involved in his son leaving home and did not like the idea of him being so ambitious while he himself was desperately struggling to hang on to his waning professional capacities. The patient also inferred that his father believed it was unfair for Mr. S. to have opportunities that would not be available to his sisters. He subsequently lowered his career ambitions as well as his academic performance level.

The patient's mother became even more grim and joyless after the father's death. She stopped having any social life and became morbidly preoccupied with other people's illnesses and suffering. Mr. S. invariably got depressed whenever he talked to his mother or visited her. She often expressed to her son a wish that he would return home, and Mr. S. was convinced that she wanted him to become her companion and replacement for his dead father.

Mr. S. became increasingly symptomatic during the years following his father's death. He unconsciously developed the belief that his development and limited successes had contributed to his father's decline. To punish himself and atone for the damage he imagined he caused his father, the patient took on his parents' suffering. In his depression and sense of futility, he was living out an unconscious identification with his failing father and his depressed mother. The patient was slowly psychologically deteriorating just as his father had deteriorated and was expecting to die at an early age just as his father had.

The patient's cognitive impairments reflected an unconscious identification with his older sister who continued to have psychotic decompensations and was never able to resume a normal life. He felt intensely guilty towards her because she had been the child who was treated the most harshly by the father, whereas the patient received the most favorable treatment. He unconsciously believed he had displaced his sister in his father's affection and thereby caused her psychological problems. She originally had been the most academically successful of the three children and was considered the most intelligent. His fear of losing contact with reality if he concentrated hard while studying reflected an unconscious punishment fantasy based on his guilt toward his sister. If he tried to succeed where she had failed, he too would become psychotic. The patient had such intense guilt about being better off than his sister that when he took himself on a very modest vacation after a few years of therapy, he ended up feeling tormented and full of self-reproach for having spent $15 on a nice dinner while his sister was living on welfare.

Mr. S.'s flat and lifeless way of relating to me not only represented an unconscious identification with his dead father but it also represented an unconscious identification with his mother that had complicated roots going back to early childhood. As a young child, he suffered from a physical handicap that required a great deal of time-consuming care from his mother. He inferred from her joyless and impersonal manner that she secretly resented having such a burdensome child, although he simultaneously felt she also had a special investment in his being defective and remaining dependent on her.

Even more significantly, he experienced his mother's coldness as a retaliatory rejection stemming from her feeling rejected by him. He imagined that she resented his closeness to his father and to other people, as well as his ability to have fun and enjoy himself while she could not. Even in recent years, his mother would express hurt feelings if she were not invited to the social events the patient attended, such as his friends' weddings. He felt that she responded to anything positive he told her about his own life by acting covertly resentful and by attempting to depress him by dwelling on her own unhappiness and on other people's tragedies. He complied with what he perceived to be her wish that he not enjoy his life away from home by making his professional training program into a joyless ordeal.

He unconsciously believed his mother's isolation and loneliness were the result of his refusal to move home and take care of her. He punished himself for abandoning his mother by becoming like her and creating a very isolated, lonely, and asexual existence. He was unresponsive to other people's friendly overtures and could take no initiative to develop a sexual relationship with a woman, even though he longed to have a girlfriend and did not lack for opportunities.

His guilt about neglecting his mother was so intense that when he made a trip home to attend his high school reunion and see old friends, he ended up spending all his time entertaining her. Instead of going to his reunion, he took his mother to a movie and then on an overnight outing. Despite his mother's words to the contrary, Mr. S. unconsciously believed that she wanted him to abandon his attempts to develop a career and a life of his own so that he could devote himself to caring for her.

THE ROLE OF UNCONSCIOUS GUILT IN THE THERAPEUTIC PROCESS

The following section illustrates the varied roles of unconscious guilt in psychotherapy. Unconscious guilt can be a source of transference or resistance as well as a source of tests carried out by the patient.

Guilt as a Source of Transference

Any kind of unconscious guilt is likely to become a source of transference in therapy. Patients worry about hurting their therapists in the same ways they worried about hurting their parents and siblings. They often try to protect and bolster the therapist by developing dependent, idealizing, or sexual transferences. Patients are typically relieved when their need to protect the therapist is interpreted because such interpretations both recognize the patient's strength and imply that the therapist does not need to be protected in that way.

The patient I described previously, Mr. S., often attempted to restore me by coming into his sessions depressed, particularly after he previously had been feeling good. As he got closer to my office, he would start to "shut down" (his expression). He would lose the pleasant feelings he had had a short while before, start to feel sleepy and lethargic, become flat and lifeless, and find himself unable to talk, particularly about anything positive. It eventually became clear that Mr. S. was responding to an unconscious conviction that I would be deeply hurt by any expression of ambition, vitality, or happiness on his part. In the father transference, he experienced me as attempting to conceal from him my slow deterioration. He believed his progress in therapy was going to be at my expense and that any display of vigor or ambition would be a painful reminder to me of my declining abilities. In the mother transference, he imagined that I resented his independence and envied his capacity to experience pleasure in ways I could not. He gave up his positive feelings before coming to his session partially as a compliance with what he perceived to be my wish that he be as joyless, drab, and grim as I was. Mr. S. usually felt relieved when I told him he was afraid I would find it disturbing for him to be energetic or in good spirits.

Other patients may be afraid that they will make their therapists feel inadequate if they show their intelligence or competence. I once had a patient who promptly forgot whatever she read because she was afraid she would make her brother look stupid (her parents called him an idiot) or her father feel less than brilliant. When she began therapy, she told me her father was the most intelligent man she had ever met, although nothing could have been further from the truth. It was initially inconceivable to her that she was trying to shield me from her intelligence. Another patient, who could not let himself succeed in anything, acted very confused, cynical, and hopeless in order to protect a schizoid father who was chronically depressed, bitter, and thought-disordered. Some patients act very insecure in an attempt to make their therapists feel self-confident, whereas others act weak in an attempt to make their therapists feel strong.

Guilt as a Source of Resistance

Guilt has been widely recognized as a potential obstacle to a cure in the psychoanalytic literature. Patients with intense unconscious guilt may feel that they do not deserve to get help in overcoming their problems. In his later writings, Freud (1923/1961, 1926/1961, 1930/1961, 1933/1961) gave increasing emphasis to the importance of unconscious guilt in psychopathology and considered it a potent resistance that could lead to a negative therapeutic reaction. He found that patients who displayed such a reaction were unable to experience pleasure, had a strong need for punishment, and persistently clung to their suffering. Treatment and recovery increased their sense of guilt, whereas illness appeased their need for punishment:

> In the end we come to see that we are dealing with what may be called a "moral" factor, a sense of guilt, which is finding its satisfaction in the illness and refuses to give up the punishment of suffering. We shall be right in regarding this disheartening explanation as final. But as far as the patient is concerned this sense of guilt is dumb; it does not tell him he is guilty; he does not feel guilty, he feels ill. This sense of guilt expresses itself only as a resistance to recovery which it is extremely difficult to overcome. It is also particularly difficult to convince the patient that this motive lies behind his continuing to be ill .... (Freud, 1923/1961, pp. 49–50)

Most discussions of the role of unconscious guilt in psychotherapy have focused on its contribution to the negative therapeutic reaction. Modell (1971) found that survivor guilt may be a powerful resistance to recovery and an important factor in negative therapeutic reactions (see also Model, 1965):

I have come to believe that the content of the guilt that underlies the negative therapeutic reaction frequently relates to the conviction that one does not have a right to the better life that would be the consequence of a successful psychoanalysis. Further, that the acquisition of something "good" from the treatment means that they will have more and that others will be depleted. (p. 339)

Searles (1958) encountered a similar type of resistance to recovery in psychiatric patients who were receiving intensive treatment in an inpatient setting. He noted that as patients began to feel better and were approaching discharge from the hospital they found it very painful leaving other sick patients, and often even the therapist, behind.

Guilt as a Source of Testing

The concept of testing has already been described in chapter 1, so it will not be repeated here. Patients continually pose tests in their efforts to master problems with unconscious guilt. The two main ways in which patients work to master their problems with guilt are by posing passive-into-active tests that allow them to identify with their therapists' capacity to not become guilty about things that make the patients feel irrationally guilty (see pages 12–17), or by posing transference tests that enable the therapist to counter the pathogenic beliefs that give rise to the patients' irrational guilt. Some common types of transference tests involve efforts to acquire an understanding of one's unconscious guilt, obtain permission to pursue reasonable goals forbidden by unconscious guilt toward other family members, or obtain protection from the harshness of one's superego.

Patients with punitive superegos will try to internalize their therapist's ability to protect them from undeserved self-punishment and self-blame. Such patients may propose doing something dangerous in the hope that their therapist will try to stop them. They may falsely accuse themselves of harboring shameful impulses or immoral motives and wait to see if the therapist agrees with or challenges their false self-accusations. Patients in self-sacrificing or self-destructive relationships may seek permission to leave the relationship without having to torment themselves with self-punishing worries and feelings. Patients commonly need help with their guilt about setting limits with abusive or exploitative partners, parents, or siblings.

Patients who harbor secret ambitions may drop hints in the hope that the therapist will give them permission to pursue a forbidden goal. I once had a patient subtly imply that she secretly wished to become a doctor. When I asked her why she had not applied to medical school, she responded with relief and immediately began requesting applications. Patients with severe separation guilt may need to repeatedly propose stopping or actually stop therapy for periods of time to prove to themselves that their wish to separate does not damage the therapist or elicit moral condemnation. In all these scenarios, patients are testing to see if the therapist will help disconfirm the pathogenic beliefs underlying their guilt.

In terms of passive-into-active testing, some patients try to master their problems by doing to the therapist what their parents did to them, thus leading to feelings of guilt. This may take the form of overtly blaming the therapist for harming or failing to help the patient, or it may take the form of quietly suffering in the presence of the therapist to see whether he or she will feel omnipotently responsible for relieving the patient's unhappiness in the way the patient felt responsible for relieving his or her parents' unhappiness. Mr. S.'s lifeless manner was not only a guilt-based transference reaction to me but it was also a form of passive-into-active testing through which he hoped to identify with my capacity to not feel guilty about being alive in opposition to his lifeless behavior. My retaining an optimistic attitude and lively manner helped Mr. S. feel entitled to become more energetic himself.

THE INTERPRETATION OF GUILT IN PSYCHOTHERAPY[2]

Almost all patients rely on their therapists to help them manage their guilt, even when they are unaware of its sources or even its existence. Sometimes patients need the therapist to take responsibility for their pursuit of normal developmental goals that make them feel unconsciously guilty, such as completing their education, pursuing career goals, getting married, or having children. At other times patients may need help in anticipating how guilty they are likely to feel if they take a certain action, such as divorcing a disturbed spouse. All patients want their therapists to protect them from doing something that would cause them to become overwhelmed with guilt. At certain moments, patients may even need their therapist to help them deny responsibility for something harmful they have actually done in order to keep them from becoming suicidal.

Freud (1923/1961, 1924/1961, 1933/1961) repeatedly noted that patients have difficulty in accepting and believing guilt interpretations. He suggested that in order for therapists to make guilt interpretations at all comprehensible to patients, they should instead interpret the patient's need for punishment:

> Our patients do not believe us when we attribute an "unconscious sense of guilt" to them. In order to make ourselves at all intelligible to them, we tell them of an unconscious need for punishment, in which the sense of guilt finds expression. (1933/1961, p. 135)

The reasons why some patients have difficulty believing guilt interpretations are varied and often quite complicated. Patients may resist guilt interpretations because they feel too endangered by the potential consequences of having some aspect of their unconscious guilt made conscious. They may unconsciously decide that becoming more aware of their guilt would be too painful or might place them in jeopardy, either in terms of feeling tempted to do something self-destructive or in terms of feeling less able to defend themselves against some feared exploitation by the therapist. They may also resist guilt interpretations because they unconsciously experience them as accusations that they have reason to feel guilty. One patient I treated many years ago was very disturbed by my guilt interpretations because she saw her disturbed mother as a very guilty woman and had resolved as a child that she would never be like her.

To be helpful, guilt interpretations must be timely and accurate. If a man is told he is struggling with unconscious guilt over his wish to leave his girlfriend when he is actually struggling with unconscious guilt over his wish to marry her, he may assume the therapist does not want him to have a successful love relationship. Highly inaccurate guilt interpretations may be very disturbing or destructive to a patient. If someone is told they are depressed because they feel guilty about their hostile impulses towards a dying family member when they actually feel guilty about surviving someone they love, they are likely to become more guilty and symptomatic.

Patients unconsciously attribute unspoken motives to any interpretation a therapist makes, and this is particularly true of guilt interpretations. The validity and therapeutic usefulness of a guilt interpretation, as with any other type of interpretation, should be judged by the actual effect the interpretation has on the patient's subsequent behavior rather than by the patient's immediate agreement or disagreement. Guilt interpretations are most effective when they are accurate, when they pass the patient's immediate tests, when they support the patient's goals, and when the therapist uses the full force of his authority in making them.

Some patients initially find even accurate guilt interpretations disturbing and may not benefit from them early in therapy, although at a later point they may welcome and utilize them. One patient, who was very afraid of her need to comply with other people's wishes, considered guilt interpretations to be my way of trying to manipulate her into complying with my agenda. After three years of proving to herself that she could resist any effort on my part to control her, she became able to derive great benefit from my interpretations of her unconscious guilt toward a disturbed boyfriend and was able to extricate herself from a dangerous relationship. Other patients are immediately helped by guilt interpretations, even though they may dismiss or ridicule them. I once had a patient scoff at a guilt interpretation I made in the first hour, only to return in much better spirits for the second session. Patients in crisis often derive dramatic benefits from an accurate analysis of the role their unconscious guilt is playing in the crisis situation.

It has been my general experience that most patients derive a considerable benefit from accurate interpretations of their unconscious guilt problems. One of the important technical implications of control-mastery theory is that guilt should generally be analyzed in terms of the unconscious beliefs from which it stems, the genetic origin of those beliefs, and the role those beliefs and the patient's guilt have in producing self-destructive and self-sacrificial behavior patterns.

Patients with severe guilt problems are often unable to defend themselves against their harsh superegos. To successfully treat such problems, the therapist should use the full weight of his or her moral authority to counter the patient's irrational guilt and protect him or her from self-destructive actions. In successful treatments, the therapist's forcefulness in helping the patient combat irrational guilt is internalized by the patient as a support against the cruelty of his or her superego. If a strong emotional bond or attachment to a benevolent and protective therapist can be developed, patients will become stronger in their ability to overcome irrational guilt, and their superegos will become less punitive.

CONCLUDING REMARKS

According to control-mastery theory, patients will derive a great benefit from therapy if therapists actively assist them in mastering problems with guilt by paying careful attention to the role unconscious guilt plays in their psychopathology, testing, and transference reactions. Therapists should help patients understand their unconscious pathogenic beliefs from which guilt stems, the genetic origin of those beliefs, and the role the guilt plays in producing self-destructive behavior patterns.

An often overlooked type of unconscious guilt is the kind that stems from patients' irrational beliefs about their power to hurt others, including the therapist, by pursuing their healthy developmental strivings and life goals. Patients commonly develop regressive, idealizing, and sexual transferences as part of their testing and their efforts to protect and restore their therapists. The difference between a successful and unsuccessful therapeutic outcome may hinge upon the degree to which the therapist passes the patient's tests and accurately analyzes the patient's problems with unconscious guilt.

ENDNOTES

1. Portions of this section are taken from Bush (1989) and are reprinted with permission of the copyright holder.
2. Portions of this section are taken from Bush (1989) and are reprinted with permission of the copyright holder.

REFERENCES

Asch, S. (1976). Varieties of negative therapeutic reaction and problems of technique. *Journal of the American Psychoanalytic Association, 24,* 383–407.

Barrett, K. C. (1995). A functionalist approach to shame and guilt. In J. P. Tangney & K. W. Fischer (Eds.), *Self-conscious emotions: Shame, guilt, embarrassment, and pride* (pp. 25–63). New York: Guilford Press.

Barrett, K. C. (1998). The origins of guilt in early childhood. In J. Bybee (Ed.), *Guilt and Children* (pp. 75–90). London: Academic Press.

Baumeister, R. F. (1998). Inducing guilt. In J. Bybee (Ed.), *Guilt and Children* (pp. 127–138). London: Academic Press.

Baumeister, R. F., Stillwell, A. M., & Heatherton, T. F. (1994). Guilt: An interpersonal approach. *Psychological Bulletin, 115,* 243–267.

Baumeister, R. F., Stillwell, A. M., & Heatherton, T. F. (1995). Interpersonal aspects of guilt: evidence from narrative studies. In J. P. Tangney & K. W. Fischer (Eds.) *Self-conscious emotions: Shame, guilt, embarrassment, and pride* (pp. 255–273). New York: Guilford Press.

Beres, D. (1958). Certain aspects of superego functioning. *Psychoanalytic Study of the Child, 13,* 324–351.

Berliner, B. (1940). Libido and reality in masochism. *Psychoanalytic Quarterly, 9,* 322–333.

Berliner, B. (1947). On some psychodynamics of masochism. *Psychoanalytic Quarterly, 16,* 459–471.

Bohart, A. C., & Stipek, D. J. (2001). What have we learned? In A. C. Bohart & D. J. Stipek (Eds.), *Constructive & destructive behavior* (pp. 367–398). Washington, DC: American Psychological Association.

Bowlby, J. (1988). *A secure base: Parent–child attachment and healthy human development*. London: Routledge.

Bush, M. (1989). The role of unconscious guilt in psychopathology and psychotherapy. *Bulletin of the Menninger Clinic, 53*, 97–107.

Bybee, J., Merisca, R., & Velasco, R. (1998). The development of reactions to guilt-producing events. In J. Bybee (Ed.), *Guilt and children* (pp. 185–213). London: Academic Press.

Bybee, J., & Quiles, Z. N. (1998). Guilt and mental health. In J. Bybee (Ed.), *Guilt and children* (pp. 270–291). London: Academic Press.

Donenberg, G. R., & Weisz, J. R. (1998). Guilt and abnormal aspects of parent–child interactions. In J. Bybee (Ed.), *Guilt and children* (pp. 245–269). London: Academic Press.

Estrada-Hollenbeck, M., & Heatherton, T. F. (1998). Avoiding and alleviating guilt through prosocial behavior. In J. Bybee (Ed.), *Guilt and children* (pp. 215–232). London: Academic Press.

Exline, J. J., & Lobel, M. (1999). The perils of outperformance: Sensitivity about being the target of a threatening upward comparison. *Psychological Bulletin, 125*, 307–337.

Ferguson, T. J., & Stegge, H. (1995). Emotional states and traits in children: The case of guilt and shame. In J. P. Tangney & K. W. Fischer (Eds.), *Self-conscious emotions: Shame, guilt, embarrassment, and pride* (pp. 174–197). New York: Guilford Press.

Ferguson, T. J., & Stegge, H. (1998). Measuring guilt in children: A rose by any other name still has thorns. In J. Bybee (Ed.), *Guilt and children* (pp. 19–74). London: Academic Press.

Fischer, K. W., & Tangney, J. P. (1995). Self-conscious emotions and the affect revolution: Framework and overview. In J. P. Tangney & K. W. Fischer (Eds.), *Self-conscious emotions: Shame, guilt, embarrassment, and pride* (pp. 3–24). New York: Guilford Press.

Freud, S. (1961). The ego and the id. In J. Strachey (Ed. and Trans.), *The standard edition of the complete psychological works of Sigmund Freud* (Vol. 19, pp. 3–66). London: Hogarth Press. (Original work published 1923)

Freud, S. (1961). The economic problem of masochism. In J. Strachey (Ed. and Trans.), *The standard edition of the complete psychological works of Sigmund Freud* (Vol. 19, pp. 155–170). London: Hogarth Press. (Original work published 1924)

Freud, S. (1961). Inhibitions, symptoms and anxiety. In J. Strachey (Ed. and Trans.), *The standard edition of the complete psychological works of Sigmund Freud* (Vol. 20, pp. 75–174). London: Hogarth Press. (Original work published 1926)

Freud, S. (1961). Civilization and its discontents. In J. Strachey (Ed. and Trans.), *The standard edition of the complete psychological works of Sigmund Freud* (Vol. 21, pp. 57–145). London: Hogarth Press. (Original work published 1930)

Freud, S. (1961). New introductory lectures. In J. Strachey (Ed. and Trans.), *The standard edition of the complete psychological works of Sigmund Freud* (Vol. 22, pp. 3–182). London: Hogarth Press. (Original work published 1933)

Friedman, M. (1985). Survivor guilt in the pathogenesis of anorexia nervosa. *Psychiatry, 48*, 25–39.

Greenacre, P. (1971). The influence of infantile trauma on genetic patterns. In *Emotional Growth, Vol. 1*. New York: International Universities Press.

Harder, D. W. (1995). Shame and guilt assessment, and relationships of shame- and guilt-proneness to psychopathology. In J. P. Tangney & K. W. Fischer (Eds.), *Self-conscious emotions: Shame, guilt, embarrassment, and pride* (pp. 368–392). New York: Guilford Press.

Hoffman, M. L. (1982). Development of prosocial motivation: Empathy and guilt. In N. Eisenberg (Ed.), *Development of prosocial behavior* (pp. 281–313). New York: Academic Press.

Hoffman, M. L. (1998). Varieties of empathy-based guilt. In J. Bybee (Ed.), *Guilt and children* (pp. 91–113). London: Academic Press.

Hoffman, M. L. (2000). *Empathy and moral development: Implications for caring and justice.* New York: Cambridge University Press.

Hoffman, M. L. (2001). Toward a comprehensive empathy-based theory of prosocial moral development. In A. C. Bohart & D. J. Stipek (Eds.), *Constructive and destructive behavior* (pp. 61–86). Washington, DC: American Psychological Association.

Jones, W. H., Kugler, K., & Adams, P. (1995). You always hurt the one you love: Guilt and transgressions against relationship partners. In J. P. Tangney & K. W. Fischer (Eds.), *Self-conscious emotions: Shame, guilt, embarrassment, and pride* (pp. 301–321). New York: Guilford Press.

Lindsay-Hartz, J., De Rivera, J., & Mascolo, M. F. (1995). Differentiating guilt and shame and their effects on motivation. In J. P. Tangney & K. W. Fischer (Eds.), *Self-conscious emotions: Shame, guilt, embarrassment, and pride* (pp. 274–300). New York: Guilford Press.

Loewald, H. (1979). The waning of the Oedipus complex. *Journal of the American Psychoanalytic Association, 27,* 751–775.

Mascolo, M. F., & Fischer, K. W. (1995). Developmental transformations in appraisals for pride, shame, and guilt. In J. P. Tangney & K. W. Fischer (Eds.), *Self-conscious emotions: Shame, guilt, embarrassment, and pride* (pp. 64–113). New York: Guilford Press.

Modell, A. (1965). On having a right to a life. *International Journal of Psycho-analysis, 46,* 323–331.

Modell, A. (1971). The origin of certain forms of pre-Oedipal guilt and the implications for a psychoanalytic theory of affects. *International Journal of Psycho-analysis, 52,* 337–346.

Neiderland, W. G. (1961). The problem of the survivor. *Journal of the Hillside Hospital, 10,* 233–247.

Neiderland, W. G. (1981). The survivor syndrome: Further observations and dimensions. *Journal of the American Psychoanalytic Association, 29,* 413–426.

O'Connor, L. E. (2000). Pathogenic beliefs and guilt in human evolution: Implications for psychotherapy. In P. Gilbert & K. G. Bailey (Eds.), *Genes on the couch* (pp. 276–303).

O'Connor, L. D., Berry, J. W., & Weiss, J. (1999). Guilt, shame and psychological problems. *Journal of Social and Clinical Psychology, 18,* 181–203.

O'Connor, L. E., Berry, J. W., Weiss, J., Bush, M., & Sampson, H. (1997). Interpersonal guilt: The development of a new measure. *Journal of Clinical Psychology, 53,* 73–89.

Searles, H. F. (1958). Positive feelings in the relationship between the schizophrenic and his mother. *The International Journal of Psycho-analysis, 39,* 569–586.

Searles, H. F. (1975). The patient as therapist to his analyst. In P. L. Giovacchini (Ed.), *Tactics and techniques in psychoanalytic therapy: Vol. 2, countertransference* (pp. 95–151). New York: Jason Aronson, Inc.

Sprince, M. P. (1971). An adolescent boy's battle against recovery. *The Psychoanalytic Study of the Child, 26,* 453–482.

Steele, B. F. (1984, October 13). *The effect of child abuse and neglect on early psychic development.* Paper presented at the San Francisco Psychoanalytic Institute.

Tangney, J. P. (1998). How does guilt differ from shame? In J. Bybee (Ed.), *Guilt and children* (pp. 1–18). London: Academic Press.

Tangney, J. P. (2001). Constructive and destructive aspects of shame and guilt. In A. C. Bohart & D. J. Stipek (Eds.), *Constructive and destructive behavior* (pp. 127–146). Washington, DC: American Psychological Association.

Tangney, J. P., Burggraf, S. A., & Wagner, P. E. (1995). Shame-proneness, guilt-proneness, and psychological symptoms. In J. P. Tangney & K. W. Fischer (Eds.), *Self-conscious emotions: Shame, guilt, embarrassment, and pride* (pp. 343–367). New York: Guilford Press.

Weiss, J. (1986). Theory and clinical observations. In J. Weiss, H. Sampson, & The Mount Zion Psychotherapy Research Group (Eds.), *The psychoanalytic process: Theory, clinical observation, and empirical research* (pp. 3–138). New York: Guilford.

Weiss, J. (1993). *How psychotherapy works*. New York: Guilford Press.

Zahn-Waxler, C., & Kochanska, G. (1990). The origins of guilt. In R. Thompson (Ed.), *Nebraska symposium on motivation: Vol. 36. socioemotional development* (pp. 183–258). Lincoln: University of Nebraska Press.

Zahn-Waxler, C., Kochanska, G., Krupnick, J., & McKnew, D. (1990). Patterns of guilt in children of depressed and well mothers. *Developmental Psychology, 26,* 51–59.

Zahn-Waxler, C., Radke–Yarrow, M., & King, R. A. (1979). Childrearing and children's prosocial initiations toward victims of distress. *Child Development, 50,* 319–330.

Zahn-Waxler, C., & Robinson, J. (1995). Empathy and guilt: Early origins of feelings of responsibility. In J. P. Tangney & K. W. Fischer (Eds.), *Self-conscious emotions: Shame, guilt, embarrassment, and pride* (pp. 143–173). New York: Guilford Press.

Part II
Therapy

5

THE ASSESSMENT OF PATHOGENIC BELIEFS

John T. Curtis and George Silberschatz

A core concept of control-mastery theory is that pathogenic beliefs are the cause of psychopathology. These pathogenic beliefs are extremely constricting, frightening, and unpleasant, and patients are highly motivated to overcome them. In order to be effective, therapists must be aware of patients' pathogenic beliefs so that they can help their patients disconfirm them. In this chapter, we will briefly review how and why pathogenic beliefs develop and how they are commonly manifested in the psychotherapeutic process. We will then describe an empirically validated and clinically tested case formulation approach, termed the Plan Formulation Method (Curtis & Silberschatz, 1997), for assessing pathogenic beliefs.

PATHOGENIC BELIEFS: AN OVERVIEW

The control-mastery model of how psychopathology develops and how psychotherapy works is presented in chapter 1. In order to provide a context for how pathogenic beliefs are assessed, we will provide a brief overview.

Pathogenic beliefs develop as a consequence of traumatic experiences. The interpretation of these traumas may be relatively "objective" (e.g., the belief that people are dangerous developing from experiences of physical or sexual abuse, or ideas that people cannot be trusted stemming from early emotional neglect) or the interpretation may reflect a misappraisal of reality (e.g., a child feeling exaggerated responsibility for the marital difficulties of parents or for the problems of a sibling). Children are especially susceptible to the development of pathogenic beliefs because of their natural egocentrism, limited life experience, and undeveloped cognitive abilities. Due to the developmental significance of the child's relationship with the parents, other caregivers, and relatives, these relationships are especially fertile ground for the creation of pathogenic beliefs.

Upon experiencing a trauma, people attempt to discern how and why the trauma occurred in order to avoid future recurrences. This assessment typically entails evaluating both one's own role in precipitating the trauma as well as the role(s) of others. This appraisal can lead to feelings of personal culpability or guilt. Weiss (1993) wrote extensively of two common forms of guilt: survivor guilt and separation guilt. Broadly stated, survivor guilt occurs when one believes, consciously or unconsciously, that his or her successes or advantages have occurred at someone else's expense. Separation guilt, in contrast, reflects an individual's belief that others are hurt by one's independence or separation from them (see chapter 4 for a thorough discussion of the role of unconscious guilt in the development of psychopathology).

Traumas can also lead to a reappraisal of others and of what can be expected from them. An abused child may come to believe that people are untrustworthy and expect rejection or abandonment. Consequently, to avoid further trauma, the child might withdraw and avoid intimate relationships, or he might behave in a masochistic, excessively ingratiating manner, believing that this is the only way to secure attention from another. More often than not, the appraisal of others is accompanied by a critical self appraisal. For instance, the abused child might develop the belief that others are critical and rejecting because the child sees him- or herself as unworthy or deficient.

Pathogenic beliefs warn the person that pursuing goals could result in danger to oneself or others. One way people avoid this danger is through pathological identifications or compliances with significant others. In fact, many of the symptoms that people enter therapy with represent pathological identifications or compliances. These identifications and compliances also serve as a form of punishment for the perceived misbehavior. The following two case examples illustrate these concepts.

A patient reported that when she was a child her mother often complained bitterly that the child spent too much time away from home playing with her friends. The mother frequently developed a variety of physical symptoms and complaints when her daughter was away. Consequently, the patient developed the belief that her autonomous strivings caused her mother's physical complaints. Her mother's complaints precipitated unconscious guilt in the patient. As an adult, she unconsciously identified with her mother by developing hypochondriacal symptoms of her own. Her "illnesses" served to prevent her from pursuing certain occupational goals, thus both keeping her from moving farther away from her mother and punishing herself for her strivings.

In another case, a man entered therapy complaining that he felt isolated and had difficulty getting along with others. He described how he frequently withdrew from others if he experienced the least tension. For example, when he got angry with his wife, he would go off to his office to work and fantasized of moving to a foreign country. As a child, the patient's mother had displayed extremely harsh reactions whenever he expressed enthusiastic or boisterous emotions. For example, whenever he displayed the smallest amount of youthful exuberance, his mother would complain of his rowdiness and tell him to "shut up and go to his room." She responded similarly, if more heatedly, whenever he argued or disagreed with her. Based on these frequent adverse experiences, he developed the belief that his feelings were too much for others to handle. His isolation and alienation from others represented a compliance with his mother's frequent demands that he be quiet and go away.

People are highly motivated to disconfirm pathogenic beliefs because these beliefs are extremely unpleasant and frustrating. However, pathogenic beliefs are often very tenacious and difficult to dispel. Their power and persistence stem from the fact that they are often unconscious. By their very nature, pathogenic beliefs can be hard to test or challenge because to do so could put the individual in a position of danger. Moreover, pathogenic beliefs typically influence and distort one's view of reality such that disconfirming experiences are likely to be ignored or misinterpreted. Certain pathogenic beliefs are difficult to disconfirm because they lead the individual to behave in a fashion that provokes trauma, thereby further confirming and strengthening the belief. For example, a person who feels unlovable may test this idea by making inappropriate or excessive emotional demands upon others. When these demands are unmet or frustrated, the belief is reinforced. It is this motivation that directs a patient's behavior in therapy. Consequently, the therapist who can identify a patient's pathogenic beliefs and understand their ramifications will be in a better position to help that individual.

ASSESSING PATHOGENIC BELIEFS

The ease with which pathogenic beliefs can be recognized and understood varies from case to case. In some instances, the patient's presenting complaints, history, and clinical presentation clearly reflect and elucidate the traumas that precipitated the pathogenic beliefs. In the following case example, a high degree of concurrence exists between the presenting problem, the childhood traumatic experiences, and the patient's therapy goals. It is a case in which pathogenic beliefs can be readily inferred.

A woman in her early thirties entered therapy because of problems getting motivated to find work. She had graduated from law school the year before and passed the bar exam. However, in the intervening time she had done little to secure employment as a lawyer. She described herself as paralyzed by fear and a lack of confidence. She imagined being bullied and humiliated by other attorneys and feared being incompetent as a lawyer. As a result, she was unable to pursue job leads, often convincing herself that she would not like the position if she got it. Instead, she took a part-time job as a receptionist and was financially supported by her parents.

As she related her history to the therapist, several key traumas quickly emerged. One occurred when the patient was 12 and her family relocated across the country due to her father changing jobs. She reported that prior to the move the family was happy and she recalled few conflicts. After the move, the patient's only sibling, an older brother, was arrested and imprisoned for several years. In addition, her parents began to have serious marital problems, and at one point, her father separated from her mother for several months. To make matters worse, no one talked about what was going on. Her parents told her nothing about her brother's problems, nor was she ever told about her parents' separation (even though she was living at home at the time).

The patient held her mother responsible for the secrecy. She described her mother as overly sensitive, insecure, and very worried about being "found out." The mother employed denial, or outright lying, to make herself or her family look better. If the patient expressed unhappiness, her mother would tell her that she was not unhappy and that she had no problems. The patient also felt that her mother tried to stifle her enthusiasm both during her childhood and as an adult. For example, when the patient was admitted to law school, her father was thrilled. By contrast, her mother said it was "nice," though she was notably low-key and complained that the patient and her father were celebrating this event too enthusiastically.

The patient was closer to her father who often acted as an intermediary between the patient and her mother. Compared to her complaining, negativistic mother, her father was warmer and more family-oriented. However, he was also an alcoholic who drank heavily during the patient's high school years. At the time the patient entered therapy, her father had admitted he was an alcoholic and had been attending AA; however, he still drank regularly.

The patient's relationships with her parents changed little as she became an adult. Although she is better able to express herself with her father than with her mother, she does not feel particularly close to him and is very critical of his drinking. She still finds her mother overbearing and prickly. She noted that since starting law school her parents have rarely asked about her studies, and she has refrained from mentioning her work to them. She explained that her parents always acted like a job could only be work and that they were critical and derisive of people who work hard at their jobs.

From this history, a number of pathogenic beliefs can be inferred. For example, the patient's problems appear to stem from identification with her weak, downtrodden parents, in particular her mother. This identification developed as a consequence of her unconscious belief that if she was assertive and successful it would intimidate and hurt her parents by highlighting their inadequacies and lack of accomplishments. Thus, on the threshold of fulfilling her goal of becoming an attorney, she was tempted to act paralyzed and fragile (like her mother) and hobble or even sacrifice her career to avoid the risk of further deflating and intimidating her parents by her success.

The patient suffered from intense survivor guilt. Following her successes in law school and on the bar exam, the patient was again threatened by the need to identify with her mother (by not pursuing employment) and to comply with both of her parents' views that to aggressively seek a meaningful and rewarding profession is wrong. Her identification and compliance was a manifestation of her belief that her success and happiness would hurt her parents. Thus, she was tempted to identify and comply with them by giving up and acting defeated.

In the preceding case, clear connections were made among the patient's history and the traumas she endured, the pathogenic beliefs that developed out of these traumas, and her presenting complaints and expressed goals for therapy. In other cases, the causal connection from traumas to pathogenic beliefs to presenting complaints is less clear or straightforward. This is particularly true in instances when the patient's presenting complaints do not reflect true therapy goals.

In a case taken from Curtis and Silberschatz (1986), a young man entered therapy with the presenting complaint that he wanted to overcome his inhibitions about intimate relationships so he could make a commitment to and marry his girlfriend. Initially, the therapist inferred that this patient had been held back from competitive successes by Oedipal anxieties and guilt, and he concluded that the patient was unable to commit to his girlfriend because he felt uncomfortable about being successful with women.

However, a careful review of the patient's history suggested a different picture. The patient described his mother as being chronically depressed and possessive, and it was inferred that he had developed separation guilt because he believed that his independence would wound his mother. Furthermore, a careful appraisal of the relationship with his girlfriend revealed that she was a poor choice for him to marry. She was demanding and unpredictable (like his mother), and they had little in common. He gave evidence that he was tied to his present girlfriend by an unconscious fear of hurting her if he chose to leave. It was thus concluded that what this patient actually wanted out of therapy was to free himself from his attachment to his mother by disconfirming his pathogenic belief that she would be destroyed by his independence. In so doing, he could overcome his omnipotent feelings of responsibility for women in general and his girlfriend in particular. Although he did want to get married, he could only do so after he had overcome his fear of being trapped by women, which in turn required his developing the capacity to leave them.

In the preceding case, the nature and power of the patient's pathogenic beliefs obscured his vision of what he wanted out of life and led him to propose what ultimately proved to be an inappropriate goal for therapy. However, a review of the patient's history and of the pathogenic beliefs that evolved out his relationship with his mother brought his stated goals for therapy into question. These doubts were sustained as the particulars of the patient's relationship with his girlfriend emerged over the course of therapy.

Some patients provide so little detail or historical information that it is extremely difficult to discern the patient's goals for therapy or their pathogenic beliefs. In such instances, the only way for the therapist to infer the patient's pathogenic beliefs is through his or her interactions with the patient. As the following case will illustrate, the therapist might monitor his or her own reactions to the patient as a source of hypotheses about the patient's pathogenic beliefs.

In another example, a middle-aged male entered therapy with complaints of debilitating anxiety and depression. The patient offered little background or history and instead focused on the extreme distress he was experiencing. The psychiatrist attempted to address the patient's symptoms by prescribing antidepressant and antianxiety medications, but with little success. The psychiatrist himself felt intense anxiety and worry about the patient's seemingly intractable symptoms and over time began to feel quite beleaguered by the patient. It seemed that nothing he had to offer was helping and that the patient was making no progress.

At one point, the patient began to complain of insomnia, and the psychiatrist suggested he keep a diary of his sleep habits. To the therapist's surprise, at the next session the patient presented him with a very thorough, well-written description of the daily circumstances leading up to his bedtime and of his bedtime routine. Based on this document, the patient identified certain behavioral changes that he thought might help his sleep. He agreed to institute these changes and at the next session reported improvement in his sleep.

Because of this success, the psychiatrist for the first time felt some relief from his worry, but this was short-lived as the patient continued to complain about his anxiety and depression. Toward the end of one appointment, the patient launched into a description of his relationship with his adolescent daughter. He reported several very heated arguments between them concerning her curfew, and he expressed great worry about the trouble his daughter might be getting into when hanging out with her friends late at night. The psychiatrist was worried about this situation but also uncertain about how to respond to it. At the end of the session, he told the patient they could discuss this issue in their next appointment and suggested that the patient think about the alternatives he might take with his daughter. The psychiatrist was left with a great sense of uneasiness, worrying that something bad might happen between the daughter and patient. He wondered if he should have done something more to help.

In the next session, the patient described in a matter-of-fact manner how he had talked with his daughter about her curfew. He set firm limits as to where she was allowed to go and when she should be home, and he established reasonable sounding consequences if she did not abide by his rules. The patient remarked that these actions seemed to have resolved the matter and that his daughter had been behaving herself. The psychiatrist was rather startled by how well it seemed that the patient had handled the matter and again felt some relief from his own worry about the situation.

The patient then began to describe a problem with a coworker and implied that the situation could threaten his job. Again, the psychiatrist began to worry but then had an epiphany that the patient might unconsciously be inviting him to do so. He speculated that the patient was behaving in a passive-into-active manner (see chapter 1) in order to work on his own issues about handling worry. The psychiatrist's speculation was reinforced by the experience of having been "invited" to worry about the patient's sleep and his relationship with his daughter, only to find out that his worries were unnecessary. He concluded that the patient wanted the psychiatrist not to worry, or not to feel omnipotent responsibility. The therapist thus engaged the patient in a discussion of various ways the work issue might be handled, leaving it up to the patient to decide what to do. Again, the patient handled the situation with aplomb.

Based on his inferences about how his own worry reflected the patient's issues, the psychiatrist began to ask the patient about his worries, now and in the past. He learned that the patient, as a child, had been traumatized by the contentious divorce of his parents. The patient recalled how he feared he had been the cause of the divorce and how he had worried about whether his parents would be able to survive on their own. Interestingly, the patient was much more forthcoming with historical information when the psychiatrist felt less worried about him. The history that emerged confirmed the psychiatrist's inferences that worry was a central issue for this patient. The patient's worry resulted from his pathogenic beliefs about his omnipotent responsibility for others.

The preceding examples have illustrated that pathogenic beliefs are manifested in various ways. In some instances, the beliefs are quite clear; the patient might even be consciously aware of and able to describe them. In other cases, these beliefs can only be inferred from the patient's history or behaviors with the therapist. In the following section, we will discuss in greater detail how to infer a patient's pathogenic beliefs.

PRINCIPLES FOR IDENTIFYING PATHOGENIC BELIEFS

In the following section, we discuss some of the general principles for identifying a patient's pathogenic beliefs. We briefly describe underlying assumptions, clinical presentation, the nature of the patient's trauma, and how pathogenic beliefs are manifested in symptoms, goals, and the patient's interactions with the therapist.

Basic Assumptions

Identifying and understanding a patient's pathogenic beliefs require a careful evaluation and interpretation of clinical material. This material is best accumulated in a clinical interview that elicits a thorough exposition of the patient's presenting complaints, current life situation, and developmental history. According to control-mastery theory, three basic assumptions inform how pathogenic beliefs will be manifested in therapy and thus underlie the clinical formulation process. First, patients come to therapy to get better. Second, a patient's true goals for therapy are improvement and development, not regression or stagnation. Third, patients want their therapists to understand their pathogenic beliefs. These basic assumptions should be kept in mind when evaluating the patient's clinical presentation. In particular, the patient's desire to be understood by the therapist will motivate the patient to explicate his or her pathogenic beliefs in the early sessions of therapy (in later sessions, while working to disconfirm these beliefs, a patient may show a less conscious awareness of them). Because of this, a therapist often can develop a very accurate and comprehensive formulation relatively early in therapy.

What to Look for in the Clinical Presentation

The control-mastery theory assumes that patients are highly motivated to make their unconscious pathogenic beliefs explicit so that the therapist can help to disconfirm them. Understanding the patient's childhood traumas, therapy goals, presenting complaints and symptoms, and the patient's interactions with the therapist are all particularly useful for identifying pathogenic beliefs.

What is the Nature of the Patient's Childhood Traumas? Childhood traumas are not limited to acute catastrophic events such as a tragic accident, illness, or death of a loved one. They also refer to events or situations that disturb or impede normal development and lead to the formation of pathogenic beliefs that in turn inhibit or prevent the individual from pursuing or achieving appropriate developmental and life goals. Although an acute trauma (e.g., the unexpected death of a parent or sibling, or a medical emergency) could well result in the development of a pathogenic belief, typically more enduring stress traumas (e.g., chronic conflict between parents or maladaptive relationship patterns within the family) are the most pathogenic.

The identification of childhood traumas requires a thorough understanding of normal developmental milestones and processes, as well as of stage-appropriate behaviors and conflicts. Not all traumas lead to the development of pathogenic beliefs, and thus it is important not only to identify what situations or events could potentially be traumatic but also to determine what impact they actually had on the patient's thoughts and actions. Identifying and understanding a patient's childhood traumas can provide clues to the probable nature of his or her pathogenic beliefs, to the dangers they foretell, to the life goals relinquished because of them, and to how the patient is likely to work in therapy to disconfirm the pathogenic beliefs. The following example illustrates the effects of childhood stress trauma on a woman's adult relationships.

A young woman entered therapy after a series of disappointing relationships with men. She reported she was the youngest of four daughters and that she had been the closest to her mother growing up. She described her mother as acting like a handmaiden to her father. The mother waited on him hand and foot, even though he never expressed any appreciation for her attention and in fact was regularly critical of her for not taking better care of him. He also expressed extreme resentment whenever he was called upon to help his wife. For instance, when he would drive her to the grocery store, he would stay in the car while she shopped and would drive home without her if she took longer than 10 minutes. Based on this reported "trauma," the therapist suspected that the patient might have difficulties being assertive, especially with men, because of a belief that she should not be happier than her mother was.

More specifically, the therapist hypothesized that the patient's closeness with her mother was an early manifestation of the patient's concern about her. The patient may have felt that she needed to stay close to her mother to protect her from her father as well as to make up for his hostility and lack of appreciation for her. Because of these beliefs, the patient came to strongly identify with her mother, resulting in the patient sharing in her mother's disappointments and maintaining her loyalty and devotion to her (by not having other fulfilling relationships). The therapist predicted that in therapy the patient would test her pathogenic beliefs by seeing if he would approve of her having a life and opinions of her own. He also expected she might address her omnipotent concerns for others by inviting the therapist to worry about her. In other words, she might act helpless or fail to address the obvious and then complain about her situation (as her mother did) to see if the therapist felt as frustrated and impotent as she did.

The following case example illustrates another instance in which childhood traumas elucidated the patient's pathogenic beliefs, despite the patient's dismissive attitude toward the traumas. A successful real estate developer entered therapy at the insistence of his wife. She had grown frustrated with his failure to address significant problems at work and at home, and offered him an ultimatum: "Go to therapy or I'm leaving." During the initial meeting with the therapist, the patient discussed his wife's reaction and the issues she felt needed to be addressed with an air of bemused detachment. He acknowledged that there were problems but downplayed their seriousness, at times even joking about them. He presented himself as a kind of lovable ne'er do well and described his relationship with his wife as one in which she was constantly on him to take responsibility, like a mother trying to get her reluctant son to do his chores. The therapist saw him as being very likable and engaging, with a quick wit and a self-deprecating sense of humor. Indeed, it was easy to get caught up in and distracted by the patient's joking style and many humorous anecdotes.

Despite the patient's tendency to minimize his problems, it became clear he was in serious trouble. His business was slipping because of his failure to attend to serious problems in his office. In a light-hearted, funny way, he described a chaotic and dysfunctional office environment in which he was surrounded by bickering, incompetent employees who failed to adequately perform their jobs. He acted as if this situation was his cross to bear, explaining how hard it was to get good employees, especially to do the tedious and boring work he required of them. He acted as if he had no right to expect more from others.

He related that an employee had embezzled enough money to significantly undermine the financial stability of his company, but he had taken no action against her. He rationalized his stance by noting that the woman in question had worked for him for many years and that she must have had financial problems of her own to do such a thing. He concluded that because she could probably not pay back the money he would just have to find some way to cover the losses. When his wife tried to get him to take action and deal with work issues more appropriately, he acted beleaguered and put-upon, accusing her of worrying too much. He acted as if there was nothing he could do to address his problems, and just wanted to be left alone.

The patient's propensity to downplay and even belittle his needs and problems was reflected in the way he reported his history. For example, he initially described his father as a successful small businessman. However, he gradually confided that his father had lost his business to hoodlums to whom he owed gambling debts. All of this was told as if reporting the humorous misadventures of a lovable buffoon. He denied any personal feelings of disappointment or outrage toward his father, even when reporting how gangsters had shown up at his bar mitzvah and taken money from him to repay his father's gambling debts.

This patient's failure to deal with the obvious threats to his security and livelihood clearly reflected an identification with his father's extremely irresponsible behaviors. His passive acceptance of mistreatment by others represented a compliance with his father's failure to protect him and the resultant message that he should not expect to be taken care of by others. The traumas that the patient endured as a consequence of his father's irresponsibility and gambling led to the development of pathogenic beliefs concerning how much control he should exert over his own life and what expectations he should have of others.

What are the Patient's Stated Goals for Therapy? Another way in which therapists can infer pathogenic beliefs is through the patient's stated goals for therapy. As noted earlier, the patient's stated goals may be influenced by and reflect pathogenic beliefs rather than true needs and aspirations. Consequently, it is essential for the clinician to thoroughly evaluate a patient's therapy goals to determine if they are appropriate to his or her developmental goals, life circumstances, and abilities. In so doing, the therapist may develop ideas about the nature of the patient's pathogenic beliefs and accommodations to them.

A graduate student in clinical psychology entered therapy ostensibly to fulfill a requirement of her program that she be in therapy for a certain number of sessions. She initially denied any problems other than being frustrated with her schoolwork. Although she expressed great interest and a commitment to psychology as a profession, she also described school as boring and irrelevant. She said she was in it just to get the degree so that she could become a therapist. All she wanted to do was "get by" and do as little as possible in school and in therapy.

The therapist's initial reactions to the patient and her stated goals for therapy were less than favorable. If her true goal for therapy was just to fulfill a school requirement, he had no interest in being party to a ruse. On the other hand, the discordance between the patient's interest in being a therapist and her professed disinterest in school suggested the possibility that the patient felt conflicted about her professional aspirations. When the patient, toward the end of the intake, requested to be seen at a reduced fee, the therapist speculated that she might be testing to see if he was comfortable taking himself and his work seriously. The therapist responded by saying he thought she should be in therapy whether or not it was required by her school. He also remarked that he suspected she had difficulties taking herself seriously and thus allowing herself to pursue her life goals, and that he would like to work with her, but that he would not reduce his fee. The patient acted disappointed, complaining that her graduate student stipend did not provide enough to pay for therapy, but she said she would think about it and get back to him. Several weeks after the initial interview, she called the therapist to set up an appointment, explaining she had been slow getting back to him because she needed to get a part-time job to pay for her treatment.

In the initial sessions, the therapist learned that the patient's father had regularly expressed great frustration in his career. At an early age, he was forced to work in his father's business, which he then inherited. He hated the work but acted resigned to it because of his need to support his family. The father was disdainful of his wife's attempts to pursue a career (as a therapist!), deriding her profession as being "flaky" and constantly criticizing her for not bringing in more money.

While growing up, the patient was also the recipient of father's criticism. He regularly accused her of wanting too much out of life and of having unrealistic or inappropriate expectations. For instance, when the patient saved her babysitting money to buy a stereo, the father accused her of wasting her money on luxuries and berated her for having a better sound system than he did. From these experiences, the patient developed the belief that others would be threatened by her aspirations, and she even questioned whether in fact her goals were inappropriate. These beliefs made it difficult for her to whole-heartedly pursue her goals.

The therapist was able to make a preliminary inference regarding the patient's pathogenic beliefs, based on the discrepancy between her stated goals (to fulfill a school requirement) and her interest in becoming a therapist. The therapist's inference allowed him to make an intervention in the first session (not reducing the fee), even though he did not gain a full understanding of the patient's traumas and the related pathogenic beliefs until later.

An appraisal of the appropriateness of a patient's stated goals cannot rest on the face value of those goals alone. Rather, it is essential to ascertain the beliefs that dictate the patient's selection of those goals. A patient may present with a reasonable sounding goal that in fact obscures other prerequisite goals. The patient described earlier who expressed a desire to overcome his fear of commitment in order to get married is an example of this. Before this individual could address this goal, he first had to get out of a bad relationship that in turn required him to resolve his issues of feeling omnipotent responsibility for others.

A more subtle variation on the theme of appropriate-sounding goals that are actually inappropriate occurs when a seemingly laudable and developmentally appropriate goal is inconsistent with the patient's true aspirations or beyond his capabilities. As the following case example illustrates, the therapist should not reach a conclusion about the appropriateness of a patient's goals (and thus the direction of the therapy) without a careful analysis of the beliefs influencing the patient's selection of goals.

A middle-aged man came to therapy because he was frustrated with his career. He was a partner in a major real estate development firm and financially successful, but he felt unfulfilled by his work and unappreciated at his job. In particular, he felt that the other partners did not value his opinions and that he contributed little to the company. In some measure, he held himself responsible for this, acknowledging that he often did not review reports thoroughly and seldom had ideas about new ventures for the firm. He wanted to understand what kept him from delving into his work and being more successful.

This patient was one of several sons born into a wealthy family that for several generations had been involved in real estate. He initially described a very warm and supportive relationship with both his parents and a very happy and pampered upbringing. Over time his story slowly changed as he revealed that his parents were in fact aloof, distant, and more involved in work and social functions than in the direct upbringing of their children. Although the patient never lacked for material goods, he was raised by nannies and had a rather formal, almost businesslike, relationship with his parents, who had little involvement or interest in his daily life. The patient spoke of his childhood with little joy and claimed to have few memories of it, other than the time he spent with his pets. The family had several purebred hunting dogs that he spent many hours with tending and training.

The patient's relationship with his parents changed little as he entered adulthood. When he visited them, he was treated more like a formal guest than a son. Although his father discussed business with him and provided professional contacts for him, he offered little direction or encouragement, adopting what sounded like a laissez-faire attitude toward his son's career. The patient took advantage of family contacts to pursue several small business ventures, but he engaged in these enterprises with little enthusiasm, and none was particularly successful. Eventually, he was recruited to join the firm with which he was affiliated when he entered therapy.

The therapist's preliminary formulation of this case focused on the effects of the parents' emotional neglect on the son. She hypothesized that the patient believed he was unimportant and that he should not expect to do well in life. The therapist considered the patient's attitudes toward his job as reflecting a compliance with the parents' apparently low expectations of him.

After several sessions, the therapist reconsidered her formulation. She came to two realizations. First, the firm had recruited the patient for his family and professional contacts, not for his business acumen, and that was the extent of the role the other partners wanted him to play in the company. Second, the patient displayed little aptitude for business and even less genuine interest in it. She learned that the patient was much more interested in the breeding and training of hunting dogs, an arena in which he was considered quite an expert.

Rather than seeing the patient's work inhibition as a compliance with his parents' neglect, she instead saw the patient's career choice as an identification with his father based on the belief that business was the only worthy profession. He was thus trapped into pursuing a career he was neither competent at nor interested in. His true goals for therapy were to leave the real estate business and pursue a career raising and training hunting dogs. To achieve these goals, he had to disconfirm the pathogenic beliefs about his unworthiness as an individual (resulting from parental neglect) and about his "right" to deviate from the family tradition of working in real estate. It is of interest that toward the end of therapy the patient revealed that he knew his father had never liked working in real estate but had been forced into it by his father.

What is the Nature of the Patient's Presenting Complaints and Symptoms?
Because a patient's symptoms are the consequences of their pathogenic beliefs, a careful evaluation of these symptoms, focusing particularly on how they fit into the total picture of the individual's life, can reveal clues as to the pathogenic beliefs underlying them. For example, in the case of the real estate developer, a clear discordance existed between certain symptoms (his difficulties holding his employees accountable

and his apparent reluctance to take things seriously) and the successes he had achieved in his career. His symptoms clearly had not prevented him from being successful, but they did distract from and limit his ability to enjoy his successes, as well as undermine the likelihood of future successes. Thus, the "role" or effects of these symptoms suggest the pathogenic beliefs about being successful and about taking himself seriously. In a similar vein, a therapist might suspect that any exaggerated needs or symptoms reported or manifested by a patient reflect the pathogenic beliefs concerning those issues. For example, the extreme desire of a narcissistic individual for attention might well reflect beliefs that he or she is undesirable or unworthy of attention. As illustrated in the following examples, discordance between a patient's symptoms and his or her apparent abilities, or between the patient's subjective experience of his or her attributes and the therapist's (more objective) appraisal, may reflect the content or consequences of pathogenic beliefs.

A middle-aged woman sought therapy to deal with the paralysis she was experiencing looking for work. The woman's husband had recently become disabled, and it was necessary for her to return to the workforce. Although she had worked prior to marrying, after the birth of her first child, she stayed at home to raise him. When confronted with the need to work outside of the home, the patient experienced extreme fear and despair, believing she was incapable of getting or holding a job. She claimed she had no marketable skills and doubted that she could acquire any at her "advanced" age.

This self-appraisal was quite at odds with the therapist's view of this individual. Her acute intellect was reflected in her thoughtful presentation of her life and in her precise and expressive use of language. She was fluent in several languages and read voraciously. Although she had not worked for pay outside the home during her marriage, she had been involved in many civic activities and private organizations. In brief, the therapist quickly hypothesized that this bright, competent individual's fears were the products of her inhibitions about being successful. The therapist suspected that the patient's inhibitions stemmed from survivor guilt toward her husband and represented an identification with this unfortunate individual.

The patient's symptoms and complaints provided the therapist with clues about the nature of the patient's pathogenic beliefs. The following example illustrates another way in which the patient's presenting complaint can indicate the nature of the patient's pathogenic beliefs.

A research scientist entered therapy at the behest of his wife because of her concerns that his angry outbursts at work could threaten his career. The patient said that he too had concerns about his anger, but he had not thought of seeking therapy until his wife suggested it. He went on to explain that at work he would occasionally yell or throw things if an experiment did not work or if he felt frustrated. When the therapist asked about the repercussions of this behavior at work, the patient acknowledged that there had been none; nobody had ever said anything to him about it. In fact, he was very highly regarded at work; he had been afforded more independence and been given more responsibilities than many other more senior and tenured scientists. However, he did not like this behavior, felt ashamed of it, and worried that it could seriously limit his career. As a result, he tried to seclude himself at work and avoid interactions with his fellow scientists lest he have a temper tantrum.

In this case, the patient did not seem to be suffering so much from his anger as he did from his worries about the meaning and possible consequences of this "symptom," which served to inhibit him and make him feel less worthy. Indeed, his concern about the consequences of his anger had actually inhibited him from expressing it, suggesting a pathogenic belief about the power or appropriateness of his feelings.

What emerged over the course of therapy was that the patient's mother was a martyr who had devoted her life to trying to raise the patient's severely developmentally disabled, destructive, and uncontrollable sister at home. As a result of her choice, the whole family suffered due to the chaos created by this unfortunate sibling. The patient's father had little patience with this daughter, and their interactions often devolved into shouting matches or physical altercations. The patient described his father as being chronically dissatisfied and full of rage, but who was impotent to effect any change. From these experiences growing up, the patient developed the belief that anger is bad and destructive, and that one should not expect to escape or find release from one's burdens—you just have to cope. As these beliefs emerged and were discussed in therapy, the patient began to address his true goal for therapy: to address his wife's alcoholism and the anger it provoked in him.

In addition to the clues that patients' presenting symptoms and complaints can provide, an awareness of the roles that identification and compliance can play in a patient's symptoms and complaints can assist the therapist in understanding a patient's pathogenic beliefs. The middle-aged housewife's identification with her disabled husband grew out of the survivor guilt she experienced because of her beliefs that she did not deserve to have a good life in general or a better life than her husband in particular. The scientist's concerns about his anger may be seen as an identification with his out-of-control father and his alcoholic wife. In turn, this identification resulted from his belief that he was doing something wrong if he did not share in others' problems or if he pursued happiness rather than wallowing in despair.

What is the Nature of the Patient's Interactions With the Therapist?

Patients enter therapy to test and hopefully disconfirm their pathogenic beliefs. Consequently, the therapeutic relationship can provide many clues about the nature and impact of these beliefs. For example, the real estate executive's garrulous, glad-handing style with the therapist reflected his inhibitions about taking himself seriously. His lighthearted interactions with the therapist (especially in light of how dire his work situation was) can be seen as a test of whether the therapist would take him and his problems seriously, as well as a reflection of his pathogenic belief that he did not deserve to be taken care of.

If properly understood, a passive-into-active enactment (see chapter 1) can provide the therapist with a profound sense of the traumas a patient has experienced. For instance, a patient who was criticized and demeaned by a parent may "share" this experience with the therapist by treating him or her in a similar fashion. From this, the therapist can learn firsthand the nature and impact of the trauma on the patient. The therapist's awareness of his or her own reactions to this behavior (e.g., feeling inadequate, threatened, or hopeless) can provide clues to the pathogenic beliefs the patient developed because of these experiences.

On occasion, a therapist's only avenue for deciphering a patient's pathogenic beliefs may lie in the transference, especially with patients who are unable or unwilling to disclose their past. A patient's reluctance to disclose history or discuss certain events might reflect core beliefs about trusting or believing in others. Another patient who downplays or makes light of seemingly distressing experiences might be manifesting a belief that he does not deserve to be taken seriously. It is important for the therapist to look beyond the patient's apparent resistance to the possible pathogenic beliefs reflected in this behavior.

A therapist can only be sure of a patient's true goals for therapy after identifying and understanding the patient's pathogenic beliefs; these beliefs determine which goals the patient has avoided and whether inappropriate goals have been substituted for them. Similarly, the patient's pathogenic beliefs dictate how the therapy should be conducted. Understanding a patient's pathogenic beliefs helps the therapist know what manner of therapy will help the patient disconfirm the beliefs. In short, an accurate appraisal of a patient's pathogenic beliefs provides the basis for a comprehensive case formulation. This will be used to identify the patient's true goals for therapy, what has inhibited the patient from pursuing or attaining those goals, the causes of these inhibitions, and the experiences or information that will help remove the inhibitions.

To determine whether a belief is pathogenic, the therapist must identify how it has inhibited the individual. To know how to address a pathogenic belief, it helps to know how and under what circumstances it has developed. We will conclude this chapter by describing a method for creating clinical case formulations that is based on identifying pathogenic beliefs.

THE PLAN FORMULATION METHOD

According to the control-mastery theory, the manner in which a patient works to disconfirm pathogenic beliefs, overcome problems, and achieve goals is called the patient's "plan" (Weiss, 1993; see chapter 1). The plan is not a rigid itinerary that the patient will strictly adhere to; rather, it comprises a general set of issues that the patient will want to work on and a description of how this work is likely to proceed. Consequently, a case formulation developed from a control-mastery perspective is often referred to as a plan formulation.

Because of the centrality that pathogenic beliefs play in the control-mastery theory, research on the clinical applications of the theory have necessitated the development of a reliable method for identifying pathogenic beliefs and developing comprehensive case formulations (see chapter 11). The research method that has evolved is called the Plan Formulation Method (Curtis, Silberschatz, Sampson, & Weiss, 1988, 1994; Curtis & Silberschatz, 1997). The Plan Formulation Method will be described here as a framework for developing comprehensive case formulations based on an assessment of a patient's pathogenic beliefs.

The Plan Formulation Method includes the following elements: (a) a description of the *traumas* the patient has experienced, (b) a list of the *pathogenic beliefs* the patient has developed, (c) the patient's *goals* for therapy, (d) how the patient is likely to *test* the therapist, and (e) *insights* that would be helpful for the patient to obtain. (The following definitions and examples are taken from the manual for the Plan Formulation Method.)

Traumas

Traumas are *experiences* that lead to pathogenic beliefs. The following are examples of traumas and the resultant pathogenic beliefs:

- During a female patient's adolescence, her mother called her a "whore" when she expressed interest in boys. Consequently, she does not enjoy sex because she believes that it is bad.
- A man's father was critical of his success at school and acted hurt when his son outperformed him (e.g., beat him at chess). Consequently, the patient does not allow himself to vigorously pursue his career because he believes to do so would hurt his father.
- A patient's mother had few friends and frequently confided in him about her disappointment with his father. Consequently, the patient has not moved away from home because he believes his mother would feel abandoned if he left.

More than one trauma may contribute to the formation of a pathogenic belief, and more than one belief may develop out of a given trauma. For purposes of a plan formulation, it is not necessary to develop an exhaustive list of all the traumas that contributed to a given pathogenic belief or to account for every pathogenic belief in the list of traumas. Rather, one must identify those traumas and the resultant pathogenic beliefs that a given patient is attempting to resolve in therapy.

Obstructions (Pathogenic Beliefs)

Obstructions are the pathogenic beliefs—and the associated fears, guilt, and anxieties—that hinder or prevent a person from pursuing his or her goals. Typically, these beliefs are unconscious in the early phases of therapy. These irrational beliefs act as obstructions because they suggest that certain undesirable consequences will occur if the patient pursues or attains a certain goal or goals. For example,

- The patient holds herself back from doing well in school because she feels her sister would be humiliated by her success.
- The patient acts aloof and distant toward her peers because she believes her mother will feel abandoned if she has friends.

- The patient stays away from people, thinking they will want nothing to do with him, because he feels he is an evil, despicable person.

An obstruction is more than just a belief in that it must in some way influence the patient's thoughts, feelings, or behavior. Thus, some negative consequence(s) must be associated with the belief for it to be an obstruction. For instance, if the previous first example were written, "If the patient is successful, she will surpass a sibling," it would not be considered an obstruction because no negative consequence is associated with surpassing a sibling (in fact, this item could just be a statement of fact). Similarly, stating that "the patient believes that if she is happily married she will leave her parents behind" would not qualify as a pathogenic belief without noting the consequences of the belief (e.g., "the patient stays away from men because she believes that her parents would be devastated if she married and left home").

Goals

The patient's goals for therapy represent potential behaviors, affects, attitudes, or capacities that the patient would like to adopt. These goals may be highly specific and concrete ("to get married") or more general and abstract ("to expand her capacity for intimate relationships"). Although at one level a patient's goal for therapy can be conceptualized as overcoming a pathogenic belief ("to overcome her belief that getting married will destroy her mother"), for the purposes of creating a case formulation, it is better to think of goals from the perspective of how overcoming a pathogenic belief might be manifested ("to get married").

The patient's presenting complaints may not accurately reflect his or her goals for therapy. He or she may not be able to acknowledge his or her true desires because, for example, they are unconscious or are experienced as being too bold or ambitious. Therefore, the assessment of a patient's goals requires a dynamic formulation of the case (e.g., the case of the patient who did not want to get married).

Tests

One method by which a patient attempts to disconfirm pathogenic beliefs and irrational expectations is by observing the therapist's behavior in response to tests. Tests are actions by the patient that are designed to appraise the danger or safety of pursuing a particular goal(s). When testing, the patient observes the therapist's behavior to see if it confirms or disconfirms an irrational expectation or false belief. For example, a patient who feels that he will hurt others if he is forceful might test this belief by observing whether the therapist is upset when the patient argues with him or acts decisive and independent. The same patient might also test by observing the therapist's reaction when the patient turns passive into active, such as acting hurt or upset when the therapist is bold or insightful.

Insights

For the purposes of case formulation, an insight is defined as knowledge acquired during therapy that helps a patient achieve his or her therapy goals. This knowledge pertains to the nature, origins, and manifestations of the patient's pathogenic beliefs and it is generally incomplete or unavailable to the patient at the beginning of therapy. A patient might obtain insight into the content of a pathogenic belief ("If I'm not perfect, nobody will love me") or into the identifications and compliances spawned by pathogenic beliefs (by pining for a man, the patient is acting pathetic and thereby not threatening, like her mother). The insight might concern the historical roots of a belief (when the patient acted independently as a child, her mother acted hurt) and or his or her therapy goals, such as the patient who wanted to feel free *not* to get married before pursuing his conscious wish to be married.

Other examples of insights are:

- A patient realizing she has inhibited herself from having enjoyable sexual relationships with men because she feels guilty allowing herself greater pleasure than her mother has experienced.
- A patient becoming aware that he has inhibited his occupational progress to avoid achieving greater success than his father.

All the elements of the Plan Formulation Method are interrelated, and each informs the others. The pathogenic beliefs develop out of the patient's responses to traumas. The beliefs serve to obstruct the patient's pursuit or attainment of goals. A patient will often test his or her pathogenic beliefs during therapy in an attempt to disconfirm them, which would free the patient to pursue his or her goals. Insights into the nature, cause, and impact of pathogenic beliefs can help in these efforts. All the different elements of a plan formulation can be seen as different ways in which the patient's pathogenic beliefs are manifested. Thus, the plan formulation sheds light on the origins and nature of the patient's pathogenic beliefs, providing valuable clinical information regarding the nature of the patient's problems and how the patient is likely to work in therapy to overcome them.

Therapists can infer a patient's pathogenic beliefs in a variety of ways. With some patients, the pathogenic beliefs are elucidated relatively quickly and form a coherent story with the patient's history and goals. In other cases, pathogenic beliefs cannot be inferred as easily, and the therapist must pay careful attention to other aspects of the patient's clinical presentation in order to gain an understanding of them. No matter what the clinical presentation is, it bears repeating that patients are motivated to make their therapists aware of their pathogenic beliefs so that the therapist can help to disconfirm them.

REFERENCES

Curtis, J. T., & Silberschatz, G. (1986). Clinical implications of research on brief dynamic psychotherapy: I. Formulating the patient's problem and goals. *Psychoanalytic Psychology, 3,* 13–25.

Curtis, J. T., & Silberschatz, G. (1997). Plan Formulation Method. In T. D. Eells (Ed.), *Handbook of psychotherapy case formulation* (pp. 116–136). New York: Guilford.

Curtis, J. T., Silberschatz, G., Sampson, H., & Weiss, J. (1994). The Plan Formulation Method. *Psychotherapy Research, 4,* 197–207.

Curtis, J. T., Silberschatz, G., Sampson, H., Weiss, J., & Rosenberg, S. E. (1988). Developing reliable psychodynamic case formulations: An illustration of the plan diagnosis method. *Psychotherapy, 25,* 256–265.

Weiss, J. (1993). *How psychotherapy works: Process and technique.* New York: Guilford.

6
CLINICAL USE OF THE PLAN FORMULATION IN LONG-TERM PSYCHOTHERAPY

Polly Bloomberg-Fretter

Twenty-five years ago, while searching for a clinical theory that would both help me organize the information that patients presented in therapy and also help them to improve clinically, I found control-mastery theory, which has proven to be a powerfully productive tool for psychotherapy. Control-mastery theory provides a rich case formulation method that is case specific, flexible, and highly empirical when applied in either a direct clinical treatment or in formal research. Although this formulation method yields a case-specific perspective of the patient, it also allows therapists to develop their own personal style for particular patients. In this chapter, I briefly review the method of case formulation, present a detailed case formulation of a patient I treated using this method, and finally present examples of interventions I made using this formulation.

THE CONTROL-MASTERY APPROACH TO CASE FORMULATION

From the first contact with the patient, the therapist focuses on understanding the patient's goals and the pathogenic beliefs blocking the achievement of those goals. Control-mastery theory provides a framework that allows the therapist to develop a rich and individually tailored formulation for each patient based on (a) the patient's own formulation of the presenting problem and goals, (b) the historic interpersonal scenarios (traumas) that seem to block the attainment of the goals, (c) the therapist's affective responses to the patient, and (d) the patient's reactions to the therapist's approach and interventions.

After the therapist attains an initial understanding of the patient's pathogenic beliefs (inferred from the patient's interpersonal history) and how these beliefs might fit with the presenting problem, the therapist observes how the patient tests those beliefs in the context of the therapeutic relationship. The therapist then attempts to disprove those beliefs, paying close attention to how the patient responds to such interventions. The continual focus on observing the patient's responses to the interventions makes the clinical formulation process highly empirical. This empirical process of theory building by the therapist continues throughout treatment as the patient reveals more pathogenic beliefs and the therapist learns how to disconfirm them.

In the following case illustration, I present a patient's background and presenting problem in detail to demonstrate the case formulation process in practice.

CASE ILLUSTRATION

The psychotherapy treatment described here was conducted as part of an investigation of long-term psychodynamic therapy for major depressive disorders carried out by the Berkeley Psychotherapy Research Project at the University of California at Berkeley (Jones, Ghannam, Nigg, & Dyer, 1993). The patient, Kathy, was diagnosed as having a major depressive disorder after an extensive assessment process that included several intake interviews by an independent evaluator as well as a battery of self-report measures. Kathy received intensive psychodynamic therapy twice a week for 2.5 years (208 sessions), and each session was videotaped. The patient and therapist completed assessment measures every 16 sessions, and a more complete evaluation was conducted by an independent evaluator every 6 months. Jones et al. (1993) noted that by all indices of patient change the treatment was very successful. At termination, Kathy no longer met criteria for either major or minor depressive disorder, and she maintained these gains at 6-month and 1-year follow-ups.

Presenting Problem

Kathy was in her mid-thirties and worked from her home as a freelance secretary when treatment began. She had three children ages 14, 12, and 10 from a marriage that ended in divorce about 8 years prior to treatment. Her ex-husband lived in another state. She and her children were living with a man with whom she had been romantically involved for 4 years. This was a good relationship for both Kathy and the children, and the couple planned to marry sometime during the year treatment began.

Her depression began 3 months prior to entering therapy when her oldest son left to live with his father. Kathy felt "devastated" by intense feelings of sadness and loss, along with debilitating physical symptoms of depression. She also experienced an intense "vulnerability" and her emotions felt "totally out of control." Although Kathy disliked the feelings of loss and the physical symptoms of depression, she highly valued this state of vulnerability because the vulnerability allowed her to feel alive and connected to people in ways previously unavailable to her. Previously, she had been closed off from her feelings, hidden, cautious, and guarded with others. During her depression, however, she somehow gained access to her feelings and allowed herself to express them. Kathy made it clear what she wanted from therapy was to be able to feel alive and open her emotions, without the accompanying debilitating depression. Currently, she could only feel one of two possible states: guarded, efficient, and functional or alive, vulnerable, and unable to function. During her son's move, she returned to "everyday functioning" and dealt with the underlying issues "by not thinking about them."

Six years ago Kathy experienced her first serious depression following the second of two abortions within a period of about a year. Prior to that time, she reported she had always been "stable and emotionally balanced." The depression hit suddenly and dramatically with debilitating physical symptoms that sent her to a psychiatrist who diagnosed her as severely depressed. Antidepressants cleared up the physical symptoms, but psychotherapy did not help.

An interesting sequence of events led up to that first depressive episode. Recently divorced, a single mother, and working full-time as a secretary, Kathy felt relieved to be free of an unhappy marriage and was involved with a new man. Although she had tolerated birth control pills well during her marriage, she discontinued using them after her divorce. She claimed she was concerned they "might be bad" for her health. She became pregnant in this new relationship due to a failed diaphragm, and a "battle" began inside her. She had always had strong feelings about abortions. She believed the fetus was a living being, a "lost soul," but she also believed in every woman's right to terminate a pregnancy. There was no way, however, that Kathy could afford to have another child, neither emotionally nor financially. After the abortion, she ended the relationship with the man, stating that his "lenient, permissive attitudes" toward abortion made her conclude he was not right for her.

Soon after, she began a 4-month-long, passionate romance with a man-about-town businessman who was "fabulously exciting" and put her "in the limelight." He treated her as an intellectual equal and described her as the smartest partner he had ever had. She felt recognized, prized, and special, and they both loved spending time together. Then one wonderfully romantic weekend she got pregnant again, the second failed-diaphragm pregnancy. "If I were superstitious I would have believed I was being punished, because I got pregnant that fabulous weekend," she remarked. It was "unforgivable" to get pregnant twice and to have two abortions: "The first time was bad enough; the second time was the breaking point." She ended the relationship, never telling the man about the pregnancy because she "feared he would be permissive of abortion rather than seeing it as the killing of an individual." Every Mother's Day since that time has been a "trauma" for Kathy. "Abortion is the antithesis of mothering," she stated. Soon her debilitating depression began.

One of the most dramatic changes the depression brought was Kathy reconsidering her feelings about mothering. Although previously she had always been intensely "fulfilled" by her children and her mothering, she suddenly felt intensely "empty" with her children. She felt resentful of what she referred to as the "surviving children." It became hard to mother them.

As in her current depression, although she disliked feeling emotionally out of control, she also cherished feeling uncharacteristically alive. She became exceptionally animated and outgoing in her social and work worlds. "I didn't feel *depressed*. I felt *crazy*. My hands would shake; I lost weight. My emotions felt out of control; I cried all the time. But I also played, had fun, and flirted with all these people. I felt very special. Then I would return home and feel lonely and miserable with the children. And I felt so guilty—here I had these three beautiful children I had always felt so fulfilled by, and I wished I could be somewhere else."

Eventually, Kathy dealt with that depression the way she was dealing with the current depression: She became functional and efficient. An external crisis developed as her ex-husband deteriorated into substance abuse. As he became irrational and threatening toward Kathy and the children, she decided to move herself and the children out of the state to the Bay Area, where they have been for 5 years.

Background

Kathy was born into a family with a brother, Dan, who was 9 years older than her and her mother's son from a previous marriage. Her parents' marriage was difficult and full of conflict. Kathy's mother was extremely passive, insecure, and dependent because of the unrelenting criticism and rejection she experienced from her own harshly "domineering" mother, Kathy's maternal grandmother. Kathy's father was also domineering. His father had deserted his mother when he was 2 years old, and his mother had died when he was 16. Kathy's father was staunchly independent and looked down upon any sign of human dependency or even normal human need. Further marital conflict derived from the fact that Kathy's father and maternal grandmother competed with each other to dominate and control Kathy's mother.

Kathy's first two years of life were relatively "abundant and full of love" as the nuclear family lived near her mother's large, extended family. However, her father's business required them to move frequently, and these frequent moves increased the marital conflict. Kathy became troubled by both her father's verbal attacks of berating criticism for her mother's social needs and her passive compliance and increasing feelings of inadequacy. As time went on, her father criticized her mother for being different from him and for not having her own opinions, at the same time he lavished praise on Kathy for being his "soulmate," looking like him, and being strong and opinionated like he was. She was the only real human connection he allowed himself since his traumatic early losses, and he used this to fight with Kathy's mother. Kathy watched in horror as her mother deflated and collapsed into further feelings of inadequacy. As she grew older, Kathy felt disturbed by the realization that the attention she received from her father caused her mother great harm and injury. She felt she was "robbing Mother of her husband."

But Mother had Dan. In fact, Kathy saw the family as "balanced" *because* Mother had Dan. These balanced alliances were crucial to Kathy's sense of fairness to her mother and allowed Kathy the closeness with her father. She required that closeness because she felt her mother was frequently bothered by her needs and often chased her away.

Kathy adored and idealized her older brother. She liked to think of him as her protector, although he laughed at her when she told him this. Although Dan "loved and tolerated" his little sister, he often teased and taunted her cruelly.

Kathy was 6 years old when her father uprooted them once again for a move that would prove devastating for everyone. None of them could adjust. The tension increased as her father competed with Dan and humiliated him in front of his teenaged friends. Dan soon found "he could get back at Father" by relentlessly teasing and taunting his little sister. Kathy felt betrayed and so hurt that she sometimes wished Dan would just disappear. Her father also began to show signs of competition with Kathy, getting upset if she beat him at a game. When she brought home a report card, he frequently told her how much better he did in school when he was her age. Kathy felt disturbed, and she noticed that now even her father seemed threatened by her doing well.

Kathy was lonely and unable to get any attention. Dan soon insisted on moving back to Texas to live with some relatives. The parents fought viciously over Dan until one day they agreed to let him move back. Although Kathy was confused by this, she thought it would be better for everyone if he left. Early one morning as she slept, he came to say good-bye to her. Kathy thought to herself, "Good. Leave me alone. Maybe I can get some attention here soon." That was the last time Kathy ever saw Dan.

Five months later, Dan died in a swimming accident. Kathy's family and life would never be the same. Somehow her father was blamed for Dan's death, especially by Kathy's maternal grandmother. The traumatic scene at the funeral was unforgettable. The entire family was literally hysterical and viciously attacked each other. The grandmother almost physically attacked Kathy's father and tried to throw herself into the grave as her beloved grandson was buried.

Kathy, however, was completely ignored. She was almost excluded from the funeral, but she begged and finally was allowed to attend. No one ever talked to her, who was now 7 years old, about any of this trauma. She was left completely alone to make sense of all that had happened and felt deeply confused. Why were they all blaming father? It made no sense. The night after the funeral, Kathy recalled the last time she had seen her brother and how she wished he would disappear so she could finally get some attention. She remembered how he had teased her until she had wished him dead. Kathy believed she "must have had something terrible to do with Dan's death," but here the rest of the family were attacking her father so viciously. Surely, she would not talk to anyone about her thoughts. Soon Kathy became convinced she was a very powerful, "evil person" who harmed others whenever she got something for herself. She also began to think about death frequently.

One day 2 months after the funeral, Kathy became "fascinated" at hearing about a little girl who died falling off a cliff. A few days later, as she swam in a swimming pool, she suddenly found herself drowning. Fortunately, someone pulled her out and resuscitated her. She felt humiliated, ran off, and never spoke about the incident to her mother. She was not sure what she feared most, that mother would be upset about the incident or that she would be upset that Kathy "had survived."

After Dan's death, Mother withdrew and stopped showing any emotion. As Kathy explained, she "functioned and did the everyday things, but she was empty inside." Her feelings were dead. Although she had never been close to Kathy, now she was totally unavailable and never recovered. In fact, the entire family never did. There were no more family celebrations of any kind ever again.

The next 6 years were some of the worst of Kathy's life. She became "invisible." No one was available to her. Mother was gone: "She died inside. ... Mother resented me and my father for surviving. There was always a tinge of punishment—maybe just in withholding." But Father disappeared too. He started drinking heavily and dove into work, rarely spending any time at all with Kathy. She could get no attention at all no matter how hard she tried. Desperately, Kathy tried to rejuvenate Mother, but she got no response. Kathy felt grimly alone and learned to be totally self-sufficient.

The family moved again when Kathy was 13, and her life turned around completely for 2 years. Mother was doing better, got involved in some community activities, and was a bit less detached. Kathy "somehow decided to just move ahead" with her own life, which became a "blossoming ... Suddenly every dream I ever had and every hope I ever had came true. I caught on academically and became very successful, but more importantly to me is that I had social acceptance for the first time. It was a dramatic change. I moved from 'unnoticeable' to 'chosen' class favorite, Valentine Miss, Homecoming Princess. I got to be the special one all the time." Those previous 6 years she had been "invisible;" now she was "chosen." Although she was a star in her own life, her parents were totally unaware of these achievements. They never asked her about her life. She also kept herself hidden because she had come to see that her getting attention and doing well were threatening to her parents.

Near the end of the second blossoming year, Kathy fell deliriously in love for the very first time. Then, abruptly and shockingly, her father suddenly sent her away to boarding school in another state, and she was ripped away from her dream-come-true world. Kathy was heartbroken and devastated. Although father claimed the change was for educational purposes, Kathy knew Father was jealous of her intense relationship with her first love and intended to stop it. He also sold all the equipment of the various sports games they used to play together. Kathy spent one miserable year in boarding school, and her father refused to even allow her visits home for the holidays, leaving her completely alone while the rest of the students returned home.

To Kathy, this banishment was clearly a punishment for her "disloyalty" to her father. For that year, Kathy remained once again socially isolated and "invisible," although she continued to do well academically. At the end of the year, however, Father still refused to let her return home. Kathy now believed she must have hurt her father badly for him to retaliate so severely. He insisted she either finish her last year at boarding school or graduate early and begin college. Kathy chose to graduate early and go to college away from home.

In college, Kathy once again "blossomed." She felt alive, happy, and successful academically as well as socially. She did not, however, allow herself to sustain this happiness for long. The summer after her freshman year, longing for her large family that had come to such an abrupt halt after her brother died, Kathy married Dave. She finished college and gave birth to three children over the next 6 years.

By this time, her marriage was growing unrewarding. Kathy's husband was competitive and envious of her accomplishments in sports and work. Kathy, though, "would have continued that way forever," because she felt so fulfilled by her children. Her husband, however, filed for divorce. Kathy and the children moved out and she found herself very relieved.

Kathy's husband did not fare very well on his own. He quit his job and began drinking heavily. Kathy, in the meantime, was going through her period of dating, abortions, and depression. Soon, in response to Dave's aggressive behavior toward her and the children, Kathy decided to move.

The Control-Mastery Case Formulation

Traumatic early life events together with inadequate parenting fortified for Kathy a deep sense of her own internal "badness" and "evil power" to hurt others. They led her to develop an intricate system of penance, which was her only method of coping with overwhelming guilt. Her normal, developmental need of feeling prized and special was severely thwarted early in life by the deep belief that her achieving recognition and attention seriously harmed, and sometimes destroyed, the people she loved. With too little adequate parenting to challenge these ideas, her childhood mind continued to interpret the events of her life in terms of her destructive power to hurt others. In the first 7 years of her life, she founded her understanding of herself and her effect on others on faulty interpretations of her causal role in others' suffering. This conviction of her "evil power" fostered in her a deep unconscious guilt toward the people she believed she was harming.

Kathy's beliefs in her destructive powers to harm others when receiving attention were seeded from birth into a conflictual family environment. Being prized by her father, who at the same time rejected and demeaned her mother, gave Kathy the distinct impression that she was "robbing Mother" of her husband. Her young child's mind was incapable of understanding the ways she was being used by her parents in their tense marriage. Instead, it looked to Kathy like Mother's weakness was a direct result of Kathy's strength.

As Kathy developed more conviction of her "harming" her mother by "stealing" Father, her growing sense of unconscious guilt triggered the beginnings of a penance system to manage this guilt. This system was founded on the one factor that allowed Kathy to bask in the needed love and attention of her father: a "balance system" that existed "because Mother had Dan." Life in the family seemed "fair" to Kathy and she was able to continue her emotional growth in the sunshine of her father's adoration as long as Mother had Dan.

By the time Kathy was a little older, however, her observations of Father's competitiveness with her fed her growing belief in her power to harm those she loved when she did well. Now her achievements appeared to hurt not only Mother, but Father as well. Soon this "destructive power" extended to her brother.

During the tense period when Dan requested to move back to Texas while Kathy was sadly neglected by both parents, as well as taunted and teased by her brother, it was only natural that Kathy "wished" her brother would "disappear" so that maybe she could get some attention. The tragic death of her brother shortly thereafter solidified for Kathy her deep belief in the connection between her getting attention and the destruction of her loved ones in the wake of her achievements.

The death of her brother, furthermore, devastated Kathy's penance system, which became heavily "unbalanced" without Dan. Kathy now came to believe she had not only "stolen" father but that she was somehow responsible for killing Dan and thereby further injuring her mother irreparably. The entire extended family fell apart and never recovered, which solidified her belief in her ability to harm others. Kathy's sense of badness and destructive power increased to intolerable proportions. Now that the balance system was broken, Kathy desperately needed to elaborate her penance system in an effort to manage her overwhelming guilt.

Shortly after the funeral, Kathy developed the concept of "trading places" with those she harmed in order to pay penance to them. In an effort to "balance" the overwhelming guilt she suffered, Kathy attempted to "trade places" with Dan. Unaware, at a conscious level, of the disturbing motivations overwhelming her, Kathy was surprised to find herself in the swimming accident that occurred shortly after she had become "fascinated with the death of another little girl." Kathy unconsciously tried to "disappear" as she had wished Dan would disappear.

Although Kathy fortunately failed in her attempts to trade places with Dan and disappear from the physical world, she did succeed in disappearing at other levels of existence. At this point, Kathy's penance system developed further intricacies in order to accommodate her overwhelming guilt. She divided or "split" her sense of self. She hid the "alive" self she had been for the first 6 years of her life and allowed "out" only an invisible self who had no feelings and achieved nothing worthy of notice. She "functioned" in everyday matters and neither caused trouble nor attempted to achieve anything. In fact, this invisible self greatly resembled how Kathy viewed Mother after Dan's death.

For 6 long and lonely years immediately following Dan's death, Kathy became her invisible self, thereby "trading places" with both her mother and Dan to punish herself for "destroying" both of them. At the end of that "sentence," Kathy's system of penance allowed her a 2-year period of blossoming, at a time when mother, not coincidentally, was doing better than she had in years. As long as her achievements were kept secret from both Mother and Father, Kathy viewed life as balanced and could come alive.

Although it was easy to keep most of her successes secret from her self-absorbed parents, falling in love for the first time proved impossible to keep secret. Father's abrupt and severe banishment of Kathy, after learning of this intense love affair, further convinced Kathy that her riches in life would inevitably harm others. Kathy was stunned at the extent of father's reaction and at the fact that their relationship never recovered. Kathy's year in isolation at boarding school feeling truly "invisible" served as penance for her crime in her now complicated guilt management system. Having "served her time," Kathy was once again allowed to be alive for a short period when she attended college away from home.

This second period of blossoming, which was allowed for only one year, was interrupted when Kathy married. The man she married turned out to be remarkably similar to her father in terms of competitiveness, vindictiveness, and alcoholism. Kathy's penance system allowed her now to feel fulfillment and connection with her children, but only as long as she remained in a miserable marriage.

When Kathy was freed after her husband filed for divorce, her penance system was thrown totally off balance. Suddenly relieved of her miserable marriage, she oddly decided to stop using birth control pills, even though there was no medical need to do so. Her pleasure in living with a new man along with her children was abruptly ruined by a failed-diaphragm pregnancy and subsequent abortion. Kathy's self-punitive attitudes with regard to the abortion further demonstrated a penance system trying to "balance" things once again with severe punishments.

Her "unbalanced" penance system, in search of a foolproof method of punishment, allowed Kathy to continue using the diaphragm after the first abortion, only to punish herself all the more severely for the "unforgivable" crime of a second abortion. Shortly after the second one, Kathy suffered the first major depression of her life. Kathy's crime had been to be alive, attractive, intelligent, and connected to a man in ways her mother could never achieve. Her punishment was to trade places with Mother by "killing" her own children, both through the abortions and her inability to mother her "surviving children," as well as to make "Mother's Day never the same again" for herself. A comprehensive attack on her mothering role was the price Kathy's penance system required in order for her to deserve the attention that she received. She did not allow herself to be in a good relationship and to be a good mother at the same time; she had to sacrifice one or the other to balance her debt to her mother.

Kathy's second major depression struck just before she sought treatment. It was triggered by her son's move to live with his father, but it also occurred in the context of being in a satisfying relationship with a man she planned to marry that year. That possible marriage once again threatened Kathy's penance system. She was not allowed to have a healthy relationship with a man and be a good mother at the same time. Her son's move retriggered the contradictory feelings of her previous depression: debilitating physiological symptoms in conjunction with the vulnerable feeling of being "alive" with the inability to mother. Her penance system was beginning to get unbalanced in various ways if she was to proceed with the good things in her life.

Kathy dealt with the second depression as she had with the first: by returning to her hidden state of being functional. Kathy's penance system hid her "alive" self since the day of Dan's death in an effort to compensate her mother and Dan for the destruction she believed she had caused. Subsequent to that time, her lively and thriving self was allowed out only after long sentences of isolation and only then for short periods of time. By the time of her second major depression, Kathy's intricate system of penance allowed her to feel alive only when concomitantly suffering a mental illness. Kathy sought therapy to reclaim the right to her "alive" self without requiring depression.

Kathy's overall goals for treatment were to recapture her right to be prized, special, and deserving of attention; to grow, achieve, accomplish, and shine; to feel alive, visible, and appreciated by others; to feel connected with others, especially with her children and her soon-to-be husband; and to have the right to focus her attention on her own life to fully develop her capacities and talents. Kathy's attainment of these goals was blocked by an intricate penance system trying to accommodate the overwhelming guilt caused by a deep pathogenic belief that the achievement of recognition for herself caused pain, suffering, and destruction to those she loved.

How the Formulation Relates to Treatment Interventions

In the first 16 sessions, Kathy worked hard to disconfirm her pathogenic belief that she did not deserve to focus on her goal to grow, feel alive, be appreciated, and to "bask in the spotlight." I helped Kathy accomplish this task in varied ways, mainly by explicitly recognizing the importance of the goal as well as by keeping it in focus throughout the treatment. Kathy continually "forgot" this goal and would ask me to keep track of it for her. I responded by sometimes summarizing Kathy's goals, sometimes questioning her difficulty focusing on herself, and sometimes pointing out how she sacrificed her own goals because of her fear of hurting others.

In the first session, as Kathy described her presenting problem and background, she also mentioned that one of the symptoms of her depression was crying. I explored the details, noting to Kathy that the crying seemed to occur when she witnessed instances of high achievements, such as when watching the Olympics. Kathy started the next session by saying, "I allowed myself the indulgence to think about what triggered my crying and I found it to be happy, joyous times that somehow mark a person's specialness, and I linked it to my earlier life in that I probably felt that way about my own life at some point." I responded by saying, "You wanted your parents to be able to share your joy, achievements, and specialness growing up." Kathy further developed this theme by describing three periods of her life when she felt "in the sunshine," none of which were recognized by her parents. These lively periods were (a) in adolescence, (b) her first year at college, and (c) the "crazy time" after the abortions.

Subsequent sessions focused on her inability to feel entitled to recapture this "aliveness." Sometimes Kathy put herself down with references to her "self-indulgence." I steadily challenged these ideas by consistently presenting contrary evidence. Kathy then explored how she "destroyed" her ex-husband by being so much more competent than he was. Patiently, I challenged her by questioning, for example, why she viewed the problem as stemming from *her* competence rather than from *his* envy and need to blame others for his own inadequacies. Kathy was relieved by such interventions and she soon realized, "I need to be more generous with myself."

These realizations, however, were often followed by feelings of unworthiness and fears of humiliation for what Kathy saw as her "boasting." "People watching the videotape at this project will think I'm tooting my own horn," she said. I replied, "On the contrary, they will see what difficulty you have tooting your own horn and they will wonder why. Maybe your parents were not comfortable or were upset when you did so." This intervention led to important work, and Kathy revealed the extreme difficulties of both parents in recognizing her achievements.

During the fourth session, Kathy began to outline some of the achievements she had made during her adolescent period. Over the next 10 sessions, however, Kathy revealed the power of her conviction that she might harm someone with her achievements by testing to see if I might be threatened. During these testing sequences, I observed that Kathy hid her achievements and required that I discover her talents as well as fight for her right to nurture them.

Two strong interventions helped challenge Kathy's belief that I might be threatened. She had been talking about a lifetime interest in writing when, a few sessions later, she made a slight reference to a book of short stories she had written. At the end of the session, I made the first of these interventions when I asked Kathy if I could read them. Although Kathy claimed the stories were "nothing special," I saw this as an opportunity to recognize a "hidden" achievement.

I was deeply moved by the stories, which gave me a disturbing sense of the sacrifices involved in Kathy's fear of harming others with her achievements. Two sessions later, when Kathy once again "forgot" her goals, I questioned why she had lost track of them. Kathy argued quite aggressively that she had changed her mind about her need to be more generous with herself. She decided she was too generous with herself and that she did not deserve any more in her life. Calmly and strongly, I made the second intervention by disagreeing with Kathy, using evidence to demonstrate the significance of Kathy's problem with self-generosity. I told Kathy how impressive the stories were in communicating her outstanding talents as a writer, storyteller, and communicator of intense emotion, especially in the face of her claim that she lacked talent, skills, or creativity. I demonstrated how Kathy's fears of her talents harming people were so severe that she required me not only to find her hidden achievements but also to argue ferociously for the cultivation of those achievements.

As Kathy developed some conviction that maybe I was not threatened and that she did need to cultivate more generosity with herself, Kathy elaborated on many of the awards she had only briefly outlined 10 sessions earlier. When I pointed out with further amazement how much she had hidden from me, Kathy admitted how fearful she had been that I might view her as "boastful," like her parents did, and retaliate or else feel uncomfortable as they had.

This long, initial piece of work culminated in Kathy solidifying her original decision to pursue her goal of recapturing the "special times." It also resulted in her announcing a decision to seek work outside the home and enroll in a drama class. The class was to help her learn to be more comfortable "in the spotlight." Kathy began the next hour revealing a previous night's dream in which she delivered the baby she had aborted in the second relationship. In the dream, she was happy because the baby was alive and all her family was present. Her thoughts immediately turned to how for the first time, a year ago, she had a vivid memory of her brother on the last day she saw him before he died. It was a memory of "remorse" in which she remembered their conversation and her thoughts of wishing he would disappear. I noted how clearly Kathy's mind associated getting attention, wishing her brother would disappear, and the abortion.

A few sessions later, on the anniversary of her second abortion, she revealed for the first time that one of her most "devastating symptoms" was a ruminating worry. Daily, Kathy imagined, in great detail, the loss of one of her children, followed by the fantasy of how she would comfort the remaining "surviving children." She would change which child died and which survived, the circumstances, and repeat the process. I asked when the symptom first appeared. Kathy replied, "As soon as James was born, I realized what Mother had experienced, and that if that happened to me, I could understand what happened to Mother and why she had refused to recover." I told Kathy she was practicing "trading places" with Mother in sympathy, and that the purpose of such mental torture was to continually punish herself because she felt responsible for Mother's loss. Kathy was visibly relieved hearing this interpretation; it helped to free her from this devastating symptom, which decreased markedly over the next several months.

Kathy next wondered why so many people she had known had died. She thought it was more than the average person. I observed that Kathy was demonstrating right there in the session her powerful belief in her destructive power. Kathy followed this line of thought by talking about her own swimming accident just after Dan died. As she described the incident, she became aware for the first time that maybe she had been trying to kill herself or disappear the way she had wished Dan would disappear. The memory of this experience was filled with intense emotion and convinced Kathy that she did feel powerfully responsible for Dan's death.

At this point in the treatment, I began to suggest that Kathy's abortions might have been a way to punish herself for harming Mother, Dan, and even her ex-husband. She began to examine why she wished her friends would be punitive and not lenient toward her regarding the abortions. She began to see how her strong reactions to her abortions served as severe punishments and how they forever changed the way she felt about herself as a mother. I took an active stance with regard to the mothering issues Kathy presented in order to demonstrate her rights to have had better mothering herself, as well as to show she had the right to be a better mother than her own had been without a fear of hurting Mother.

At an early point in the treatment, her son James returned to live at home following a disastrous attempt to live with his father. His father's alcoholism had increased to the point that he was unable to adequately care for his son while blaming Kathy for all his failures. James returned home feeling severely depressed, rejected, and angry at Kathy. As she described the situation, I noted a total absence of any advocacy on Kathy's part for her own position, and I encouraged her to stand up for herself. I showed Kathy how her irrational feelings of destructive power were distorting her ability to protect herself and her son from alcoholic blame and denial. She then spoke of feeling paralyzed and incapable of even comforting her son. When she said, "I've been as bad a mother to

James as my mother was to me," I showed Kathy she was acting like her mother in order to make her mother's inadequate mothering look better. I then explicitly directed, "You must comfort James, no matter how angry he is at you." I role-played with Kathy the ways this could be done, demonstrating how, for the well-being of her son, she could be a better mother to her son than her mother was to her. Kathy successfully followed these suggestions and made excellent progress in comforting James over the next several months.

Somewhat later, Kathy needed to learn the limits of how far she should go in helping James. Kathy's ex-husband, in a distraught frame of mind, frequently phoned to talk to his children, complaining what a mess his life was. James reacted badly to these phone contacts, as he felt excessively responsible for his father's misery. Depressed and withdrawn, James began to have serious school problems. I took an active stance again, teaching Kathy how to take appropriate levels of responsibility without overstepping those levels.

During a particular period, James remained severely depressed and refused all Kathy's efforts to comfort or help him. Kathy then became severely depressed herself. I noted how this situation was similar to her mother's depression after Dan died and Mother rejected Kathy's attempts to console her. I told Kathy that if James "refused to recover" Kathy should attempt to comfort him, but if he persisted she was to show him that she could both love him and still maintain a separate mood from him. She was to teach James that she could tolerate his pain without feeling overwhelming responsibility for it: "Try to reach James and if he refuses, let him be. Go ahead and be happy with the rest of the family."

At first, Kathy claimed that such actions felt mean and cruel. I then explained that James needed to learn to go on with his own life despite his father's alcoholism, and that he could learn that best if Kathy modeled appropriate separating with James's depression. Kathy then began to remember vividly her own trauma after Dan died, when her entire extended family fell apart and never recovered. At this point, Kathy was convinced of the importance of teaching James to go on with his life. She proceeded successfully with James and was able to maintain consistently good mothering. James, who showed excellent progress by improving academically and socially, later told his mother how much he appreciated her steady love and support, which had enabled him to face his father's alcoholism.

SUMMARY

This chapter illustrated the control-mastery method of case formulation, which provided a highly case-specific perspective on the goals Kathy sought in treatment and which pathogenic beliefs blocked the attainment of these goals. The intervention examples demonstrated my own particular style of disproving those beliefs, which is fairly active and direct. A different therapist treating Kathy could have used the same formulation to disconfirm the identical pathogenic beliefs utilizing a distinctly different therapeutic style. For example, a therapist with a more indirect, exploratory style might periodically pose questions about the patient's thoughts or motives. Such an approach might have been equally effective as long as the exploration and questions were directed at helping Kathy disconfirm her pathogenic beliefs. Control-mastery theory provides a case-specific approach to formulating the patient's problems and a flexible approach for accommodating a wide variety of therapeutic styles.

REFERENCE

Jones, E. E., Ghannam, J., Nigg, J. T., & Dyer, J. F. P. (1993). A paradigm for single-case research: The time series study of a long-term psychotherapy for depression. *Journal of Consulting and Clinical Psychology, 61,* 381–394.

7

TREATMENT BY ATTITUDES

Harold Sampson

THE PATIENT'S AND THE THERAPIST'S ATTITUDES

A young woman, Miss Snow, decided to ask her uncle, a psychiatrist, whether to seek psychotherapy. She was experiencing difficulty in establishing close relationships, especially with men. Might psychotherapy help? If so, whom should she see? Her uncle suggested that she meet with a therapist for a few sessions to help her answer these questions, and he recommended she consult with Dr. M. He told her that Dr. M. had been one of his teachers, and he thought highly of him. Her uncle warned her that Dr. M. might be too busy to add a patient, but he was sure Dr. M. would make time for a consultation.

Her uncle then called Dr. M. and left a message about the referral. He hoped Dr. M. would at least see her for a consultation. He added that he believed his niece had a "rejection problem." Her father was a "workaholic" who had never been very available to her, and that may have been a factor in her problem.

In the first two sessions with Dr. M., Miss Snow described her problem exactly as she had to her uncle. She then expressed some skepticism about the usefulness of therapy. She said she did not find it easy to talk about herself or to express her feelings. Her manner in both sessions was reserved. She presented no history even when invited to do so.

In the third session, when the therapist was expected to make his recommendation, Miss Snow declared that she had almost decided not to seek therapy, at least for now. She repeated her doubts about its usefulness and again emphasized her dislike of self-disclosure and of talking about feelings. She added a new obstacle: The commute to Dr. M.'s office took nearly half an hour. If she did decide on psychotherapy later, maybe she should find a therapist closer to home.

Dr. M., for reasons we will examine later, replied that he believed therapy would be helpful to her and he recommended she begin now. He would be pleased to work with her if she was agreeable to doing so. Without hesitation, Miss Snow exclaimed, "That's great! I'm very pleased to have the opportunity to work with you—my uncle recommended you highly. I can start whenever you can see me." Her manner was animated, and she smiled for the first time.

After a brief pause, her thoughts turned toward her father, who was on the East Coast working on a large research project. She had planned to go to visit him. When she phoned him several days ago to discuss the visit, he could talk for only a minute. He told her he was very busy but could probably see her for one or two dinners during her visit. She had become aware of feeling a "twinge of disappointment." She teared momentarily, then composed herself, and added that she probably had more feelings about his unavailability than she had let herself realize. Over the next several weeks, she brought forth many painful memories of feeling unimportant to him. She thought it was because she was uninteresting and dull.

The beginning of this therapy had a paradoxical quality. The patient defined a reasonable problem for beginning psychotherapy. She had talked it over with her uncle and followed up on his recommendation to consult with Dr. M. She was cautious and distant in the first two hours with Dr. M., though she defined a relevant problem that seems potentially amenable to psychotherapy. But in the third hour when a recommendation would presumably be made, Miss Snow said she had almost decided not to begin, at least for now, and probably not with Dr. M.

Dr. M. did not respond by suggesting a further investigation of her doubts, or by a tentative interpretation of her reluctance to start, but by recommending therapy, now and with him. Surprisingly, Miss Snow enthusiastically agreed. She expressed pleasure at the opportunity to work with him and wanted to start as soon as possible. She then spontaneously mentioned painful feelings about her father's unavailability and her conviction that it was probably because she was not a very interesting person. She continued to explore her relationship with her father over the following weeks and months.

Dr. M. was not surprised by the patient's positive responses to his somewhat unorthodox intervention. He had seriously considered her uncle's idea that she had a rejection problem that was possibly based on her relation to an unavailable father. He believed it was a useful hypothesis. He thought her initial reserve and caution with him might be explained by her fear of rejection. She might have feared getting involved with Dr. M. in the absence of any commitment from him to continue to work with her. He took her somewhat rejecting attitude in the beginning of the third session, their last agreed upon meeting, as also confirmatory of the hypothesis.

Dr. M. then acted on this hypothesis by making a commitment to her in the form of a recommendation that she begin therapy with him, and that they begin as soon as they could arrange to do so. Her enthusiastic acceptance of the recommendation, her spontaneous exploration of her feelings about her father's unavailability, and her pathogenic belief that her father's lack of interest in her was due to her being uninteresting seemed consistent with Dr. M.'s hypothesis and with his rationale for the recommendation.

What gave Dr. M.'s intervention its power? Its power cannot be convincingly explained as based on compliance on her part, because he had not spoken to her about her father or about rejection as an issue in her life. The intervention derived its power by conveying the *attitude* that the therapist wanted to work with her and would not ignore or reject her, as she believed her father had done. Dr. M.'s attitude began to disconfirm her beliefs about her inherent rejectability and unworthiness. This attitude made her feel safe enough in relation to Dr. M. to begin psychotherapy, to feel enthusiastic and hopeful about doing so, and to begin spontaneously to examine her painful feelings in relation to her father.

In addition to illustrating treatment by attitudes, this vignette is also an example of "crying at the happy ending" (refer to chapters 2 and 3). Miss Snow's expressed reluctance about therapy may also have been a passive-into-active test, that is, an unconscious attempt by Miss Snow to find out how Dr. M. would respond to *her* rejecting attitude toward him. Dr. M. responded by recommending that she start therapy now and with him. In doing so, Dr. M. consciously or unconsciously modeled a useful attitude that *she* might want to acquire, an attitude that expressed a willingness to pursue a relationship even at the risk of possible rejection and disappointment.

Several other characteristics of this example of treatment by attitudes warrant further examination. First, Dr. M.'s intervention was case specific. It was based on his hypotheses about her psychology. If Miss Snow had been concerned not with rejection but with freeing herself from parental control, Dr. M.'s intervention would have been endangering to her rather than increasing her sense of safety about beginning therapy.

Second, Dr. M. used all the information available to him in deciding how to respond in the third session. His knowledge of the patient's history came from Miss Snow's uncle, rather than from the initially reticent patient. He used his observations and affective reactions to her behavior with him, and he understood that behavior in terms of his own life experience, intuitions, emotions, clinical experience, and his sensibilities.

Third, the intervention Dr. M. made fit his hypotheses, but it is not the only response that might have been compatible with these hypotheses. We may assume that the specific intervention he made was based on his own style of doing therapy, as well as his personal sense of what would be most useful to Miss Snow.

Fourth, as suggested by the preceding comments, treatment by attitudes is *not* ordinarily a rote, mechanical, or formulaic process. Nor is it a contrived or inauthentic process. It is based on personal judgments, sensibilities, and beliefs that reflect the therapist's convictions about how to help the patient. The intervention may be planned and premeditated, as well as simultaneously spontaneous and genuine, not unlike many ordinary interactions in everyday life (e.g., a teacher giving special attention to a particularly insecure student).

Finally, treatment by attitudes is usually understandable in terms of familiar human experiences. Miss Snow's hesitance to commit to therapy before the therapist indicated he would work with her was based in part on her wish to avoid disappointment, feelings of rejection, and possibly humiliation. She anticipated (unconsciously feared) that the therapist would not see her. I assume this was not only because he was reputed to be busy and hence would not have a free hour, but also because she unconsciously believed a man would not be interested in making time for her. In order to avoid the painful disappointment of rejection by a man whom she unconsciously wished would be interested in her, she was cautious about investing emotionally in the possibility of working with him. When Dr. M. committed to working with her, he conveyed an attitude that contradicted her beliefs about rejectability and unworthiness. This attitude enabled her to feel more positive and hopeful about therapy, as well as safe enough to make a commitment to it. This patient's initially cautious approach was prevalent in relational dramas outside of therapy, such as dating, which involves a real and meaningful danger of rejection, and sometimes, painful disappointment.

THE ROLE OF THE THERAPIST'S ATTITUDES IN PSYCHOTHERAPY

Treatment by attitudes is a ubiquitous, though often unnoticed, part of all psychotherapies. Every therapist, whatever his or her theoretical orientation, inevitably conveys attitudes about the patient. The therapist does so by interpretations, by silences, by what is attended to and what is ignored, as well as by his or her manner and way of being. In short, the therapist conveys significant attitudes about the patient in all the varied conscious and unconscious ways people convey attitudes in everyday life.

The patient, for his or her part, is highly motivated, unconsciously as well as consciously, to detect attitudes relevant to his or her goals, pathogenic beliefs, hopes, and fears. The patient will construe the therapist's attitudes in terms of his or her own psychology and the immediate concerns in treatment. For example, a patient who is working to be free from what he or she perceives as controlling parents may construe much that the therapist says and does in terms how it reflects the therapist's attitudes toward the patient's struggle to feel more autonomous. The therapist may convey relevant attitudes implicitly as well as explicitly, unintentionally as well as intentionally, and unconsciously as well as consciously.

Therefore, treatment by attitudes refers both to a process that commonly takes place outside the conscious awareness of either of the participants, as well as a process that may be used intentionally by a therapist to facilitate treatment. In the case of Miss Snow, the therapist's inviting, friendly attitude was intentional. The next case example illustrates a treatment by attitude that is less consciously intentional.

Mrs. W.[1]

Mrs. W., who was treated by a colleague, was a 33-year-old, highly successful lawyer who seemed unusually conscientious in therapy as in life. She was always helpful toward friends and associates, and unconsciously felt responsible for solving their problems. She sought treatment because, in spite of business success and a good marriage, she felt driven, derived little pleasure from anything, and occasionally felt vaguely depressed. This feeling did not interfere with her functioning, but it made her aware of how dissatisfied she felt. During her childhood,

Mrs. W. had developed an unconscious belief that she was responsible for making her chronically dissatisfied mother happy. She worked hard to do so but did not succeed. She unconsciously inferred that she was not doing enough for her mother.

Mrs. W.'s initial manner in therapy was relentlessly earnest, hard working, almost grim. She was completely task oriented. She focused determinedly on addressing her problems, as well as her feelings and ideas about them, but she continued to feel dissatisfaction. She implied from time to time that the therapist was not doing enough or not doing the right thing, but she denied any interpretations that she had such feelings.

The therapist noticed that he had adopted, without premeditation, an unusually chatty, informal style with Mrs. W. He talked in an unhurried manner. His interpretations were casual and a bit lengthy. Sometimes he digressed from the immediate task or joked a little. After a few months, he noticed a change in the patient's behavior. She began sessions with a few comments about the weather, the traffic, politics, even football. The therapist responded conversationally, and they would frequently chat for a few minutes. The patient then shifted back to her earnest, dissatisfied manner. The therapist offered observations and interpretations freely, and she worked on them diligently but without any sense of pleasure or progress.

One day she began in her customary way with chatty items of the day and then said, "Ever since I began to work—or before, even in law school—I've worked through my lunch hour without a break. Yesterday I went out to lunch with a friend, and I enjoyed it. I thought to myself, you (i.e., the therapist) don't seem to work too hard here. You seem to be enjoying yourself." There was a long pause, and then she continued. "You don't seem to feel responsible for my problems and dissatisfactions to the same extent that I do with my friends' problems. I wonder why I have to be so driven, so responsible."

In the following sessions, she became both more relaxed and more productive. She became aware that she had felt critical of the therapist during the first few months for not working harder and taking more responsibility for her unhappiness. But what surprised her was a different reaction: She had also felt relief when he continued to work in an easy, relaxed way, offering interpretations without a feeling of urgency or pressure to satisfy her. She also began to remember more about how dissatisfied her mother had always seemed. She became conscious of a childhood feeling of desperate urgency to make her mother happy, and of how she always felt she should be trying harder. She realized she had that same feeling toward her husband, her friends, and her business associates.

In this vignette, the therapist's demonstration of a relaxed attitude, of a sense that he was not irrationally responsible for making her feel satisfied, began to disconfirm her unconscious belief that she was responsible for making her chronically dissatisfied mother happy. This enabled her to feel a little less irrationally responsible and driven. She became able to go out to lunch with friends and enjoy herself. She also began to make conscious and resolve an important aspect of her transferences to the therapist.

CORRECTIVE EMOTIONAL EXPERIENCES AND TREATMENT BY ATTITUDES

The concept of treatment by attitudes is not new. It was described explicitly and systematically more than 50 years ago by Alexander and French (1946, pp. 66–70). They introduced the concept of the "corrective emotional experience" and recommended that the therapist should infer from the patient's childhood relationships and current behavior these attitudes that the therapist should manifest in order to provide the patient with the corrective experience.

Alexander and French's formulation of corrective emotional experiences and treatment by attitudes provided a significant advance in the understanding of how psychotherapy actually brings about change. However, these new concepts were for the most part condemned by the psychoanalytic community. They were criticized as manipulative, inauthentic playacting, and not leading to a genuine analytic change. In recent years, Alexander and French's ideas have been cautiously rehabilitated.

Although Alexander and French's concept of corrective emotional experience and treatment by attitudes is similar to the concepts presented here, some very distinctive differences must be mentioned. First, we do not view the patient as a passive recipient of the therapist's interventions. The patient actively attempts to discern the conscious or unconscious attitudes of the therapist that bear on his or her goals, fears, and the pathogenic beliefs he or she is struggling to overcome. The patient may also "coach" the therapist (see chapter 9) by presenting precisely that material that will help guide the therapist to convey those attitudes that may disconfirm pathogenic beliefs. Moreover, the patient may unconsciously test the therapist in order to determine his or her attitudes toward the patient's pathogenic beliefs. In recognizing the patient's active role in eliciting what he or she needs from the therapist, we provide a more accurate, as well as a more comprehensive, understanding of the therapeutic process than provided by Alexander and French. Control-mastery theory recognizes that psychotherapy is a process in which both participants interactively attempt to create conditions for progress, unconsciously as well as consciously.

Second, the recognition that treatment by attitudes often takes place outside the *conscious awareness* of *either* participant transforms the concept from that of *only* a *technique* to a way of *following closely and understanding* often overlooked change processes. For instance, if a therapist observes that a patient has made progress in the absence of interpretations or other deliberate interventions, he or she may be able to discover how *other* aspects of the patient's behavior have conveyed attitudes that made it safe for the patient to progress in a particular area. In a case that I supervised, for example, a strikingly inhibited young man had begun to be less inhibited and more assertive. We inferred that the therapist's implicitly self-confident, bold, and free-wheeling attitude had reassured the patient that if *he* were freer and more assertive he would not threaten the therapist, as he believed that such strong behavior would have threatened his weak and fragile father. This understanding of *how* the therapy was actually working enabled the therapist to help his patient not only by his attitudes but also by intensive exploration and interpretation of the patient's childhood relationship to his father.

Third, we redefine the corrective emotional experience as a powerful relational experience, often based on treatment by attitudes that challenge and begin to disconfirm a pathogenic belief held by the patient. The disconfirmation of the pathogenic belief increases the patient's sense of safety. As Weiss emphasized (refer to chapter 3), an increased sense of safety is the essential precondition for therapeutic progress.

CONCLUSION

I have argued that treatment by attitudes is an understandable and lawful process that may be employed by a therapist to disconfirm pathogenic beliefs and thereby enable the patient to feel safer and make progress. It is a process that often takes place unconsciously, and knowledge that it does so may enable the therapist to study and understand otherwise unexplained changes in the patient. Treatment by attitudes is one important component of the relational aspect of psychotherapy and provides the therapist with an additional understanding of how the therapeutic relationship may affect the patient's progress. It works by providing an experience that may discomfirm a patient's pathogenic beliefs.

Finally, there are a number of people—and these are by no means the most severely impaired or dysfunctional clients—who can *only* be helped by treatment by attitudes. They are unable or unwilling to comply with most conventional psychotherapies. Often they have seen several therapists and have dropped out quickly. They may, however, continue and thrive in what Weiss and I have referred to as "unusual therapies"—successful, often lengthy treatments in which there are no interpretations, confrontations, or analysis of defenses, and little explicit discussion by the therapist of the patient's psychology. These are treatments in which the therapist accommodates to the unique requirements of the patient by manifesting an attitude that is helpful to the patient (for examples of such cases, see Weiss's discussion of Samir and Gordon in chapter 3, and Pryor's case presentation in chapter 8).

In conclusion, therapists—regardless of their theoretical orientation, conscious awareness, or intent—inevitably convey attitudes about the patient's beliefs, relationships, goals, expectations, hopes, and fears. The patient construes these attitudes in terms of his or her own psychology and immediate concerns. These attitudes may prove helpful in the patient's struggles to overcome the pathogenic beliefs that block the patient from achieving important goals.

ENDNOTE

1. This vignette is taken from Sampson (1991) with permission of the William A. White Institute.

REFERENCES

Alexander, F., & French, T. M. (1946). *Psychoanalytic therapy: Principles and applications.* New York: Ronald Press.

Sampson, H. (1991). Experience and insight in the resolution of transferences. *Contemporary Psychoanalysis, 27,* 200–207.

8

A LONG-TERM THERAPY CASE ILLUSTRATING TREATMENT BY ATTITUDE

Kathryn Pryor

This chapter describes the 9-year treatment of Ruth, a 32-year-old, highly traumatized woman. Although many themes arise in this case, it is most strongly distinguished by Ruth's overwhelming feelings of responsibility, identification, and compliance with her profoundly depressed mother and Ruth's consequent terror and avoidance of close relationships. Ruth benefited substantially from the therapy, and we both agreed this was a very successful treatment. This case illustrates a "treatment by attitude" (chapter 7) in that the most curative element of the therapy was my relationship with Ruth. My overall approach and attitude were designed to provide a corrective emotional experience that would enable Ruth to understand and overcome her pathogenic beliefs about herself and her world. Ruth was able to identify with my behaviors and attitudes and use them to develop new relational capacities within herself.

Following an introduction by way of the first sessions, I will describe Ruth's therapy in three phases: phase one, the first 18 months; phase two, from 18 months until year four; and phase three, from year four to year nine. In the first phase, Ruth frequently and vigorously tested the safety of the therapeutic relationship to assure herself that she was not going to be retraumatized. During the second phase of treatment, many important previously inaccessible experiences and memories emerged due to Ruth's increased feeling of safety. She was able to bring the anxieties fueled by her pathogenic beliefs into the therapy and test them out with me so that I could help her disconfirm them. Finally, in the third phase, Ruth, freed from the grip of her pathogenic beliefs, made great progress and attained many of her therapy goals while continuing to work on disconfirming her pathogenic beliefs.

THE FIRST TWO SESSIONS

Before detailing the three phases of the therapy, I would like to begin with some of my initial impressions of Ruth and several details from our first two sessions. This will be followed by a brief summary of Ruth's history and a case formulation.

In her first phone call to me, Ruth requested help with "a few small problems." She emphasized that she needed a flexible therapist who would be okay with many missed sessions because her work involved a lot of travel. Furthermore, she requested an evening hour. I told her I would like to work out a flexible schedule with her, but that I didn't have evening hours. I suggested the possibility of an early morning or lunch hour, adding that if that didn't fit her schedule, I could refer her to someone who might have evening hours. Sounding quite put off, she said she would try once to come in during a lunch hour.

This phone conversation primed my expectations for our initial session. First, she sounded extremely anxious. I thought she might be feeling frightened and ashamed of needing help, and I decided a relaxed approach on my part might be most useful to her. Second, although I believed she actually did need some flexibility due to her work schedule, her manner in requesting this suggested there was likely more to this than her actual need. Because her annoyance and dissatisfaction were palpable, I wondered if this might represent a passive-into-active test. I began with a hypothesis that Ruth might be rigidly bound by a set of fears and was asking me to be flexible and patient in order to model a way of freeing herself from them. I also felt that her need for flexibility in the time and frequency of our sessions would provide her with a necessary feeling of control. Finally, I suspected it would take her a long time to feel safe with me, and we might therefore need to proceed very slowly. These first thoughts about the case helped shape my attitude toward her before we met in person.

At the initial session, Ruth appeared extremely self-conscious and ill at ease. She was very attractive and meticulously groomed. Although she smiled continuously, she appeared guarded and uncomfortable. She sat on the edge of her seat, and her anxiety was apparent. Ruth told me she was a positive person and wanted to focus on positive things. She said she didn't like anything that sounded like weakness. She proudly described herself as a perfectionist and said she worked best with very definite goals, wanting the focus of the work to be on behavioral change.

When I questioned her about the changes she wished to make, she hesitated. With considerable embarrassment, she reported that she had been in therapy several years ago for a panic disorder, which had begun right before her marriage and had lasted until her divorce a year and a half later. During the course of that therapy, she had taken medication to control the panic attacks. She said she found her previous therapy useful, so she was willing to try again.

During the session, I noticed that she scrutinized me closely. Even though I had thought I was prepared after our phone conversation, it was far more difficult to adopt a casual, relaxed stance than I expected. I had the feeling that there was absolutely no room for mistakes on my part. Ruth told me she particularly liked the matter-of-fact style and behavioral approach of her first therapist, because it had made her feel normal. When I probed into her therapy experience, she became visibly annoyed and repeated that she preferred focusing on present issues.

Throughout the session, Ruth bristled at most of my questions. She stated she had already learned from her first therapy that her father's womanizing was at the root of her problems. Immediately after her marriage, all her "father issues" had been rekindled. When I asked about her mother, she dismissed it as irrelevant. She said she already understood her family's influence on her and that it would not be useful for us to explore it any further.

I noticed that when I simply listened silently Ruth shared more information. Near the end of the session Ruth told me that several months earlier she had moved to the Bay Area from the Midwest. Her new marketing position required frequent sales presentations in front of large groups and she was terrified of public speaking. She wanted me to help her overcome a "panicky, sick feeling" that she was about to be "exposed."

Then, almost as an aside, Ruth mentioned she felt quite ashamed of an eating disorder she had developed. She was bingeing and purging at least once a day. She couldn't understand her growing obsession with food because she had always been, and still was, a healthy, physically fit woman. She ran marathons and ate "meticulously" well. She also added proudly that she was successful at work. Most men found her to be an ideal woman, and most women were jealous of her because of this. It was puzzling and upsetting to her that food had become her "lover and best friend."

Ruth described in detail the elaborate plans she made each day for her "health food" binges. She also admitted drinking more wine than usual. She said she had never had problems with eating in the past. She learned about bingeing from her last boyfriend, and she subsequently added the purging because it dawned on her that she might get fat. She had met this boyfriend immediately following her divorce. Instantly, they fell "madly in love" and spent a lot of their time planning binges. After ending the relationship because her boyfriend was "too needy," Ruth moved to California and continued the habit. Ruth carefully watched my reactions to what she was telling me and seemed somewhat more relaxed when I didn't appear upset.

At the end of the first session, Ruth told me she would be traveling during the next 3 weeks and after that would like to come in every other week to accommodate her work schedule. She asked, "Could you be kind enough to extend yourself for a short period of time and see me for an evening appointment?" She requested this in a way that made me feel as if I were being manipulated or shamed into giving her the desired hours. I replied that I could work around her travel schedule and would like to work with her, but that I didn't have evening hours and my latest afternoon hours were filled. Vexed, she said she might call for an appointment when she returned from her trip. She added that she felt quite disappointed in me, especially because the woman who had referred me to her had been so positive about her experience with me.

Reflections on the First Session

The following themes emerged during the first session: (a) autonomy and Ruth's need to be in control; (b) perfectionism and a dread of weakness or failure; (c) shame, because Ruth didn't feel normal and was terrified about being exposed (e.g., bulimia); (d) anxiety and panic; (e) difficulty in relationships with men (her father was a womanizer and she had a failed marriage) and with women (their jealousy); (f) dissatisfied, annoyed, and provocative presentation; (g) and severe suffering.

Control-mastery theory was very useful in understanding and treating Ruth. Especially important was its emphasis on childhood trauma in the development of false beliefs about the self and the world, the importance of establishing conditions of safety in therapy so that the patient could feel free to work on these beliefs, the concept of testing the therapist as a way of disconfirming pathogenic beliefs, and the importance of the therapist's general attitude. Immediately, I had the sense that Ruth had been severely traumatized. Her intense annoyance and provocative presentation communicated to me the profound anxiety she experienced when vulnerable. At first, it was important for me to focus on establishing conditions of safety and security for her. I paid particular attention to her "coaching" (see chapter 9), that is, her communicating what she needed in order to feel safe with me. Ruth appeared to need to control the pace and frequency of the therapy, to control what was revealed without additional probing questions on my part, and, most importantly, to feel normal rather than impaired. Her intense, annoyed initial presentation was likely a test to see if I could tolerate her anger and her distance.

I began thinking strategically about how I might approach Ruth so that she could begin to feel safe with me. It appeared that a calm, matter-of-fact, unflappable attitude coupled with a refusal to worry would be most useful. Even though she described serious symptoms of depression and bulimia, it appeared that, at first, listening was all she could tolerate from me. I remained calm and friendly, even when she expressed her deep disappointment in me. I felt empathic and supportive, but believed it would be best for Ruth if I expressed this only in a carefully titrated manner. Finally, I was aware that often the most helpful thing a therapist can offer patients is simply to listen to them without imposing interpretations on them.

Ruth seemed dissatisfied at the end of the first session and was unsure when she would return. I wondered if I had failed an important test by asking too many questions. In fact, I thought that Ruth was unlikely to return for a second session and didn't even open a permanent file for her. However, when I sent the bill, I did include a note encouraging her to come in. I repeated sending a bill with a note for the next 4 months with neither a response nor a payment. I wondered if Ruth's not responding was a test to see if I was truly interested in helping her and if I could tolerate her setting the pace.

Four months later, on December 31, Ruth called. In her message she said, "Why haven't you sent me a bill? I would like to come in as soon as possible." The tension in her voice and the fact that it was New Year's Eve suggested she was suffering considerably.

At the second session, Ruth had just returned from a visit home for the holidays. She told me she had made a New Year's resolution to work on her eating disorder, which had gotten worse. She was eating from the time she arrived home from work until bedtime, and throughout weekends, in between marathon training and weight lifting.

Our interaction was similar to that of the first session. When I asked her if she had any idea why the eating disorder had gotten worse or how her family visit went, she seemed very annoyed and dismissive, but did curtly mention feeling lonely and stressed. Ruth said that holidays were always difficult for her. She felt exhausted from dividing her time between her parents and three older sisters and their families, whom she described as all very needy of her attention. She admitted feeling "slightly depressed," because this was the first time in her life she was alone and didn't have a boyfriend. January the first was the anniversary of her divorce.

She then demanded that I do something about her eating disorder immediately. I suggested coming in more frequently and, remembering that she had been helped by medication for her panic disorder, that we consider medication along with psychotherapy. Ruth stiffened and, shaking her index finger, admonished me, claiming I should be ashamed of myself for frightening her with my outrageous suggestions. I calmly asked how my suggestion had frightened her. She replied that, as a professional, I should know that taking medication implied that something was seriously wrong with her. She did agree that coming in more frequently might help, and again brought up the issue of scheduling, requesting an evening hour. I repeated that I didn't have evening hours but could see her midday. Offended, Ruth again wondered what kind of therapist I was if I couldn't provide her with the hour she needed. Once again, I offered to help her find a therapist who might have the time she wanted. Even more upset, Ruth asked, "Don't you want to work with me? I want to see you." I expressed my desire to work with her and added that together we would find a suitable time. Although I never did have an evening hour, I agreed to establish a flexible schedule (once a week with flexibility around her work travel).

Reflections on the Second Session

Ruth's wish to reveal her problems, as well as her intense anxiety and fear of doing so, were strikingly apparent in this session. This conflict, I believe, contributed to her difficulty in coming in for a second session, her not paying her bill for months, and her prickly and adversarial style with me. Her description of her interactions with her family over Christmas led me to hypothesize that Ruth probably had a long history of feeling responsible for her needy family. I also hypothesized that Ruth suffered from unconscious guilt over separation/individuation and from survivor guilt.

I began wondering how her eating disorder and panic attacks might have resulted from identification with a dysfunctional family member. Guilty about separating from her family and leading a successful life, Ruth unconsciously might have developed these symptoms in order to remain loyal to her family. Her chronic state of unhappiness and pain relieved her unconscious guilt

From a control-mastery perspective, the primary task of the therapist is to disconfirm the patient's pathogenic beliefs. One important way the therapist does this is by interacting with the patient in a way that passes the patient's tests of those pathogenic beliefs. I suspected that Ruth's urgency in this session was a passive-into-active test to see if I would join her in her panicked state and experience her problems as catastrophic. I hypothesized that Ruth was behaving toward me in the traumatic, panicked way her mother behaved toward her. She was unconsciously hoping I would not be as upset by her as she was by her mother. It appeared that I mainly passed her test by remaining calm and reassuring. However, I somewhat failed her test when I suggested medication, which frightened Ruth. When I realized this and backed off, she became more relaxed.

HISTORY

Before turning to my description of the three phases of treatment, I will present a summary of Ruth's history (which emerged over the course of several years) followed by my case formulation.

Ruth is the youngest of four daughters of Eastern European parents and was raised Catholic. She was her mother's favorite. Her older sisters—by 6, 8, and 10 years—were relieved that Ruth captured their mother's attention so that they were free to escape from their mother's chronic depression. Ironically, all three older sisters married young and live close to their parents. Ruth is the only child who moved far away. Ruth described her sisters as impaired and needy, like her mother. They constantly phoned her with their problems, and she often lent them money, which they rarely repaid.

One of the first pieces of information Ruth revealed in therapy was that when she was 4 years old her father "turned against her." She said she had been the apple of his eye. What had actually happened was that her great-grandmother who lived with them had just died, and her mother became profoundly depressed. Her great-grandmother had played an important role in raising Ruth during her first 4 years by taking care of her when her mother was too depressed to do so and by mediating within the parents' constant fighting in order to shield Ruth from some of the trauma. After her great-grandmother's death, Ruth was left alone with her mother. Her father who had been unable to tolerate his wife's depression "escaped" by avoiding home as much as possible and having relationships with other women. Ruth was left alone with her mother, and she believed she had been delegated the role of mother's caretaker. During the first years of therapy, the only facts Ruth would convey about her father was that he was a womanizer. For Ruth, this fact seemed to define her relationship with both her father and mother.

Her father had been a soldier in an Eastern European army corps and was captured by the Nazis. At that time, he witnessed his brother's execution and was incarcerated in a concentration camp. He escaped from the camp and fled to the United States where he met his wife at a church function. Ruth's father coped with his traumatic past by adopting a happy-go-lucky, carefree attitude. He was extremely charming and seductive outside the home, but angry and unhappy inside. Ruth described him as "phony." Both her parents instructed her to always look perfect in front of others and to never reveal family problems. She had memories of the family's weekly attendance at Sunday Mass where her father was an active participant in church services. The congregation admired her perfect family. At first, Ruth attributed her problems, including an excessive preoccupation with appearance, her intense jealousy of other attractive women, and her extreme self-doubt, to her father. She often described moments of intense longing for him. He never attended any of her school events. She remembered being out with him and feeling incredibly hurt because he would stare at beautiful women and not notice her. Strange women would often approach her and tell her how lucky she was to have such a wonderful father.

Ruth's mother was severely traumatized while growing up. At the age of 9, Ruth's mother spent a year in a TB sanatorium. One month after returning home, her father died of emphysema. Shortly thereafter, her only sibling, a sister, died of rheumatic fever and then her mother died of poisoning from ink that was used in a factory where she worked. Consequently, Ruth's mother suffered from chronic major depression. At times, she was hospitalized and received electroshock therapy.

Ruth described her mother's need to impress upon her family the dangerousness of the world in general, and of disease and illness in particular. Her mother responded to routine childhood mishaps as if they were major catastrophes and withdrew whenever Ruth or her sisters were ill.

Ruth's mother became fanatical about food in an attempt to ward off disease and death. She followed a rigid regimen and insisted that the family eat a stringently healthy diet. Ruth learned early that it was extremely dangerous to be sick and that she would be responsible for hurting her mother. On one occasion, her mother beat Ruth because she went to school during a winter storm without wearing pants under her skirt. Her mother believed Ruth would contract pneumonia and die. Because the slightest sign of vulnerability heralded disaster, Ruth concluded danger was always present, and that if she could learn to be perfect, she might be able to avoid it.

Ruth's mother also taught her that the course of life was totally outside the realm of human control. Ruth, she said, had been born under a lucky star, and because of that everything would be perfect for her. Any sign of imperfection meant that her mother might have been wrong about her lucky star. Implied was the fact that Ruth's mother was not so lucky and could only be saved by remaining close to Ruth. Her mother believed that learning anything new or any attempt to control one's destiny was futile. You got through life by luck, magic, or God's blessing.

At puberty, Ruth began getting attention for her good looks. She imitated the popular girls at school as well as the "phony" seductive style of her father. She felt she didn't know how to act in the world, so she chose people who looked successful and used them as role models. This gave rise to a persistent feeling that she was playacting and was a fraud.

Ruth never learned how to study. She cheated in school and got by on natural intelligence and manipulation. After graduation from high school, Ruth attended nursing school and thrived on the family-like atmosphere. However, because she didn't study, she failed her final exams. Ruth thought, "You get through life by snowing people—it's who you know rather than what you know." She always believed that that there were naturally smart people and the rest who faked their way through. Ruth felt she was clearly a member of "the rest." A nursing supervisor, who liked her, pointed out that Ruth never took notes and often daydreamed in class. With a lot of help, she was able to retake her exams and pass. She liked working in the hospital emergency room so that she could take care of patients in crisis and then have them leave.

Although Ruth was exceptionally loyal to her mother, she simultaneously dismissed her as helpless, pathetic, and histrionic. Until she was 12 years old, Ruth slept in the same bed with her mother while her father slept in another room. Ruth felt that her job was to protect her mother from jealousy and to keep her company. She described an incident one

Valentine's Day when she hid the card her father had given her in order to protect her mother from jealousy. She described the hangup phone calls her family received from her father's girlfriends. She would run to answer the phone to protect her mother from the call, or to protect herself from her mother's tirades if her mother answered. Ruth had her first panic attack after one of these phone calls.

She began having sexual relationships at age 13 and exchanged her mother's bed for that of her boyfriends'. Her mother, in an attempt to prevent her daughter from separating from her, decided to support her daughter in her amorous activities. She set few limits and even encouraged her to do dangerous things like drive at age 14. Ruth felt totally unprotected and believed she was responsible for her mother's well-being. She once described this as "the blind leading the blind." When she got her first job in high school, her mother waited in the car all day outside her workplace, clearly unable to tolerate the separation.

Ruth consistently chose boyfriends who were exceedingly handsome (an absolute requirement) and either very clingy and needy, or independent and rejecting. Her first husband was the latter type. She described him as a perfect man, and the two of them as the perfect couple. She married him because everyone was jealous of her great catch and because her family strongly opposed the marriage. Her mother, in particular, warned her that this man was no good. While planning her wedding, she began experiencing panic attacks. She could not envision herself walking down the aisle and being so exposed. She felt terror and shame about being seen. After her marriage, she began identifying with her mother more intensely and became extremely jealous of other women. If her husband even glanced at an attractive woman, she would dissolve into a rage. This happened so often that he wanted to end the marriage after one year. Feeling very ashamed and responsible for the divorce, Ruth moved to another state in January, right after her divorce became final. She immediately found the boyfriend who taught her how to binge. She stayed with him for 3 years and moved to the Bay Area largely to escape him.

CASE FORMULATION

My case formulation describes how I understood Ruth's conscious and unconscious goals for therapy, the pathogenic beliefs that impeded her from attaining those goals, and the testing strategies that would help her disconfirm her pathogenic beliefs.

Ruth's conscious goal was to experience love, happiness, and success. Specifically, she wanted to have a good marriage and a successful career. Another conscious goal was to alleviate her terror of imperfection and illness. She wanted to experience the world as a safe place so that she could expose her genuine self and be free from the chronic pain of hiding. Unconsciously, Ruth entered therapy primarily to free herself from her mother. She wanted to overcome the powerful sense of guilt she felt as a consequence of separating from her mother and to attain more happiness, love, and success than others in her family. Ruth developed many unconscious pathogenic beliefs related to her guilt and shame:

- The world is not a safe place.
- It is dangerous to exhibit any vulnerability or flaws.
- I have little control over my life because all life events, including goals or accomplishments, are results of magic, destiny, fate, or God's will.
- I can neither be helped nor be taught how to help myself; my only recourse is escape or, at times, manipulation.
- It is dangerous to love a man. I will lose him like my mother lost my father.
- I will either be abandoned or engulfed in a relationship; therefore, intimacy is forbidden and dangerous.
- I must be negative, jealous, and lonely like my mother.
- If I am not the "perfect woman"—extremely beautiful and desirable—I will be shamed, humiliated, and pathetic.
- If I separate from my mother, I will hurt her.
- If I am angry or disappointed with my mother, I will hurt her.
- I am omnipotently responsible for people's unhappiness, especially my mother's.
- I do not deserve a happier life, marriage, or career than my parents.
- I am an imposter and have no real value or abilities.

In her attempts to overcome these pathogenic beliefs, Ruth employed both transference and passive-into-active tests.

Transference Tests

In order to determine if I would be like her mother, she tested to see if:

- I would excessively worry about her and transform her problems into catastrophic events.
- My thoughts or problems would be more important than hers.

- I would be angry and deeply wounded when she attempted to separate from me.
- I would find her anger, disappointment, and occasional dislike of me intolerable.
- I would find her refusal to answer questions intolerable.
- I would be unable to help her with her problems.
- I would be unable to protect her from her destructive behaviors and teach her more effective ways of coping.
- I would be negative and pessimistic.

Passive-Into-Active Tests

Behaving (unconsciously) like her mother, she tested to see if:

- I would be able to tolerate her anxiety, depression, anger, pain, criticism, and rejection without becoming overwhelmed, guilty, and/or compliant.
- I would be helpful and protective without becoming submissive and compliant.
- I could remain optimistic in the face of her anger, despair, and grim presentation.
- I would be overly concerned with being perfect at all times.

DESCRIPTION OF THERAPY

Having described Ruth's initial presentation, her history, and my case formulation, I will now turn to a description of the therapy. I am going to summarize the first 18 months of therapy, focus on the middle and most therapeutically important period of therapy, and finally summarize the last 3 years.

Phase I: First 18 Months

The first months of treatment were difficult for me because there seemed to be little progress and Ruth was still suffering. It was helpful for me to understand this case from a control-mastery perspective because it emphasized that Ruth was motivated to overcome her problems that had developed from the severe traumas she suffered as a child. I also understood that Ruth felt extremely anxious about exposing her vulnerabilities because she unconsciously believed she was flawed, and that she would need time and many passed tests on my part to feel safe enough to do so. However, in spite of this understanding, at times I felt discouraged because I had little sense of a positive alliance and little indication that Ruth was getting better. In the very beginning, it would have been easy for me to let her go. I found myself working unusually hard to remain receptive and tranquil, even though I understood she needed to provoke me in order to keep me at a distance so that she could remain separate and safe. I also felt that Ruth's provocative behavior was part of her unconsciously testing my ability to take care of myself.

As she had warned me, Ruth's travel necessitated many cancelled appointments. During sessions, she focused on difficulties at work and with friends, and on her eating disorder and exercise schedule. She tolerated almost no exploration of her feelings, and I often felt that I was doing everything wrong. She barely acknowledged me and, when she did, appeared to dislike me. During this first period of therapy, Ruth needed to keep me at a distance. She was testing me to see if I would be okay with her negativity and rejection. Unlike her mother, I did not need her to share all her thoughts and feelings with me. In addition, I could tolerate her anger and dislike of me. Her mother would either burst into tears if Ruth didn't share everything with her or lash out and attack her. Ruth also needed to feel in control of how much she would reveal in order to feel safe with me.

Often, I felt caught in a bind. If my attention appeared to be even slightly more than casual, Ruth became agitated because, I believe, she experienced me as intrusive or worried that I (like her mother) was overly dependent. If my attention wandered or if I misunderstood her, she became upset and reproached me for not understanding. I noticed that if I calmly acknowledged my misunderstanding and didn't look upset at her reproach, Ruth picked up the thread of what she had been talking about. Therefore, I knew that I was passing most of her tests by remaining calm and receptive. Also, I was aware that even though Ruth did not appear to be getting better, she had been so severely traumatized as a child that it would take some time for her to feel safe with me. The fact that Ruth diligently kept returning to therapy served as a useful reminder that she was motivated to get better.

On one occasion, Ruth was describing her interaction with a young salesperson at a bagel store. This young woman had brought Ruth the wrong bagel, and Ruth launched into a diatribe against her. As she was describing the waitress's ineptness, I found myself momentarily feeling sorry for the bagel girl and then wondering how Ruth herself might have been subjected to such treatment. At that moment, Ruth turned to me and accused me of not getting it. I nodded and asked her to help me understand. She spoke about how destructive incompetent people were. Then, for the first time, she began describing her mother's incompetence—how she never knew what to do for Ruth when anything went wrong. She told me she was disappointed in me for having to ask her to help me understand—wasn't this my job? I told her that I hadn't understood until now how much she had suffered due to her mother's incompetence. I began to realize how unprotected Ruth had been and how, in order to survive this, she had developed an illusory system of self-sufficiency. This was actually one of the very few times during this first period of therapy that Ruth manifestly experienced me as helpful.

Cancellations were frequent and how I handled them was extremely important. I quickly learned that if I appeared fine with the cancellations, she calmly made another appointment. If I commented on them or on their frequency, she either withdrew or became agitated. She was hoping I didn't need her to come in and that I could let it go without repercussions. On one occasion, Ruth didn't show up for an appointment and I charged her for it. Very upset about this charge, Ruth began talking about how unfair it was for her to have to be responsible for everything. At first, she insisted it was my mistake and that she had called to cancel. Then she said it was possible she had forgotten this one time, but why couldn't she ever be given any slack? She asked me if I would consider erasing the charge this one time. I said okay, there was room to make mistakes. Ruth never missed a scheduled appointment after that. At first, I thought she might have been testing me to find out if I would keep my boundaries and charge her for the missed session. However, it appeared that she was testing to see if she could "be given some slack" and didn't have to be so responsible and perfect all the time.

Ruth gradually became more relaxed during the next few months of therapy, but she continued to need me to remain far in the background. Although, as before, my comments and interpretations were usually ignored or challenged, her protestations were weaker. As I listened to Ruth, I noticed that if I exhibited too much empathy she would become upset. At these times, I was failing a test by acting like her mother who would cry with her whenever anything was wrong. During this initial period of the therapy, I found it best to tell her what I thought only when she asked.

Ruth usually spent the sessions describing her physical condition. Every ache and pain was reviewed, magnified, and often resulted in increased anxiety that something catastrophic might occur. She was relieved when I, unlike her mother, listened in a relaxed, nonworried manner and offered reassurance. She became more constricted and angry when even a flicker of concern crossed my face. She needed to feel assured that I understood how healthy, strong, and desirable she was. She filled her sessions with details of what she ate and of her running and exercise schedule. It was striking how her tension would dissipate when she was describing her love of running, which made her feel free, powerful, and alive. She lived to run and eat. When home alone or out with others, all she could do was eat.

Ruth had been raised in a world where food and its consumption were areas of potential disaster. It was no wonder she had developed an eating disorder. For Ruth, bulimia represented an unconscious identification and compliance with her fragile, defective mother. Bingeing was an attempt to restore her mother when Ruth felt unconsciously guilty about separating from her. When "in danger" of developing a close relationship with a man, Ruth unconsciously either began having panic attacks, as she did with her husband, or used compulsive eating and vomiting as a barrier to intimacy and a means of staying loyal to her needy mother.

Ruth often talked about God, whom she described as the sole positive force in her life. Raised as a Catholic, she went to church several times a week. She attributed her suffering to God's will. She felt she was meant to be special and that God must have some kind of plan that she didn't quite understand. She relied on God to help her and frequently prayed when upset. This helped relieve some of her feelings of omnipotent responsibility, guilt, and shame. More subtle but powerful was a fear that God might punish her for her sins.

The theme of jealousy and competition echoed throughout her description of interactions with friends and colleagues. She seemed to devote a lot of time to friends who were very needy like her mom. Whenever she befriended a healthy person, he or she immediately became a competitor like her father's girlfriends. Ruth operated under the rigid interpersonal assumption that people were either needy or jealous. Because she could never count on anyone to listen to her and actually want to help her get what she needed, Ruth never learned how to be direct. She also believed that if a person knew what you actually wanted, you would surely not get it. Furthermore, if you didn't want to comply with someone else's needs, it wouldn't be safe to be direct. Therefore, Ruth had learned that manipulation was the only safe means of interaction and that you couldn't count on anyone but yourself. Basically, she felt she had to trick someone into fulfilling her needs in order to avoid filling their needs.

Ruth tested me frequently to be certain I was not hurt by her success. Once, she remembered winning the "Miss Congeniality" contest in high school and her mother responded, "Aren't you the stuckup one?" So when she would brag about her beauty, successes at work, and athletic ability, I would genuinely admire and support her.

Ruth also needed to be sure I was neither worried about her nor about myself. On one occasion, having sprained my ankle, I was limping as I walked to my office from the waiting room. She ignored this and seemed relieved and more relaxed that I did not appear to be bothered either by my sprained ankle or by her ignoring it.

By the end of the first year, it was clear that my initial hypothesis, formulated after the first phone conversation, was correct. I was passing most of Ruth's tests by remaining calm, reassuring, and respectful of both her boundaries and her need to remain in control of the pace of therapy. At about this time, I began to learn much more about her history and inner life. Some of it, of course, was revealed between the lines as she was talking about eating, running, God, and work, but most of what I learned came from the many pages of writing she gave me each session to read later. Writing appeared to be safer than telling me directly. I had passed enough of her earlier tests so she was feeling bold enough to begin to reveal more.

The writing began after about 9 months of therapy in which at least half the sessions were cancelled, usually due to work. Ruth came in one day very upset, complaining that her eating disorder wasn't any better. I repeated that bulimia was a symptom she had developed to avoid something dangerous. Over time we would better understand what was troubling her and the symptom would gradually improve. I suggested again, as I had done in the past, that if she could pay attention to her thoughts we would have a clearer understanding of her dilemma. Perhaps she could start observing these thoughts more closely and write them down, especially during those times when she felt the urge to binge and purge. As usual, she appeared somewhat disgruntled by my suggestion, but at the next session she began the weekly practice of giving me pages of her observations and ponderings. At first, she mainly wrote about what she was eating and the attempts to control herself, but it became apparent that this solitary exploration suited her well.

For a while, the unspoken rule in our sessions was that Ruth gave me her writing and asked me to read it later. At first, she preferred that I made little or no reference to her writing. As before, during our sessions Ruth focused on the details of her eating, running, work, and needy friends, and I simply listened with interest and without worry.

Gradually, the content of her writing shifted from her eating disorder, and Ruth began testing my reaction to her confessions. In one of her first writings, she described stealing communion hosts from the church so that she and her friends could play priest. She wrote about her great fear of being caught and punished. On another occasion, she described cheating in school. She never actually read a book but would write her reports from Cliffs Notes. She did make some reference to this in the session, which was unusual, and I casually responded by saying that she had found a clever compromise to her dilemma. She had been afraid and guilty about triggering her mother's jealousy by being successful and at the same time she had a healthy part of herself that wanted to be successful. She was clever enough to compromise and actually achieve some success, but remained unable to enjoy it because she thought she had cheated. The fact that she could actually pull this off most of the time was striking. I admired her determination to find a way to be successful in her world. Ruth liked this interpretation. This was different from her usual response that my interpretations were "crazy."

This confession was an important test because she needed to know I wouldn't blame, criticize, or humiliate her or become overly worried, wounded, or undone. She was also beginning to show an interest in understanding how she had developed her pathogenic beliefs and behaviors. She felt relief whenever she realized she had adapted to a very traumatic childhood in the best way she could. She began to understand through my interpretations that she was motivated to attain healthy goals but was deeply conflicted about it because of her strong sense of unconscious guilt about having a better life than her mother (survivor guilt). She enacted this conflict by taking advantage of opportunities while at the same time finding some way to punish herself.

As I review the first 18 months of therapy, several things are evident. First, Ruth persisted in therapy and never gave up. Second, feeling safe with me was our primary task. To feel safe, Ruth needed to test me to be certain I could function well without her, that I didn't need her for my own purposes, that I didn't see her as sick or in danger, that I respected her autonomy, and that I could tolerate her negative emotions and still be available to respect, care for, and help her. Understanding some of Ruth's more offputting behaviors as adaptive and as attempts to overcome pathogenic beliefs helped me pass many of Ruth's tests. Finally, I was aware of feeling great admiration, respect, and caring for Ruth.

It is difficult to do justice to the richness and subtlety of our relationship. I believe that this growing intimate connection was a critical element in the therapy. It seemed to help give her the courage to proceed with her therapeutic work. As she became more relaxed and less angry, Ruth seemed more receptive to my influence. I was able to help her understand more about her shame, guilt, and symptoms of anxiety, depression, and bulimia. Also, gradually it appeared that her eating disorder was becoming less of a problem. In fact, Ruth was now rarely bulimic and this symptom has only occasionally resurfaced during periods of great stress.

In sum, certain themes emerged during my first sessions with Ruth: autonomy and the need for control, perfectionism and the dread of weakness or failure, shame and the fear of not being normal, bulimia, severe anxiety and panic, difficulties in relationships, a preoccupation with health concerns, and severe suffering. All these continued to be major issues in our work together, but several important changes occurred. Ruth's symptoms of bulimia and depression were reduced. Due to a growing sense of trust, Ruth had also begun to develop a close relationship with me.

Phase II: Eighteen Months through Five Years

After about 18 months of treatment, Ruth began working for a new boss, a stern, unfriendly man who did not like her. She became increasingly tortured with the feeling that no matter how hard she tried, she could not please him. He was European and spoke with an accent similar to her father's. His presence gave rise to memories (mainly revealed in her journal) of desperately trying to please her father, only to be rebuffed. At the same time, she began to remember occasions when she actually won her father's attention. This, however, caused her to feel intensely conflicted because even though she desperately wanted her father's attention she worried her mother would feel hurt and angry. The guilt Ruth felt was exacerbated by her mother's displays of jealousy. For example, her mother would comment that Ruth used to be a pretty child, but it was too bad she had lost her looks.

Ruth's difficulties with her new boss occurred about the same time she was expressing interest in finding a boyfriend. She was having great difficulty and worried that she would never find a loving man. In therapy, she was beginning to understand the connection between her relationship with her parents and her relationship with men. Ruth began to understand that she felt guilty and unconsciously feared she would hurt her mother if she formed a good relationship with a man. She relieved her guilt by not allowing herself to have one, and in this way she remained loyal to her mother.

Ruth's conviction that her boss wasn't pleased with her work terrified her for another reason. She believed the discovery of any flaw in her would open a Pandora's box of imperfections that would leave her feeling shamed and humiliated.

About 6 months after his arrival, Ruth began one of her sessions by announcing she thought it would be in her best interest to take a new job. I knew this was a result of her feeling exposed, shamed, and rejected by her new boss. She had also been revealing a lot more in her writings, and I wondered if she had become uncomfortable with the exposure. The job she was considering involved spending 2 to 3 weeks per month in Europe, and this would clearly interfere with our therapy.

I struggled with the dilemma this posed. If I encouraged her to stay here and continue her work, I wondered if I would be curtailing her freedom to separate from me. At first, I tried to explore her thoughts and feelings about this move. Then I suggested she look for a new job that would allow her to continue her therapy. Claiming that she felt much better and was no longer depressed and bulimic, Ruth insisted that I needed to let her go because this new job was important to her and she wanted an opportunity to live abroad. I encouraged her to consider allowing herself a trial period on this job before she formally accepted it. She spent a month in Europe and decided she was going to take it. She asked me to be happy for her. She also added that she had thought a lot about how important therapy was to her and that she planned to continue it the last few weeks she was in California.

After arriving, Ruth extended her stay in Europe and joined a hiking group for a vacation. While hiking, she broke her wrist, which necessitated her coming home for surgery. Although relatively minor, the surgery was traumatic for Ruth. As part of a powerful, unconscious identification with her mother, she became terrified she would be left an invalid. She was unable to run. She then discovered that her wrist wasn't healing properly and she needed a second surgery. Her feelings of terror escalated. Despite her desperate pleas, no one from her family would come out to help her. This gave rise to a flood of memories of how her family either ignored or abandoned her whenever she needed their help. She felt her sole role in the family was always to be the caregiver and never the care receiver.

Ruth phoned me right before our first session following her surgery. She said she felt terrified, almost paralyzed, and could not leave her house. I tried unsuccessfully to convince her to come to her session, but she then pleaded for me to come to her home for the session. She lived only a couple of blocks from my office; with some misgivings but an intuitive sense that this might be helpful, I agreed to go.

At Ruth's home, for the first time, I clearly saw the depth of her anxiety and despair. She was crying and shaking because she believed she was crippled and would be permanently incapacitated. Ruth thought that I needed to hospitalize her because she said she couldn't cope. She even added she might need electroshock therapy. At first, I felt extremely concerned and for part of the hour wondered if hospitalization might be necessary. I was experiencing an unusually powerful feeling of doom. I experienced this momentary but terrifying feeling with Ruth often during this period. However, I found myself responding strongly, insisting that she would be okay and that I would help her through the crisis. I then noticed that although her home was quite lovely and beautifully decorated, all the shades were drawn and it was incredibly dark inside. When I commented on this, Ruth looked stunned and commented that she always left the blinds shut. She then began to calm down and asked me if I would like a tour of her home. I commented on how lovely I thought it was. She asked me if she should open the blinds, and I agreed that she should try it out. At the end of the session, although somewhat calmer, she said she still felt unable to leave the house. I told her firmly that she needed to be able to leave the house, and that we would meet tomorrow at my office. She listened to me and seemed to feel relieved.

We repeated variations on the previous scenario in my office and thus began a very prolonged and intense period of passive-into-active testing. Ruth was struggling to free herself from her powerful identification with her mother who had terrorized her with her suffering. She was also trying to overcome her feelings of omnipotent responsibility for her mother's suffering. She tested me by attempting to frighten and overwhelm me with her suffering as her mother had done to her. I passed her test by remaining calm, helpful, and reassuring her that she would be okay.

Over the next few months, Ruth began recalling significant childhood traumas. For instance, she described summers at home with the curtains drawn because her mother couldn't stand the light and needed to sleep. She remembered she had had no friends as a young child and used to stay at home to take care of her mother who was lonely and profoundly depressed. She would feign illness to miss school so that she could keep her mother company. She would hear children playing outside and longed to join them. At times, children would make fun of

Ruth. When she tearfully related this to her mother, her mother would start crying too, telling Ruth that she would be her friend and that she didn't need any other friends.

She then remembered times when, as an older child, she would have a friend or accomplish something in school, and her mother would respond negatively, often with fits of jealousy. Especially as an older child, Ruth learned to hide anything positive from her mother in order to protect herself from her mother's jealousy. Up until this point, Ruth had described her mother as depressed and "pathetic." She was now describing her mother's abusive rages. Ruth frequently used the expression "my mother wanted to kill me." She often felt that her mother was almost blaming her for her father's disloyal behavior.

From here on, Ruth brought her terrors into the therapy room and often described herself as living in a "black hole." As she did this, she became more and more receptive to me. At first, she seemed to find my calm stance soothing. Soon after I began to talk, she seemed to relax. Gradually, my comments and interpretations became useful to her as well. She liked me to be active, strong, and protective. It was also important that I convey with utmost certainty that everything would be okay. Her terror was palpable and her depression so intense that I at times I struggled to hide my worry. If even a flicker of concern crossed my face, she panicked. I usually remained calm and reassuring that this was not a black hole, that life had stressors that were normal and that she would be okay.

Ruth reported a dream in which she was outdoors, paralyzed in a lightning and thunderstorm. A heavy, translucent plastic divider was separating her from the people on the other side of the divider playing in the sunshine. I proposed that for most people life was about being able to go back and forth across the divider. This plastic divider became a positive symbol for her, and Ruth often referred to it. She developed a meditative self-soothing technique of envisioning herself passing back and forth through openings in the plastic divider.

During this period, Ruth was often in a panic and began calling me for extra sessions. We would either talk on the phone or schedule an extra session. Although her distress was intense, she usually seemed soothed just by my tone of voice. At the beginning of our sessions, she would frequently coach me, telling me that she needed reassurance that everything would be okay and that she was not an invalid. As her terror escalated, she also began to experience a whole host of body pains, which prevented her from running. She was convinced she had cancer, arthritis, or some other terrible disease. Ruth began to think God was punishing her for her sins. On one occasion, after noticing that bulimia had been replaced with a host of somatic terrors, she became extremely agitated by the thought that she was trapped in an endless cycle of suffering. Calmly, I told her she was making a lot of progress and that eventually I was sure most of her symptoms would disappear. I told her she was identifying with her mother because she felt too guilty to have a better life than her mother had.

This last example was one of Ruth's many tests to see if I would become discouraged. She often seemed to be getting worse, reaching states of hopelessness and desperation. I felt she was testing me to see if I would join her in despair. I passed these discouragement tests by remaining absolutely convinced she would be better. Although she found interpretations more useful at this point, she also benefited from direct reassurance that she would be okay. My attitude remained calm, friendly, caring, and extremely reassuring.

Another major event occurred at this time. While recuperating from her broken wrist, Ruth met a man she liked. He was a teacher who was kind, thoughtful, and very different from her former boyfriends. She had not been in a relationship for almost 2 years. This new relationship seemed very positive, and Ruth was terrified of the intimacy. Identifying with her mother, she was convinced no man would remain loyal and loving to her. What she described as her "Jezebel" side emerged and lasted for at least a year. Her intense jealousy of other attractive women gave rise to vicious attempts to tear them down. She described many interactions in which she was manipulative, angry, and accusing. During therapy, she frequently criticized her boyfriend and tried to convince me he was no good and that he preferred other women. She also constantly complained about other attractive women and accused them of being incompetent and weak or manipulative. When I listened to her outpourings, she accused me of siding with them. If I attempted to understand her feelings, she would berate me, and if I remained neutral she accused me of being critical and judgmental. I held firm with my conviction that she deserved to have a good relationship with a man. I understood this behavior as another example of passive-into-active testing. Ruth was treating me the way her mother had treated her, but I never became discouraged and maintained my belief that she deserved to have a good relationship. We continued to explore how having a better relationship with a man than her mother had had with her father provoked Ruth's survivor guilt. She was attempting to reduce that guilt by identifying with her mother and not allowing herself to experience a good relationship with a man.

Ruth continued to elaborate on memories of her mother's resentment, rage, and "attempts to rip other women apart." She also remembered feeling afraid of her mother's physical and verbal abuse. Ruth often admitted hating her mother intensely. These feelings gave rise to increased guilt that she was hurting her mother by hating her, and her panic attacks had also returned. They were occurring several times daily and were interfering with her ability to work. Ruth resisted my suggestion to take medication to relieve the panic attacks because of her conviction that taking medication meant she was very sick and that she was like her mother. It took many months to convince her otherwise. Ruth was phoning me daily at this point, and although we usually met twice a week she couldn't tolerate a regularly scheduled second session. Ruth said that this made her feel trapped, a feeling she continued to find intolerable.

One incident that occurred during this period proved to be a turning point in the therapy. Ruth usually felt devastated when I was on vacation. It helped when she knew where I was going and exactly when I would return. She had been considering medication for her panic attacks for some time. One Saturday, after I returned from vacation, she phoned and asked if I had any time to talk to her before I returned to the office the following Monday. I called her back while doing my laundry and we spent about a half hour on the phone. She said I sounded so relaxed and calm that she felt normal. She also remarked that I must care for her a lot if I would phone her on a Saturday after just returning from vacation. She then felt that perhaps it was okay to try some medication and that it might help her. With medication, Ruth did receive much needed relief, and she only needed it for about 6 months.

Another important sequence of events occurred around this time. Ruth had spent a weekend with her boyfriend and his family, which included a 4-year-old niece who was enthralled with Ruth's "movie star looks" and began following her around. Ruth described the little girl as selfish because she wanted all of Ruth's attention and mentioned her fantasy of hurting the child. She had been verbally mean and looked to me for approval of her behavior. Ruth noticed a look of concern on my face, which may have triggered Ruth's own worry that she had done something wrong. It was the end of the session, and I commented that it would be really important to understand what she was feeling and to think about this.

The night following this session Ruth had a dream in which she murdered someone. Alarmed, she awoke in a panic and phoned me early the next morning. She was worried to the point of hysteria that this dream meant she had murdered someone in her past. I told her I didn't believe that she had actually murdered anyone. I added that I wasn't worried and that I knew we would handle and make sense of whatever came up. She came in for an emergency session. Very ashamed, she confessed she was remembering some terrible things she had done.

Thus began many sessions filled with confessions. When she was 10 years old, she had tried to poison her best friend by lacing her soda with her mother's Valium. She was angry and jealous because her friend had been spending time with another girl. She remembered waiting for the phone call, informing her of her friend's death. With horror and shame, she remembered how she often pinched babies. She would smile and look attentive, and then when no one was looking she would hurt them. With deep shame, she described the pleasure she got from this. She remembered cheating in school and trying to get competitors in trouble. She remembered manipulating teachers. She wrote:

> I've been trying to think about the past as I meditate and today am very bothered by what I'm feeling. I realize that I've had this dream all of my life that I've either killed somebody or helped kill somebody and the whole dream is how I'm trying to act normal, like nothing happened, but I start to panic because I know that I'm gonna get caught. I remember having that devastated feeling like, okay, you just have to act like nothing's happened and forget it. It brings me back to the situation with T. [the friend she tried to poison]. I think it probably blew me away when I realized what I was doing. I know that I never wanted to feel pain and instead of letting myself feel badly about it, I tried to just forget that it happened. I've since unconsciously tortured myself over and over. I get so panicked because I wonder if I'm really trying to suppress something horrible. I think that this panic is rooted in extreme fear of my mother. I was always so conscious when we were little of holding on to the family secret [father's affairs] so I wouldn't embarrass us. Every time I got caught doing something wrong [playing with matches, teasing the handicapped] she'd go crazy.
>
> I really was a nice kid. I just was so confused. I am still so sad with how I picked on poor Mrs. K. and that little Mexican girl down the street. I pray that she didn't have lifelong problems because of me. I'm so horrified and ashamed of what I did. It seems like all throughout my life, mostly prior to my divorce, I

would get really ashamed if I acted jealous, snobby, short-tempered, anything less than perfect. I would try to make up for it by being extra, extra nice.

Feeling terribly guilty and monstrous, Ruth repeatedly tried to end her relationship with her boyfriend. I challenged her assumptions about herself by helping her understand how she had been identifying with her mother. I encouraged her to forgive herself for doing some of the things she deeply regretted and strongly supported her continuing her relationship with her boyfriend. I assured her that even though they had conflicts they could continue trying to work them out and that I would help her to do so. Most importantly, I repeatedly emphasized that she deserved to have a loving relationship with a man. Around this time, Ruth jokingly began to occasionally call me "Mom." This was a very good thing for Ruth. She was experiencing a new relational capacity with me. I was hopeful that she would be able to extend this new capacity to her boyfriend.

While all this drama was occurring in therapy and in her personal life, Ruth's work was actually going well. Following the accident, she had decided not to take the job in Europe but to stay with her company. Her division was launching a new product, and her boss put Ruth in charge of presenting it. Ruth's fear of public speaking took center stage in her conscious life and that was what she talked about in her sessions. She desperately wanted to feel successful and proud of herself. As the date of her big presentation neared, Ruth experienced heightened anxiety and a resurgence of the panic attacks. She once again was convinced she was suffering from a major illness and that she needed a break from all the anxiety with a disability leave. When I tried to convince her that she didn't have a major illness, that it was in her best interest to complete her job, that she deserved to be successful, and that her anxiety was a manifestation of her survivor guilt, she began escalating her distress signals. Insisting on her need for a leave of absence, Ruth pleaded, "Don't I deserve a break, just once?" "Not in this way," I replied. I was passing Ruth's tests by insisting repeatedly that she was capable and that she deserved to enjoy success. Each passed test resulted in another more rigorous test. Her guilty pathogenic belief that she didn't deserve success was so severe that repeated vigorous testing was needed to alleviate it.

Ruth intensified her passive-into-active testing even more. One morning, profoundly distraught, she phoned me and said she had the papers for the disability application all filled out. All she needed was my signature, which she begged me to provide. I flatly refused and firmly replied, "Ruth, I just don't buy it." It became apparent once again that insisting that she stick with her work was very beneficial. Ruth then began remembering all her school failures. She realized she had never learned how to prepare for anything. We talked about how guilty and disloyal she would feel whenever she was successful. Ruth began to allow herself adequate time to prepare for her presentation. She realized that successful people worked hard, so with great fear and trembling she made her big presentation that resulted in a successful launching of her company's new product.

From this point on, Ruth became noticeably different. Debilitating anxiety was replaced with relatively symptom-free, manageable stress. The dramatic passive-into-active testing quieted down. What gradually emerged was a focus on her work and an interest in how people lived meaningful lives. She began to express healthy, altruistic goals. She wanted to feel successful at work by helping people be better. She decided she really did want to leave her company and look for a job that would make her happier. Consequently, Ruth found a more rewarding job and actually began to enjoy working hard. Her new position combined hands-on nursing with business sales. She felt it was a way to both help others and feel good about herself at the same time. Her success was rewarded with a quadrupling of her income, which made her very proud. Once she felt free enough to allow herself to enjoy this success, she decided she would like to try to feel good about herself even when she wasn't number one.

Ruth's relationship with me also took on an added dimension. At the beginning of one session, she announced she had been struck by a comment one of her friends had made about me. Ruth had referred this friend to me for psychotherapy. She discovered that her friend knew some personal details of my life that she did not. Ruth commented that she had actually liked not knowing anything about me because it got in her way, but now she wasn't so sure. She gradually began to show some interest and curiosity about me. For example, she asked how I chose my career and what being a psychologist meant to me. I would answer her questions, but I was still careful not to say too much. I believe that all the passed tests had heightened her sense of safety in our relationship, and she no longer needed me to remain as far in the background as I initially had been. Now having let me come a little closer, she could focus on developing a healthier, more autonomous relationship with her boyfriend.

Ruth's relationship with her boyfriend continued to be, at times, a struggle for both of them. However, despite many attempts on her part to sabotage the relationship, it gradually became more rewarding. Ruth invited me to help her figure things out. What was particularly impressive was how they were both able to tolerate their conflicted feelings, actually discuss them, and often reach some resolution.

Here she describes some of her conflicted feelings about her boyfriend and how she struggled with them:

> I'm feeling very depressed. It's very hard for me to believe that I'm ever going to get out of this. It's a sunny day and I feel almost paralyzed. Last night I really got out of hand with J. I got really hurt because he didn't rant and rave over my chicken shish kebabs. The feeling was so intense that I knew that it must have been some relation to my childhood. I snapped at him because he said it was good instead of really making a fuss over it. Afterwards he stopped me in my tracks and made me tell him what was wrong. ... I told him that it wasn't really about the food, but that I felt that he would really love the meal and would show me. I told him that I just needed a little bit of attention. It turned out all right, but I now see more to this. It seems that I get to a certain point in a relationship and I start getting my feelings hurt about everything. I think that what I end up doing next is whining and manipulating the man into showering me with attention. ... I think that I have always had that manipulative way with men and therefore my barometer is off to where I think that J. is totally unappreciative because all the others adored me sooooo much. It also makes me realize that there is a really selfish side to me with my generosity towards my boyfriends. I give and give and then want that adoration in return. ... It brings up a sad memory of my mother when she was yelling at me and crying ... I think that I was home from college ... and she was screaming, "I don't know what else to do with you kids, I try to be so nice to you, I buy you things just so you'll like me." I thought about how she used to let me take the car at 14 and stay out late ... all manipulation so that she would get my love and attention. I think that is what I do. When J. said, "God I thought I really knew you, but I realize that there is so much more to learn," that broke my heart and terrified me because I imagined that I was about to be discovered and that he would find out who the real me was. This bumbling, insecure idiot who needs his love and adoration. I realize that whenever J. makes any comments, I feel that it is severe criticism and it makes me very self-conscious I think that this is a form of self-sabotage.

It is clear from Ruth's writing how much she had changed and how devoted she was to her boyfriend. She even convinced him to begin his own therapy. It was a great relief for her that he was able to help himself and that she wasn't responsible for doing it all. She was also developing confidence that she actually could have a very positive effect on people. Ruth and her boyfriend began to talk about marriage. She relived with me the trauma of her first marriage and in particular her deep shame about her divorce. She worried that her problems with her boyfriend would escalate after marriage and that he would be unfaithful to her. I convinced her that although there would continue to be conflicts, we could work out anything that came up. She deserved to have a good marriage.

During the fourth year of therapy, Ruth and her boyfriend were married. Shortly after their marriage, she struggled with feeling smothered by him. In particular, she had difficulty sleeping in the same bed with him. After describing critically how he hogged the bed, she began remembering what it had been like sleeping with her mother for the first 12 years of her life. She remembered her mother yelling and slapping her if she tossed and turned.

Finally, Ruth gradually began to let go of the pull of her mother and her family. She described her preoccupation with them as futile and exhausting, and she decided she wanted to have very little to do with them. She stopped calling them so often (she had been calling several times a week) and sending money as she had done in the past. She told them they all needed to go to therapy and work out their own problems. Ruth's survivor guilt was greatly reduced.

Ruth began expressing a strong, altruistic need to help people the way she had been helped, because she was beginning to believe she could actually be effective. Her experience with her husband contributed to mastering an old trauma: She realized she couldn't help her mother, who was too impaired to allow herself to receive any help. She then began to express enormous gratitude to me for my help. She decided she wanted to become a counselor and enrolled in an evening master's degree program while maintaining her job. She wanted to go to school to actually learn. She began to think she could be successful while helping people at the same time. I agreed. She decided that, rather than work with illness, she preferred to focus on wellness.

About a year after she was married, Ruth began talking about having a baby. She was surprised because in the past she had never wanted children. She felt that now she had a chance of being a good mother. It was very important to her that I also believed that she would be a good mother, and I did. Three months later, she became pregnant.

Pregnancy resurrected a host of conflicts centered on her anxiety about feeling out of control, being fat and ugly, being smothered and entrapped, identifying with her mother, and becoming an incapacitated mother. She felt every change in her body in a magnified way, but responded more readily to reassurance that everything was okay and that she would be a good mother. During our sessions, she often spoke to her baby in a very loving way. She asked me if I was a mother, and she began to question me about my own experiences. Her attitude toward me became tender and loving.

Once during her pregnancy, she made an extra appointment. Worried that she was unable to sleep and that the lack of sleep might harm the baby, Ruth announced she wanted to focus on developing more flexibility. She knew she still had a hard time when things weren't perfect. Because she would be caring for her baby, it would be a good idea to work on becoming more flexible. Paradoxically, she had been reading in one of her baby books about infant feeding schedules, and she said she planned to train the baby right from the start to be good and follow a schedule. I told her I disagreed with some of what she was saying. She thought I was wrong, that modern baby wisdom dictated that infants do better on fixed schedules. I said that although that was in part true, it was also true that babies flourished when their cries were answered. I reminded her how we set up our appointments. We only loosely followed our schedule. Today had been an example of that. She had called in distress and I made time. If she had to wait, she would have been okay, but most of the time we are able to meet or at least talk on the phone. I believed this might be a useful model of how she might want to raise her baby. What followed was a memory of her mother saying that she used to be a good baby until her aunt arrived from Europe to live with them. Her mother mentioned that the aunt supposedly turned baby Ruth into a demanding monster by picking her up whenever she cried. Ruth was relaxed at the end of the session, however, and called me the next morning to say she had slept well. She said that she had gotten a dose of Vitamin "K."

Phase III: Years Five Through Eight

At our first session following the birth, Ruth brought the baby in. The baby was relaxed and beautiful, and Ruth was tired and worried. She said she was having many nightmares about her mother. In one dream, her mother was dressed in baby clothes and Ruth had to help her into the bathroom. She was washing her mother's hands and noticed a sign above the sink that said BEWARE OF THE HOT WATER. She was terrified that her mother's hands would get burned. When associating to the dream, she said she was always worried about her mother, felt on the edge of disaster at all times, and was afraid she wouldn't be able to protect her. She then talked about all the attention the baby needed and how she reminded her of her mother. At the end of the session, she looked at me and said, "I'm afraid I'm going to drop the baby." I told her she wasn't going to drop the baby, that she was a good mother, and that the baby was not her mother.

Ruth had another dream—a vampire dream. She was in bed with her mother who was dressed in the baby's clothes. Her mother wriggled over to Ruth and began sucking on her neck. Ruth woke up but then fell asleep again and resumed the dream in which her mother crawled over to her again. Ruth was working on individuating from her mother and seeing her baby as separate from her mother.

During this period, Ruth continued to take notice of me, which now included expressions of empathic compassion and worry. Soon after Ruth's baby was born, I was leaving to take my son to college. Ruth knew this. She said she felt so sad for me because she had a brand-new baby and I would be losing my baby. We talked about how precious an infant can be but also how wonderful it was to watch a child grow up and develop his own life. This was one of the many opportunities I had to model healthy separation. Ruth's freedom to bring her worries out into open meant they were simply less compelling.

Ruth continued to benefit from therapy during this period. Her childhood traumas were very severe and she continued to rework them. Her tests were familiar and easy to pass. Talking to someone she trusts reinforced her therapeutic gains, and her pathogenic beliefs were far less influential. In fact, about a year after the birth of her first child, Ruth became convinced she was an excellent mother and decided to become pregnant again. She and her husband are the proud parents of two healthy children.

CONCLUSION

Over the course of therapy, Ruth has made substantial progress in several areas. First, she is increasingly able to handle conflict. She analyzes herself and demonstrates the capacity to recover very quickly. Her process goes something like this: She brings in an undesirable emotion or thought, produces related dreams and memories, analyzes them, and subsequently feels better. She frequently relies on me to bear witness to her struggle and to support and encourage her. Second, Ruth has been able to talk about her parents' traumatic childhoods and feel sadness for them, along with an appreciation of their suffering and its untoward effect on the family. In the past, it would have been too risky for her to feel understanding and compassion because of her profound survivor guilt. However, now that she is free from some of her survivor guilt, she is increasingly able to appreciate some of her parents' positive traits and acknowledge that they were impaired because of their own horrific traumas. She has been free enough to love them and at the same time feel comfortable with minimal contact. Finally, some freedom from her guilty identification with her mother has allowed her to appreciate her own true self. She realizes that the reality of her childhood was often grim and brutal, and many of her attitudes and behaviors were adaptive means of survival. She describes herself aptly as a warrior woman. Relief from the chronic pain of hiding has helped her achieve a greater sense of authenticity.

One day, while reviewing her progress in therapy Ruth said, "In a nutshell, I would define my therapy with you as an attempt to get safe enough to be with the people I love."

9

HOW PATIENTS COACH THEIR THERAPISTS IN PSYCHOTHERAPY

John Bugas and George Silberschatz

INTRODUCTION

This chapter focuses on a clinically important topic that has not been specifically addressed in the psychotherapy literature: the different ways and reasons patients *coach* their therapists during psychotherapy. In the most general sense of the word, to coach is to train someone, to give special instruction, to help prepare someone for an examination or an event. We use the term *coaching* to refer to those patient behaviors and communications that serve to attune the therapist to essential aspects of the patient's problems, conscious or unconscious treatment goals, and how the therapist can best help the patient attain these goals. When coaching, patients provide special information or instruction in order to help their therapists more effectively help them.

With the exception of recent work by Casement (1991) and Bohart and Tallman (1999), we found no specific references to patients coaching their therapists. Casement, borrowing concepts from Bion, Langs, and Winnicot, suggested that patients may unconsciously prompt and guide therapists to be more helpful. He proposed that therapists need to adopt an attitude (or an internal supervisor) that renders them more receptive to these unconscious communications from patients. Bohart and Tallman viewed the activation of the patient's self-healing capacities as essential to successful therapy. Their book includes empirical research and clinical material that supports their self-healing model of therapy. They believe patients (or clients in their lexicon) have inherent capabilities for self-healing and creative problem solving that are fundamental to the therapeutic change process. It is incumbent upon therapists to intervene in ways that support, stimulate, and mobilize their patients' capacities and inner resources. Bohart and Tallman contended that a significant (if not the most significant) common patient variable in a successful outcome across different therapeutic modalities is active self-healing. Therapists help their patients by coaching them to engage in creative problem solving and other self-healing activities.

The concept of coaching presented here is derived from and unique to control-mastery theory. A central tenet of this theory is that humans have an innate striving toward adaptation, growth, and mastery. Traumatic childhood experiences interfere with and often thwart these developmental strivings. Such traumatic life experiences, according to control-mastery theory, are internalized in the form of conscious as well as unconscious pathogenic beliefs. For instance, if a child is treated abusively by a parent, the child typically develops the (unconscious) belief that he or she deserved to be mistreated. Such a belief frequently leads to repetitive, maladaptive relationships in adulthood, and hence Weiss (1993) refers to these as pathogenic beliefs (refer to chapter 1).

Pathogenic beliefs are grim and highly distressing; they interfere with the pursuit of normal developmental goals, generating inhibitions, symptoms, and self-destructive behaviors. Patients who seek psychotherapy are highly motivated to overcome pathogenic beliefs and they work in therapy to disconfirm them. According to control-mastery theory, psychotherapy is a process in which patients, with the help of their therapists, actively seek the knowledge and experiences that will enable them to disconfirm pathogenic beliefs.

One of the primary ways patients work to disconfirm their pathogenic beliefs is by testing them in the therapeutic relationship (Silberschatz & Curtis, 1986; Silberschatz & Curtis, 1993; Weiss, 1993; see chapter 1). Tests are trial actions carried out by the patient (often unconsciously) to appraise the danger or safety of pursuing certain crucial goals. Consider, for example, a patient whose parents were unable to tolerate her childhood strivings toward autonomy and independence. This patient developed the pathogenic belief that her independence was intolerable or upsetting to the people in her life that cared about her (friends, lovers, teachers). The patient worked in therapy to disconfirm this pathogenic belief by experimenting with behaving independently with the therapist (e.g., by disagreeing with the therapist, coming up with her own insights) to see if the therapist (unlike her parents) could comfortably tolerate her independence. (For a further discussion of testing, refer to chapter 1.)

Each patient has specific pathogenic beliefs stemming from particular traumatic life experiences. According to control-mastery theory, the primary motive of patients in psychotherapy is to solve their problems. Weiss (1993) proposed that patients enter therapy with an unconscious plan to disconfirm their pathogenic beliefs and attain desired goals (see also Curtis & Silberschatz, 1997, and chapter 1 for further discussion of the plan concept). Patients unconsciously make and carry out plans for solving problems by attempting to disprove the pathogenic beliefs that underlie them. They work to disprove these beliefs by testing the beliefs with the therapist in the hope that the therapist will not respond to the tests as the beliefs predict (Silberschatz & Curtis, 1993; Weiss, 1993).

COACHING AND THE PLAN CONCEPT

The coaching paradigm presented in this paper is based on the control-mastery conception of the patient's plan. The plan conception is a hypothetical construct used to explain a broad range of patient behaviors during therapy. It contains three interrelated components: goals, pathogenic beliefs, and tests.

The first component refers to the patient's goals for therapy. These goals represent potential affects, attitudes, or capacities the patient wants to achieve. They reflect the direction (or series of directions) patients want to go during therapy. Goals may be specific and concrete (e.g., to change a career) or more general and abstract (e.g., to have a fulfilling life). Migone and Liotti (1998) suggested that goals are innate dispositions and values toward different states of interpersonal relationships (e.g., attachment, caregiving, competition, cooperation, and sexuality) that have been relinquished because of pathogenic beliefs. Throughout therapy, patients experience their therapists' interventions as demonstrating either sympathy, opposition, or indifference to their goals. The degree to which patients are conscious of their goals at the beginning of therapy depends to a large extent on how dangerous and forbidden they believe them to be.

The second component of the patient's plan formulation concerns pathogenic beliefs. Control-mastery theory proposes that psychopathology is a product of irrational pathogenic beliefs about self and others acquired from early traumatic experiences with parents and siblings.

These beliefs warn patients that if they attempt to gratify certain impulses or seek specific developmental goals they will risk the disruption of their all-important parental ties. Pathogenic beliefs impede the pursuit of normal developmental goals and strivings, and they typically generate inhibitions, symptoms, self-destructive behaviors, and maladaptive interpersonal relationships for example:

> *Carl was an exceptionally bright, inquisitive man who was traumatized as a child by his parents' inability to tolerate his incisive questions and unrelenting intellectual curiosity. For instance, as a young child, he asked his father to explain the solar system; when he pushed his father to provide more details, the father apparently felt threatened and became increasingly frustrated, irate, sullen, and emotionally withdrawn. Carl's mother blamed him for the father's reactions and pleaded with him to stop asking so many questions; with extreme disdain and harsh disapproval, she frequently chided him for being too smart for his own good. Carl developed the pathogenic belief that his intelligence was dangerous and needed to be suppressed. Thus, despite a superior IQ, he became a mediocre student and dropped out of college after his first year.*

Patients suffer from these beliefs and the feelings they engender and are highly motivated (both consciously and unconsciously) to change them (for a further discussion of pathogenic beliefs, see chapter 1).

Tests comprise the third component of the patient's plan. As previously mentioned, tests are experimental behaviors and attitudes that patients present to their therapists in order to appraise the relative danger or safety of pursuing valued goals. Patients may test by either "transferring" or by "turning passive into active" (Weiss, 1993, see chapter 1). When patients test by transferring, they repeat the behavior from childhood that they believe provoked their parents to traumatize them in order to see how the therapist will react. When patients test by turning passive into active, they identify with the parents and repeat the parental behavior they experienced as traumatic. By repeating the past in either a transference or a passive-into-active test, patients are actively seeking experiences with the therapist that will help them disprove irrational expectations and false beliefs (Silberschatz & Curtis, 1986).

Research has shown that when therapists "pass" key tests (i.e., intervene in a manner that is compatible with the patient's treatment plan), patients will be relieved and emboldened, and they will make significant therapeutic progress. When therapists "fail" key tests (i.e., intervene in a manner that is incompatible or at cross-purposes with the patient's treatment plan), patients become anxious and constricted, and they retreat from the therapeutic progress (Silberschatz & Curtis, 1993; see chapter 11 for an overview of research on testing). While testing, patients closely monitor their therapist's behavior and attitudes to see if they confirm or disconfirm pathogenic beliefs.

Patients want therapists to understand their plans and help them master their problems. They are highly motivated to directly or indirectly communicate the relevant and pressing aspects of their unconscious treatment plan to their therapists. Coaching behaviors serve to provide therapists with the information necessary to understand various components of the patient's plan. This includes information about treatment goals, pathogenic beliefs, the ways the patient wants to work with the therapist, and the therapists' attitudes and interventions that are most likely to be helpful. Patients coach in order to make their plans clear to therapists, to get therapists back to the plan if they stray, and to keep therapists focused on how not to traumatize them the way their parents did. Unconscious considerations of safety significantly influence the clarity and directness of the patient's coaching communications. Because patients vary with respect to the intensity and pervasiveness of their pathogenic beliefs, it follows that patients differ in their coaching ability and effectiveness.

CASE ILLUSTRATIONS

Patients may employ coaching strategies at any given time during therapy. However, coaching tends to be prominent on three specific occasions: (a) at the beginning of therapy, (b) before, during, and after presenting significant tests to therapists, and (c) when patients want to change the therapeutic relationship.

Coaching at the Beginning of Therapy

Control-mastery theory emphasizes that it is the patient rather than the therapist who sets the agenda in psychotherapy. By coaching at the beginning of therapy, patients directly and indirectly convey how they would like therapists to work with them. Coaching allows therapists to infer the goals their patients want to pursue and the pathogenic beliefs that have prevented them from attaining these goals.

Empirical studies indicate that a significant number of psychotherapy patients manifest a great deal of self-awareness and insight at the beginning of treatment (O'Connor, Edelstein, Berry, & Weiss, 1994; Weiss, 1994). These findings underscore the unconscious importance patients give to orienting therapists to their plans. Indeed, some patients may begin therapy with clear and direct verbal summaries of their treatment plan, as the following example will demonstrate.

> Out of guilt, Jill felt compelled to invite her mother to come live with her, even though she knew it would not work out. Her mother accepted the invitation and moved in with the predicted disastrous results. Jill began a brief (16-session) psychotherapy saying, "My mother is driving me up the wall. I mean that's my prime concern. You know, the other things are security of my home and financial problems. But as great as they are, and as horrible as they are, and they are surmounting like you wouldn't believe, what is really getting me down and making it harder to cope with things is the problem with my mother." Jill then said she wanted her therapist to help her overcome her guilt so that she would be able to follow through on her plan to move her mother to a retirement community. She wanted to understand the source of her guilt and suggested that encouragement and support would help her attain her treatment goal.

More frequently, patients begin therapy by coaching therapists in more indirect ways. These include the use of exaggerations and striking contradictions in verbal content, attitude and behavior.

> Doris began therapy by presenting an emphatic case against herself. She claimed she was stupid, weak, and profoundly psychologically impaired. She recounted story after story that seemed to support her case. However, her behavior was relaxed, her attitude confident (even cocky), and she spoke in a coherent and intelligent manner. Moreover, towards the end of the session, she briefly mentioned she had applied to and was accepted by a top university (one that is highly selective and difficult to

get into), but she had turned it down because her mother thought she was too dysfunctional to go. The mother wanted Doris to live at home and attend a local vocational school to become a hairdresser, something Doris had no interest in, but did anyway to satisfy her mother.

The patient's ability to directly convey pertinent information about his or her treatment plans at the beginning of therapy is primarily determined by how bound the patient is to pathogenic beliefs (Weiss, 1993). Jill was able to communicate her plan clearly and directly to the therapist despite her pathogenic belief regarding her sense of omnipotent responsibility for her mother's welfare. Doris employed more indirect coaching methods that were still powerfully effective in orienting the therapist to her unconscious plan. She presented exaggerations and contradictions that helped the therapist to accurately infer her tendency to obscure strengths and sacrifice goals as a compliance, out of pathological loyalty and guilt, to her mother. The patient demonstrated that she wanted to begin working with the therapist by inviting him to view her as incapable and impaired in the hope that he would not accept her invitations at face value. This way she could begin to use her strengths and abilities while pursuing the goal of becoming independent of her mother.

Coaching and Tests

During therapy, patients work to disconfirm their pathogenic beliefs by testing their validity in the therapeutic relationship (Curtis & Silberschatz, 1986; Sampson, 1990, 1994; Silberschatz & Curtis, 1986; Silberschatz & Curtis, 1993; Silberschatz, Curtis, & Nathans, 1989; Weiss, 1993; Weiss, Sampson, & The Mount Zion Psychotherapy Research Group, 1986). Tests are trial actions by patients designed to assess the danger or safety of pursuing treatment goals. Throughout therapy, patients are primarily concerned with how therapists respond to tests. They closely monitor their therapists' behavior in response to tests to see if it confirms or disconfirms irrational expectations and false beliefs. By testing, patients work to create a relationship with the therapist that makes it safe for them to lift repressions and pursue previously forbidden goals (Weiss, 1990).

However, testing is a risky activity. There is no guarantee that therapists will pass the patients' tests (i.e., intervene in plan-compatible ways); indeed, they may even confirm pathogenic beliefs by failing key tests. Thus, because of the inherent risks involved, patients may coach their therapists on how to pass upcoming tests. The unconscious (and conscious) education therapists receive from their patients' coaching behaviors often allows them to pass tests with a sense of ease and an enhanced confidence in the validity and helpfulness of their interventions. In addition, therapists' spontaneous plan-compatible interventions are usually good indications that they have been successfully coached.

> Neal devoted an entire session talking about his difficulties saying no to his son's unreasonable demands. When the session was over, he tried to engage the therapist in a discussion of various self-help books. The therapist immediately reminded the patient that the session was over and they needed to stop. In the following session, Neal reported he was able to say no to his son's excessive demands.

Neal wanted his therapist to demonstrate the capacity to set limits with him so that he could begin setting limits with his son. He provided the necessary information to help the therapist understand and respond appropriately to his attempt to extend the session.

> During the hour, Bill talked about his father's cold, critical, and rejecting attitude toward him when he was a child. He then began to talk about his inexplicable tendency to suddenly withdraw from the people he enjoys and feels are important to him. Bill began the following session saying that he had decided to quit therapy. He was reassured when his therapist suggested the two of them take whatever time was necessary to understand his sudden decision to end therapy.

Here Bill wanted his therapist to help him overcome his fear of rejection and continue with therapy. He prepared the therapist for a sudden rejection test (i.e., he would reject the therapist before the therapist rejected him) by providing him with sufficient information to understand the test. Bill was then able to become aware of and explore his pathogenic belief that he deserved to be rejected. In both of the previous cases, the therapists felt at ease and confident with their interventions.

> When Carl (the man previously mentioned who believed his intelligence should be suppressed) started therapy, he was significantly underemployed as a grocery store clerk and was generally unhappy with his life. In the early phases of the treatment he vigorously tested to see if the therapist would condemn his intelligence. For instance, he resumed his college education and presented numerous intellectual and academic accomplishments in a veiled manner to see if the therapist could acknowledge him. These tests were relatively easy to pass because the therapist not only recognized but also genuinely admired Carl's incisive intellect and the breadth of his abilities. As Carl developed a greater sense of safety and confidence in the therapeutic relationship, he intensified the testing process and made it more immediate and personal. He began to read numerous articles and books on psychoanalytic theory and therapy (a field in which he saw the therapist as an authority) and then engaged the therapist in theoretical discussions. Carl was particularly astute at zeroing in on topics of considerable controversy, and on several occasions he clearly pushed the limits of the therapist's knowledge. Nonetheless, the therapist pursued these discussions in a friendly, respectful, and collegial manner, for he saw them as an integral part of Carl's testing to see if he would be threatened by his inquisitiveness and his brilliance, as his parents had been. Carl was clearly pleased by the therapist's ability to comfortably tolerate and even enjoy these theoretical dialogues. After one of these, Carl began to recount several poignant memories of his parents' rageful outbursts at him asking his father to explain how gravity worked. With considerable insight and emotion, he began to articulate how inappropriate, abusive, and stifling his parents had been.

This vignette illustrates the interplay between coaching and the testing process. Early in the treatment, Carl informed the therapist about his parents' inability to respond to his intellectual prowess; in so doing, he was educating the therapist how to pass important tests. As Carl developed increasing confidence in the therapist, he began to intensify the testing process in order to disconfirm his most deeply held pathogenic beliefs.

Sometimes, while testing, patients become uncertain about how to understand or interpret their therapist's responses:

> A patient who feared that the analyst would reject him tempted the analyst to do just that by announcing abruptly that he had decided to discontinue the treatment. When the analyst remained silent, the patient became increasingly anxious. He feared that the analyst would permit him to terminate, and so he coached him by saying, "Whenever I do something impulsive, I regret it later." (Weiss et al., 1986, p. 104)

When therapists' interventions are consistently antiplan, patients may escalate their coaching activity and utilize any relevant material to get their therapists more attuned to their plans:

> *Jill (the patient from the first vignette who wanted to overcome her guilt so she could place her mother in a retirement community) provided clear and direct communication of her treatment plan to the therapist during the first two sessions of therapy. However, he continued responding with antiplan interventions. She began the third session by presenting a dream about a man who misunderstood her and was unable to help her solve a problem.*

Therapists who persist in failing critical tests place their patients in difficult and traumatic situations. Under these circumstances, the very act of coaching may become a key test:

> *Fran began a brief (16-session) therapy with the unconscious goal of extricating herself from a destructive marriage. The therapist, however, viewed her as having problems with intimacy. His interventions focused on her dependency needs, fears of abandonment, and desire for a closer relationship with her husband. Because of Fran's exaggerated sense of responsibility for others, she felt compelled to mostly comply with her therapist's interventions in order to protect and restore him. Late in the therapy, she began a session by boldly stating she had just*

> *returned from a great vacation and was able to enjoy it because she went without her husband and didn't feel burdened by having to take care of him.*

This vignette illustrates Fran's last attempt to get her therapist to be helpful. She presented the therapist with information that challenged his formulation of the case. Unfortunately, he was not receptive to the patient's coaching behavior and persisted in making the same antiplan interventions regarding her unconscious conflicts over dependency needs and fears of abandonment. The Fran case had the poorest outcome of the brief psychotherapy cases studied by the San Francisco Psychotherapy Research Group (Silberschatz, Curtis, Sampson, & Weiss, 1991).

Patients may also coach after passed tests. This coaching behavior informs therapists that their interventions are helpful and that the patient wants to continue working in the same manner:

> *Alice had been working in therapy on extricating herself from an abusive relationship with her boyfriend. In the session after she had ended the relationship, Alice said she was worried about how the boyfriend was taking the breakup. She felt he really needed her and was probably devastated by her leaving. She began to consider going back to him. The therapist interpreted Alice's concern about her boyfriend as a product of her exaggerated sense of responsibility for his welfare. She became immediately less anxious and began to talk about her admiration for independent women. She then added that a friend of hers had to break up many times before she could finally leave her abusive boyfriend.*

Alice's last two comments informed the therapist that his interventions were helping her move in the direction she wanted to go, but that she had more work to do on the problem of leaving her boyfriend. She wanted the therapist to continue responding to her tests in the same plan-compatible manner.

Coaching to Change the Therapeutic Relationship

Therapists help patients change by pro-plan interpretations and passing tests. Pro-plan interpretations (i.e., interpretations that are compatible with the patient's plan) enable patients to gain insights into their pathogenic beliefs and the resulting problems. By passing key tests, therapists help patients feel safe enough to confront the dangers foretold by their pathogenic beliefs and to pursue the goals these beliefs have prevented them from attaining. In this way, direct plan-compatible experiences with the therapist leads to significant therapeutic progress (Sampson, 1992; for clinical illustrations, refer to chapters 6, 7, and 8).

Passing tests often requires a great deal of flexibility in the therapist's approach. During the course of treatment, patients may want to test in a variety of ways or work differently toward achieving a new goal. When patients' unconscious plans necessitate changes in the therapeutic relationship, they frequently coach therapists on the specific experiences, capacities, and knowledge they will need to make progress in.

> Neal's therapist had been working with him in an analytic, interpretive mode when the patient began a session presenting new material about his father's inability to protect him from his abusive, alcoholic mother. In the following session, he reported he had resumed an old, dangerously destructive pattern of behavior. The therapist responded by actively enjoining the patient to cease the self-destructive behavior.

The previous vignette illustrates Neal's need to have his therapist demonstrate the capacity to effectively protect him. This allowed the patient to feel safe enough with his therapist to stop the self-destructive behavior and become aware of the false belief that he did not deserve protection. Information given in the preceding session enabled the therapist to understand the new test and provide the patient an almost effortless pro-plan intervention.

> Dan began treatment focused on overcoming an urgent relationship problem with his lover. Except for a few interpretations (which the patient found helpful), the therapist was mostly silent during this time. After the relationship problem was resolved, Dan began talking about his inability to pursue his interests in film. He presented new material concerning the parental indifference and neglect he experienced in childhood, and then resumed talking about his work inhibitions. The therapist began to actively engage the patient in discussions of film and encouraged him to pursue his goal of becoming a film

director. During this time, the patient made steady progress in undoing his work inhibitions and pursuing his goal. Moreover, he developed key insights into his problems with little or no interpretations from the therapist.

Here Dan coached the therapist on his need for encouragement and reassurance in order to confront the dangers predicted by his pathogenic belief. He had inferred from his parents' neglect and indifference that his interests upset them and were dangerous to pursue. The therapist's active engagement and encouraging attitude countered the belief. It was clear from the successful treatment outcome that the patient benefited greatly from the new experiences acquired in the relationship to his therapist.

CONCLUSION

Previous psychodynamic formulations of therapists learning from their patients have focused on the patient's unconscious perceptions of, and constructive responses to, the therapist's countertransference-based behavior. Searles (1975) and Langs (1975) contended that patients are powerfully motivated to help (or cure) their therapists. The concept of coaching presented here is different from these previous formulations in that, while coaching, patients are not concerned with helping solve the therapist's unresolved intrapsychic conflicts. Instead, coaching behaviors serve to inform and educate the therapist on relevant and pressing aspects of the patient's unconscious treatment plan.

An essential (and refreshing) characteristic of control-mastery theory is that the hypotheses derived from its underlying propositions have been, and continue to be, rigorously studied by formal empirical research. The reliability and predictive validity of the plan concept has been demonstrated in numerous studies (e.g., Curtis & Silberschatz, 1997; Curtis, Silberschatz, Sampson, & Weiss, 1994; Silberschatz et al., 1991; Silberschatz & Curtis, 1993; for an overview of this research, see chapter 11). Empirical studies of psychotherapy conducted by the San Francisco Psychotherapy Research Group have demonstrated a high interrater reliability for patient plan formulations (Curtis & Silberschatz, 1997). Moreover, these studies show that the degree to which therapists' interventions are compatible with patients' plans is predictive of both patient progress during therapy and the therapy outcome. The idea of patients coaching their therapists is deeply embedded in the plan concept. Indeed, coaching refers directly to the communication of specific components of the patients' plan. A close examination of psychotherapy transcript material shows that coaching plays a vital role in orienting therapists to the patients' unconscious plans at the beginning of therapy, and coaching then helps keep them attuned to and in accordance with the plan throughout treatment. Even therapists who are not familiar with control-mastery theory and its plan concept may be significantly influenced (albeit unconsciously) by their patients' coaching behaviors.

REFERENCES

Bohart, A., & Tallman, K. (1999). *How clients make therapy work: The process of active self-healing.* Washington, DC: American Psychological Association.

Casement, P. (1991). *Learning from the patient.* New York: Guilford Press.

Curtis, J., & Silberschatz, G. (1986). Clinical implications of research on brief psychodynamic psychotherapy: I. Formulating the patient's problems and goals. *Psychoanalytic Psychology, 3,* 13–25.

Curtis, J. T., & Silberschatz, G. (1997). Plan formulation method. In T. D. Eells (Ed.), *Handbook of psychotherapy case formulation.* New York: Guilford.

Curtis, J. T., Silberschatz, G., Sampson, H., & Weiss, J. (1994). The plan formulation method. *Psychotherapy Research, 4,* 197–207.

Langs, R. (1975). Therapeutic misalliances. *International Journal of Psychoanalytic Psychotherapy, 3,* 77–105.

Migone, P., & Liotti, G. (1998). Psychoanalysis and cognitive–evolutionary psychology: An attempt at integration. *International Journal of Psychoanalysis, 79,* 1071–1095.

O'Conner, L., Edelstein, S., Berry, J., & Weiss, J. (1994). The pattern of insight in brief psychotherapy: A series of pilot studies. *Psychotherapy, 31,* 533–544.

Sampson, H. (1990). How the patient's sense of danger and safety influences the analytic process. *Psychoanalytic Psychology, 7,* 115–124.

Sampson, H. (1992). The role of "real" experience in psychopathology and treatment. *Psychoanalytic Dialogues, 2,* 509–528.

Sampson, H. (1994). Repeating pathological relationships to disconfirm pathogenic belief—commentary on Steven Stern's "needed relationships." *Psychoanalytic Dialogues, 4,* 357–361.

Searles, J. (1975). The patient as therapist to his analyst. In P. Giovacchini (Ed.), *Tactics and techniques of psychoanalytic therapy, Vol. II: Contertransference.* New York: Jason Aronson.

Silberschatz, G., & Curtis, J. T. (1986). Clinical implications of research on brief dynamic psychotherapy: II. How the therapist helps or hinders therapeutic progress. *Psychoanalytic Psychology, 3,* 27–37.

Silberschatz, G., & Curtis, J. T. (1993). Measuring the therapist's impact on the patient's therapeutic progress. *Journal of Consulting and Clinical Psychology, 61,* 403–411.

Silberschatz, G., Curtis, J.T., & Nathans, S. (1989). Using the patient's plan to assess progress in psychotherapy. *Psychotherapy, 26,* 40–46.

Silberschatz, G., Curtis, J. T., Sampson, H., & Weiss, J. (1991). Research on the process of change in psychotherapy: The approach of the Mount Zion Psychotherapy Research Group. In L. Beutler & M. Crago (Eds.), *Psychotherapy research: An international review of programmatic studies.* Washington, DC: American Psychological Association.

Weiss, J. (1990). The nature of the patient's problems and how in psychoanalysis the individual works to solve them. *Psychoanalytic Psychology, 7,* 105–113.

Weiss, J. (1993). *How psychotherapy works.* New York: Guilford Press.

Weiss, J. (1994). The analyst's task: To help the patient carry out his plan. *Contemporary Psychoanalysis, 30,* 236–254.

Weiss, J., Sampson, H., & The Mount Zion Psychotherapy Research Group. (1986). *The psychoanalytic process: Theory, clinical observation and empirical research.* New York: Guilford Press.

Part III

Research and Integration

10

A DEVELOPMENTAL BASIS FOR CONTROL-MASTERY THEORY

Robert Shilkret and Sara A. Silberschatz[1]

Many of the important ideas in control-mastery theory are supported by research and theory from developmental psychology. One of the key developmental assumptions of the theory is that early experiences, including those during infancy, exert a strong (and generally unconscious) influence on later personality and psychopathology. Beyond this basic assumption, several other ideas in control-mastery theory also reflect important concepts from developmental psychology. For example, a key assumption underlying the development of pathogenic beliefs is that young children make inferences and construct theories about their experiences. In this chapter, we will address some of the important ideas and supporting research that provide the basis for the developmental assumptions of control-mastery theory. Our review of the developmental literature is not intended to be comprehensive; we focus on those aspects of the research that are particularly pertinent. The discussion will be organized in four broad areas: (a) social interactions and expectations in infancy, (b) attachment theory, (c) early cognition and the development of pathogenic beliefs, and (d) prosocial behavior, empathy, and the development of guilt.

SOCIAL INTERACTIONS AND EXPECTATIONS IN INFANCY

One of the fundamental ideas in control-mastery theory is that psychopathology develops in the context of relationships and is ameliorated in therapeutic relationships. Research in developmental psychology has shown that infants are socially oriented beginning at birth and that they are motivated to engage in social interactions with caregivers. These early social interactions go beyond simply receiving necessary nurturance and physical care. Infants engage in complex interactions with caregivers during which they develop expectations about their interpersonal world, and they modify their behavior in accordance with these expectations. Although infants do not possess the level of cognitive development required to form pathogenic beliefs, expectations that are formed based on negative patterns of interaction with caregivers can be considered a precursor to pathogenic beliefs.

The control-mastery view of infants as active participants in social interactions has considerable support in developmental psychology. Contemporary research portrays the infant as naturally geared for social interaction, as naturally evocative of social responses from the world, and as able to regulate behavior in response to both the physical and interpersonal environment. The infant's social capacities and natural inclination toward social interaction are clearly documented in an edited volume of infant research, *The competent infant* (Stone, Smith, & Murphy, 1973). This and much other work suggests that the visual, auditory, and olfactory capabilities present shortly after birth allow and encourage the infant to be socially oriented. For instance, infants like to look at their mothers' eyes while nursing or being held (Stone et al.), 3-day-olds recognize and prefer their own mothers' odor over that of another nursing mother (MacFarlane, 1975), and 4-day-olds prefer the sound of their own mothers' voices over the voice of another mother (DeCasper & Fifer, 1980).

The program of research by Beatrice Beebe and her colleagues (e.g., Beebe & Lachmann, 1992) shows the exquisitely well coordinated interactions that occur between infant and caregiver very early on. Using fine-grained analyses of slowed-down video and audio recordings of interactions, Beebe has shown that long before the utterance of the first word, infant and caregiver engage in a complex dialogue of vocalize-stop-listen-vocalize again. Sometimes these exchanges are successful (i.e., coordinated or "matched"), whereas at other times they are not well matched. For example, the mother may "chase" the infant by her gaze and head movements, leading the infant to "dodge" in order to avoid such intense face-to-face encounters, perhaps to modulate or "down-regulate" her own inner affective state. Beebe's work suggests that infants are not merely passive participants; rather, they take an active role in social interactions.

A body of work by Tronick (1986, 1989; Cohn & Tronick, 1987, 1989) examined the ability of infants to repair "mismatches" in their interactions with caregivers. Tronick and his colleagues explored interactions between mothers and 6-month-old infants. They found that infants actively participate in the interaction to regulate their own affect level and to achieve a desired response from their mothers. Detailed analyses of face-to-face interactions between infant and mother have shown that coordination between mother and infant (for example, mutual eye contact) normally occurs only about one third of the time. The interaction frequently moves from mutually coordinated, matched states to mismatched states and back again to matched ones. The infant by 6 months has learned a lot about how to control those interactions (e.g., vocalizing to bring the mother back to eye-to-eye contact; averting eye contact to "down-regulate" a too intense inner state). The mother's unique patterns of social responsiveness come to be anticipated and remembered by the infant by 6 months or earlier, and over time infants form expectations about caregiver responses based on these patterns.

A case study from the classic paper, "Ghosts in the nursery" (Fraiberg, Adelson, & Shapiro, 1975) illustrated how everyday patterns of interaction can eventually become the basis of pathogenic expectations. One of the cases presented in the paper described a 3-1/2-month-old infant who displayed different interaction patterns with his father and his mother. The mother was extremely conflicted about caring for her infant and had turned over all responsibilities to her husband. By the time the infant was 4 months old, he had developed differential expectations toward his mother and father such that he generally acted solemn and withdrawn with his mother, whereas he was able to be responsive and engaged with his father. Later research by Cohn and Tronick (1989) reported similar results regarding the effects of differential caregiver interaction styles on infant behaviors.

Control-mastery theory posits that the formation of pathogenic beliefs is not limited to infrequent or extreme traumatic events. Many of the expectations infants develop based on everyday preverbal interactions could be considered precursors to or rudimentary forms of later, more verbally organized pathogenic beliefs. Certain patterns of interaction between caregiver and infant may prevent the infant from realizing an important developmental goal and lead to later psychopathology. For example, a pattern in which the infant is neglected or is consistently responded to in a way that is inappropriate or unresponsive to his or her needs and emotional state is likely to be traumatic. Additionally, the expectations that infants develop about interactions with caregivers can become pathogenic if the infant develops a narrowed range of behavior and is unable to modify the interaction pattern beyond the original relationship in which it occurred. In summary, a wealth of research and theory highlights the early and complex interaction patterns between infants and caregivers, as well as the potential negative expectations of infants based on their experiences. These findings are congruent with the assumption underlying control-mastery theory about the importance of early social interactions as laying a basis for the eventual development of pathogenic beliefs.

ATTACHMENT THEORY

Control-mastery theory emphasizes the importance of an infant's relationship with caregivers in the development of personality as well as in the development of psychopathology. Indeed, control-mastery theory posits that the infant's or child's motivation to preserve the tie with the caregiver subsumes other drives or motivations. This basic tenet of control-mastery theory has strong empirical and theoretical support in attachment theory, which addresses the ways in which infants continually modify their behavior toward caregivers in order to preserve the attachment bond (Bowlby, 1969, 1973, 1980; see also Cassidy & Shaver, 1999; Karen, 1998; Thompson, 1998). Attachment research has identified four attachment styles or tendencies: (a) insecure–avoidant, (b) insecure–resistant (also called ambivalent), (c) disorganized, and (d) secure (Ainsworth, 1973; Ainsworth, Blehar, Waters, & Wall, 1978; Cassidy & Mohr, 2001). These attachment styles reflect specific adaptations that the infant has made in order to optimize the amount and type of caregiving received. Mary Main (1995) argued that infant attachment styles persist throughout development into adulthood, and she articulated corresponding adult attachment categories including "dismissing of attachment" (a later version of avoidant attachment in infancy), "preoccupied with attachment" (resistant), "disorganized attachment, and secure/autonomous."

In control-mastery theory, specific attachment styles are likely to influence the type and content of pathogenic beliefs in adults. Infants who experience caregivers as unresponsive or rejecting of the infant's dependency needs are likely to develop insecure–avoidant attachments.

Avoidant behavior toward the caregiver minimizes the importance of the attachment relationship, which lowers the infant's anger, sadness, and distress at being rejected (Cassidy, 1994). Adults who have avoidant or dismissing styles minimize the importance of attachment issues; they often idealize parents unrealistically and seem aloof as part of an effort to ward off feelings of rejection. Unconscious pathogenic beliefs associated with avoidant or dismissing attachment styles might include, "I can't get close to my wife because to do so would be disloyal to my mother, who was not close to me," "I dismiss expressions of love from my children because my parents never told me they loved me," and generally "Depending on others drains them." These pathogenic beliefs keep the individual from being overly close to others, a closeness that the person unconsciously thinks might endanger the relationship with his or her parents or other loved ones.

Infants who have received inconsistent or minimally available care have a tendency to form insecure–resistant attachments. For these infants, the importance of the attachment relationship is heightened, and they express more negative emotionality in an effort to receive more consistent responses from the caregiver. In adults, insecure–resistant/preoccupied attachment styles are characterized by wanting to be closer to others than others would like and by persistent conflict surrounding parents. Some examples of pathogenic beliefs that could result from this attachment style are "I feel every lover I get involved with is going to leave me because I couldn't rely on my parents to be there for me when I really needed them," "I can't relax and enjoy my children because my mother worried excessively about me," "I am furious with my children too often because the only time my mother would pay attention to me as a child was when I had tantrums," or more generally "I'm not interesting unless I'm emotionally intense." These pathogenic beliefs result in overly dramatic behavior, which often does get an inconsistent parent or partner to pay more consistent attention.

The disorganized style in infancy is characterized by the absence of a consistent strategy for interaction; it most typically results from a parent who unpredictably frightens the infant or is frightened by the infant (Cassidy & Mohr, 2001). In adults, a disorganized attachment style is characterized by a lack of a consistent strategy in relationships or by great variability in how one relates to others. The following are some examples of possible unconscious pathogenic beliefs for disorganized attachment: "To expect consistency in my relationship with my husband is dangerous because I might be taken by surprise," or "To show any initiative is dangerous because it might frighten my mother." Such pathogenic beliefs frequently drive others away and thereby ensure the person's loyalty to a fragile or inconsistent parent. Disorganized attachment is correlated with more severe psychopathology (Solomon & George, 1999).

Secure infants are those whose caregivers usually respond sensitively and promptly to the infants' signals. Securely attached infants learn that they can reliably and effectively get their needs met by caregivers when they cry or express discomfort. Research in attachment theory has shown that individual differences in the four infant attachment styles often continue through childhood, adolescence, and adult life where they describe important aspects of interpersonal expectations and behavior take place. The idea that adult relational styles can be traced to infancy provides strong support for control-mastery theory, which argues that early relationships and interactions with caregivers are often a source of pathogenic beliefs and psychopathology later in life.

Attachment styles develop based on infants' expectations and internal representations of their relationships with caregivers. Bowlby introduced the construct of the internal working model (IWM) as the mechanism by which attachments develop. The IWM refers to a young child's internal representation of early caregiving relationships and is used as a model for subsequent relationships, or what Bowlby described as plans for interpersonal interaction (Bowlby, 1969, 1973, 1980). Through interactions with caretakers, Bowlby proposed the young child develops IWMs of both self and important others. The IWM allows the child to predict the behavior of the attachment figure so the child can plan responses and interact more effectively with caregivers. Bowlby's construct of the IWM is particularly relevant to control-mastery theory because these early relational models often persist into adulthood and can be a source of pathogenic beliefs.

The IWM becomes even more powerful as a mechanism for developing pathogenic beliefs with the onset of language. Representation in language means that a word or phrase (e.g., "bad") comes to have significance beyond the immediate circumstances in which it was used (Werner & Kaplan, 1963), and this can occur by the second year. For example, if an infant can think "Janie bad," that IWM of self can apply far beyond the specific situations that gave rise to a parent's saying this to a child.

The following case study of Mr. S. (Weiss, Sampson, & The Mount Zion Psychotherapy Research Group, 1986, p. 79) illustrates a pathogenic belief that was formed by the patient preserving an attachment to his parents. Briefly, Mr. S. was sent away without warning at 2 1/2 years of age to stay with an aunt and uncle for 3 months because his brother had contracted measles and his parents feared his contracting the disease. Mr. S. was given no explanation of why he was being sent away. Before leaving, among other things, he had been provoking his parents by mischievous, rowdy behavior. A later analysis revealed that he had inferred this was the reason for his banishment. At his aunt and uncle's, he stopped being rowdy and became a "model boy." When he returned home, he was less playful and outgoing than before and remained so for many years.

In therapy at age 30, he reenacted some of the elements of the childhood situation. He became mischievous and began to have numerous affairs, and he feared the analyst would punish him by rejecting him. As these behaviors were analyzed in treatment, Mr. S. began to remember more clearly the childhood situation described earlier, and he eventually confirmed his memories by asking his parents about his behavior before, during, and after his separation from them. Many other factors contributed to Mr. S.'s difficulties, but his central pathogenic belief was that unless he was good, he would be punished by rejection. This case shows how Mr. S. modified his behavior in order to preserve his attachment with his caregivers and how pathogenic beliefs can arise from early attachments. His pathogenic belief was based on the original attachment style with his parents and then generalized to an overarching relational style.

According to control-mastery theory, pathogenic beliefs are stable. They are held in place by the desire to maintain attachments to loved ones and by conscious and unconscious feelings of guilt. The individual consciously or unconsciously believes he or she deserves the grim fate contained in his or her pathogenic beliefs (refer to chapter 4). Many examples of this can be found in the control-mastery literature, and we will cite only one type of example here. A child's compliance with a parent's negative view of her (e.g., a parent's excessive criticism or shaming of the child), when it leads to the child adopting this view of herself (that she deserves her fate), is grounded in the assumption that the child wants to maintain the relationship with the parent. This formulation is consistent with attachment theory, which emphasizes the child's active efforts to adapt to the caregiver and maintain the attachment. Control-mastery theory further assumes that the child thinking positively about herself would be defying her parent's views, and this could be threatening to the parent and/or to the relationship.

The importance given to early infant–caregiver relationships in control-mastery theory has strong support in attachment research and theory. The development of various attachment styles illustrates the assumption that infants are motivated to adapt in ways that preserve the relationship with caregivers. Research on the disruption of early attachments and on the development of pathological attachment styles can provide insights into the origins of pathogenic beliefs.

EARLY COGNITION AND THE DEVELOPMENT OF PATHOGENIC BELIEFS

Children's logic and ways of understanding reality differ in important respects from adults'. One of the basic premises of control-mastery theory is that from infancy onward we form and test hypotheses about our world and that some of these hypotheses ultimately lead to pathogenic beliefs. Research and theory on childhood cognitive development have shed light on how these pathogenic beliefs are formed and why pathogenic beliefs often originate in childhood. Particularly, this body of research has identified some of the specific qualities of children's cognitive processes that lend themselves to the formation of pathogenic beliefs.

One of the fundamental characteristics of young children's cognitive development originally discussed by Piaget (1955) is egocentrism, or seeing things primarily in terms of oneself and the inability to take another's point of view. A second related characteristic is omnipotence, which refers to a child's exaggerated sense of power regarding his or her ability to influence the thoughts and actions of other people. Consequently, young children often make inferences that tend to exaggerate their own significance and ability to affect others. Egocentrism and omnipotence are a normal result of limited cognitive and social development. They can, however, lead to pathogenic beliefs. For example, children who grow up with a depressed parent frequently feel their parents' unhappiness was their fault.

The child's recognition that other people have thoughts and feelings different from his or her own and that can be influenced by his or her behavior (Gopnik, Meltzoff, & Kuhl, 1999) is a cognitive prerequisite for the development of pathogenic beliefs. This has been called "theory of mind," and research suggests that children develop this capacity around 3 or 4 years of age. Because theory of mind research has relied primarily on tasks with dolls and imagined situations and has not investigated the child's theory of mind with respect to real people who are well known to the child (e.g., family members), it is possible that these abilities (the recognition that one's behavior can affect another's thoughts and feelings) may occur even earlier than the literature suggests.

More specifically, theory of mind research has important implications for the development of pathogenic beliefs about excessive responsibility and the negative influence of one's actions on others. As children develop a theory of mind, they may begin to form pathogenic beliefs about how their behavior hurts parents and loved ones. For example, a preschool-aged child may conclude that her excitement about going to school causes her mother to feel rejected and sad. The child may then subsequently feel compelled to develop negative feelings toward school or have difficulty separating from her mother.

Pathogenic beliefs are generally based on actual experiences. Because children lack the cognitive abilities that develop later on, they are unable to accurately understand and interpret traumatic experiences. They are also prone to certain types of cognitive "errors." These kinds of mistakes are a normal part of development, but they also make children particularly vulnerable to forming pathogenic beliefs. From studies of how young children explain things in the world, Piaget articulated in detail the qualities of the child's logic and how it differed from those of the adult (Piaget, 1951; Cowan, 1978). These included: (a) inferences such as "If A is like B in one respect, it is like B in all respects," (b) the reversal of cause and effect (e.g., "I was bad and therefore I was punished" becomes "I was punished and therefore I am bad"), and (c) the imprecise use of "all" and "some" (e.g., a particular instance implies that this will always occur). These characteristics of the young child's reasoning are commonly seen in pathogenic beliefs and even in those of adults.

Another quality of children's thinking that is also seen in many pathogenic beliefs is what Piaget (1955) called "syncretism." This refers to the tendency to connect a series of separate ideas into one undifferentiated whole, assigning a similarity to disparate things. Extending this concept, a child who does poorly in math may generalize this weakness and believe that she will do poorly in all areas of school or, even more generally, that she is stupid. In the development of a pathogenic belief, specific instances of behavior called "bad" may become a holistic (or syncretistic) self-conception of badness. Although these forms of reasoning can occasionally be found in adult logic, such reasoning is far more typical of thought earlier in development than later. These ways of thinking can often be seen in the logic of unconscious pathogenic beliefs.

Our claim is not that the young child's thought is solely of this kind; only that such characteristics of thinking are normal attributes of the young developing child. Such thinking normally is adaptive in the life of the child. It represents a considerable advance from the sensorimotor schemas of earlier infancy and enables the child to understand the phenomena he or she encounters in a new and more general way. Problems may emerge when such normal and adaptive schemas encounter particular kinds of environmental events, such as the kinds of trauma or patterns of parental behavior discussed earlier.

An important characteristic of the young child's thinking is symbolic representation, which Piaget linked to the transition between his or her sensorimotor period (infancy) and his or her preoperational period (early childhood). Symbolic representation makes it possible for children to generalize both correctly and incorrectly about their experiences. Control-mastery theory also assumes that pathogenic beliefs are based on real experiences, and with symbolic representation these experiences become more powerful, for good and for ill. For example, when a parent says, "If you do that again, I will kill you" often and seriously enough, and does in fact lose control, the child may well take his parent literally. He may come to develop the grim belief that (a) the parent can in fact kill him and may want to, and (b) that his behavior was so heinous that he deserves to die. Because children often overgeneralize the inferences they make beyond the original experience in which the inference was most adaptive, the inference can easily become global (e.g., in this example, the pathogenic belief might become, "I am so bad, I deserve to die").

Although control-mastery theory holds that pathogenic beliefs can be formed at any point developmentally (including in adulthood if the trauma is sufficiently powerful), we still might expect that particular kinds of pathogenic beliefs are characteristically related to different stages of development. Heinz Werner (1961) defined development as an increase in differentiation and hierarchic integration. From that viewpoint, one might expect pathogenic beliefs formed earlier in development to be more global and less specific than those formed later (e.g., "I'm a bad person" is more global than "I'm bad at mathematics" or even "I'm a bad parent"). Earlier in development less differentiation and hierarchic integration take place.

For example, the significant people in one's world are not seen as being as different from each other as they will be seen later. For this reason, a belief in one's omnipotence or ability to influence and harm others formed earlier during development may be more pernicious and more pathogenic than a similar belief formed later. Earlier on, it might be seen as potentially affecting everyone, whereas later it might be limited to certain situations or specific people. This can be subtle, because many beliefs are formed from specific experiences involving specific individuals. A young child's belief may seem to be linked to his father, but if he fails to differentiate his father from other men, for example, it might actually be more far-reaching. Likewise, beliefs about one's own worthlessness would be more pathogenic if formed earlier and prior to important differentiations in how one thinks about oneself later as good in some respects but bad in others.

PROSOCIAL BEHAVIOR, EMPATHY, AND THE DEVELOPMENT OF GUILT

A wealth of research and theory in the past two decades has been devoted to the early development of prosocial emotions, including empathy, concern for others, guilt, and helping behavior. As in the field of cognitive development, a theme of many findings has been that many of these prosocial capacities are present at an earlier age than was previously thought. We will highlight only a few points of this area of work that are particularly relevant to control-mastery theory.

Regarding the appearance of concern about and empathy for others in distress, evidence shows that a child around 2 years of age is interested in the feelings and experiences of others, particularly those who are important to him or her. Further, a child this young is aware of the suffering or difficulties of others (Barrett, 1998; Hoffman, 1982, 1998, 2000). Children who are 2 and 3 years old are also capable of experiencing guilt, which is seen as an interpersonal phenomenon (Baumeister, Stillwell, & Hetherton, 1994).

As noted previously (and discussed in chapter 4), the concept of unconscious guilt is central to the formulation of many pathogenic beliefs in control-mastery theory. Thus, work on the early origins of guilt is of considerable interest. Carolyn Zahn-Waxler and her colleagues at the National Institute of Mental Health (NIMH) have eloquently demonstrated the early origin of guilt (Zahn-Waxler & Radke-Yarrow, 1982; Zahn-Waxler & Kochanska, 1990; Kochanska, Gross, & Lin, 2002). This work has used several different methodologies to uncover the young child's abilities in this area. These include semiprojective procedures (story narratives), interviews, observations of children's reactions to naturally occurring as well as simulated problems, and experimentally arranged "mishaps." These studies have shown that the very young child has the capacity to be concerned, even upset, by the mishaps of others. When the child is old enough to have developed a theory of mind, he or she can conclude that his or her own actions can influence others, occasionally to their detriment. The child's inferences about his or her influence on others are highly adaptive in that they allow the child to account for progressively more of his or her experience, beyond the simpler associational connections of infancy. However, these inferences can lead the child to exaggerate his or her ability to affect other people.

Zahn-Waxler cited some responses of children between 1 and 2 1/2 years of age to the distresses they caused others. She noted the expressions of concern, anxiety, remorse, reparation, and acknowledgement of responsibility in situations of wrongdoing or accidental harm (Zahn-Waxler & Kochanska, 1990). Such statements indicate the capacity of the very young child to experience feelings of guilt. Mothers (trained as observers) made these recordings in their own homes:

> *61 weeks*—Child is pounding with cup and accidentally hits Father hard in the nose. (Father gives loud "ouch.") Child drops cup, looks very serious, leans forward to Father for a kiss. (At 81 weeks when child accidentally kicks Father and Father responds [with "ouch"], the child immediately gives him a big hug and pats him.)
>
> *62 weeks*—Child repeatedly turns milk cup upside down. (Mother starts to hit child's hand, but then takes the cup away and calls her a bad girl.) Child whines and calls herself "bad."
>
> *75 weeks*—Child pulls hair of another child and hits her face. (Mother becomes angry, scolds, and explains why it was bad.) Mother leaves room and child follows her saying, "Me," pulling her own hair and hitting herself in the face. Then she returns to her playmate, kisses her, and plays nicely for quite a while until the fight erupts again later.
>
> *93 weeks*—Child throws favorite doll very hard out of the crib, slamming it into the toy chest and looking defiant. She then looks at doll and says sympathetically (looking sad) that the "baby" is crying. (Mother says, "You probably hurt her.") Child asks Mother to get doll, then hugs it, and says "Baby hurt foot"

and kisses foot, sings, rocks, wraps it in blanket, and tries to give it a bottle. [Note in this example the child's "pretend" reparation, that is, the symbolic representation of reparation.]

98 weeks—Mother is angry with child's whining and scolds. He bursts into tears and says, "Mommy, I love you. Do you love me?"

109 weeks—Child bites playmate. (Mother explains, scolds, is judgmental, comforts playmate, tells child to say sorry.) Child does say sorry, with all the emotion of a wet fish. Later she says "sorry" with a little more sympathy in her voice, in the presence of the playmate's mother. And later she told her father, "Pam cry, I bad." (pp. 247–249)

These examples are representative of the behavior of the 24 children of normal mothers in this study. In another report (Zahn-Waxler, Radke-Yarrow, Wagner, and Chapman, 1992), it was found that spontaneous pro-social behaviors like helping, sharing, and providing comfort emerged and increased in variety and frequency between 1 and 2 years. Likewise, during the same period, expressions of concern and attempts to understand another's plight increased, as did reparative behaviors after causing harm to another. By 2 years, children in this study were most responsive to distress in their mothers but showed some sensitivity to strangers. Children at this young age even discriminate and respond differently to distress that they themselves caused versus distress they did not cause. A child will seem more upset when he or she has been the cause of parent's distress.

Research studies by the Zahn-Waxler group and others have noted a greater incidence of guilt responses among the children of clinically depressed mothers as compared with nondepressed groups. Zahn-Waxler noted that the child may come to feel he or she has caused the mother's depression. We would extend the argument, noting that not only depression but any misfortune befalling a loved one may be interpreted by the child as having been caused by him or her, even in the case of a very young child. It is from such inferences that pathogenic beliefs are built.

The results of this line of work are congruent with the developmental assumptions of control-mastery theory. The child's relative egocentrism seems apparent: He or she often blames him- or herself for harm done, even when this is not accurate. Egocentrism is apparent also in reparative attempts that employ solutions that would soothe the child but are unlikely to soothe an adult (except by amusement and delight in these "childlike" attempts). The attempt to help, however, is not egocentric in itself; rather, it is socially oriented and clearly indicates the child's understanding that there are others in the world with differing experiences. It seems that actual physical hurt to others elicits the earliest expression of empathy and guilt.

Beyond these studies showing the origins of interpersonal guilt in very young children, research in social psychology has demonstrated that adults experience guilt even without causing harm to others. People can feel guilty simply because they are better off than others (Baumeister et al., 1994, pp. 252–253 and p. 260). The early origins of such survivor guilt have not yet been explored fully in the developmental literature, but we might speculate that it is a form that develops later than guilt about actually causing harm to another or seeing someone else harmed, given both the earlier focus of the child on physical integrity and also adult strictures against harming others. It might be useful to conceptualize a developmental sequence of guilt. For example, Martin Hoffman's (1982, 1998, 2000) work on the early origins of guilt suggested that guilt over physical action comes first, followed by guilt over inaction or omission, and finally guilt over contemplating a harmful act (see also Zahn-Waxler & Kochanska, 1990, p. 17).

To summarize briefly, the developmental implications of the control-mastery theory are that guilt is common as early as 2 or 3 years of age, and that such early guilt can become the basis for symptoms and later psychopathology (refer to chapter 4). As described earlier, the developmental research points out that inferences involving irrational guilt can be formed quite early, significantly earlier than the Oedipal onset of guilt suggested by psychoanalytic theory. A commonly recognized example is the pathogenic belief formed around the parent directly mistreating the child. The young child often blames him- or herself for the mistreatment or for causing the parent to be sufficiently upset to harm him or her (refer to chapter 4). Beyond these more specific examples involving early guilt, the child is assumed to be altruistic both by control-mastery theory and much research in early prosocial emotions. Coupled with the attachment style developed during infancy, as the child's cognitive capacities increase, he or she often feels responsible for the well-being of the parent, a concern reflecting his or her altruism.

CONCLUDING REMARKS

Control-mastery theory emphasizes the role of early relationships in the development of psychopathology. Research and theory from developmental psychology clearly support the importance of these early relationships and indicate that the infant may have a much more active role in these relationships than previously thought. Many pathogenic beliefs might be considered to originate with expectations and IWMs formed during infancy. In addition to early relationships, theory and evidence from developmental psychology show that many pathogenic beliefs may form during childhood due to specific qualities of children's logic and reasoning. Cognitive abilities are now being attributed to children considerably younger than was the case even a decade ago. Work on the earliest origins of the child's theory of mind might even underestimate its origin, because the studies in that area have not yet examined the child's thinking about those who are most important to him or her: family members. One would expect the child's thinking to be further developed regarding family members than the hypothetical situations child participants typically encounter in the research laboratory. As we have seen in the family-based research of the Zahn-Waxler group, concerns about family members, attempts to make reparations for imagined harm done to them, and feelings of guilt for transgressions visited upon them, imagined or real, have a very early appearance.

In summary, we have presented an overview of research and theory from four areas of developmental psychology that are particularly germane to control-mastery theory. A wealth of support exists in the developmental literature for the central ideas of control-mastery theory.

ENDNOTE

1. This chapter is based on ideas developed by the first author (R. S.). An earlier version was presented by him at the conference of the San Francisco Psychotherapy Research Group, March, 1991. Cynthia Shilkret contributed to the development of these ideas and her contribution is gratefully acknowledged.

REFERENCES

Ainsworth, M. D. S. (1973). The development of infant–mother attachment. In B. M. Caldwell & H. N. Ricciuti (Eds.), *Review of child development research, volume 3* (pp. 1–94). Chicago, IL: University of Chicago Press.

Ainsworth, M. D. S., Blehar, M. C., Waters, E., & Wall, S. (1978). *Patterns of attachment: A psychological study of the strange situation*. Hillsdale, NJ: Erlbaum.

Barrett, K. C. (1998). The origins of guilt in early childhood. In J. Bybee (Ed.), *Guilt and children* (pp. 75–90). San Diego, CA: Academic Press.

Baumeister, R. F., Stillwell, A. M., & Heatherton, T. F. (1994). Guilt: An interpersonal approach. *Psychological Bulletin, 115*, 243–267.

Beebe, B., & Lachmann, F. M. (1992). The contribution of mother–infant mutual influence to the origins of self and object representations. In N. J. Skolnick & S. C. Warshaw (Eds.), *Relational perspectives in psychoanalysis* (pp. 83–117). Hillsdale, NJ: Analytic Press.

Bowlby, J. (1969). *Attachment and loss. Volume 1: Attachment.* New York: Basic Books.

Bowlby, J. (1973). *Attachment and loss. Volume 2: Separation: Anxiety and anger.* New York: Basic Books.

Bowlby, J. (1980). *Attachment and loss. Volume 3: Loss: Sadness and depression.* New York: Basic Books.

Cassidy, J. (1994). Emotion regulation: Influences of attachment relationships. In N. A. Fox (Ed.), *The development of emotion regulation: Biological and behavioral considerations. Monographs of the Society for Research in Child Development, 59* (2–3, Serial No. 240, pp. 228–249).

Cassidy, J., & Mohr, J. J. (2001). Unsolvable fear, trauma, and psychopathology: Theory, research, and clinical considerations related to disorganized attachment across the lifespan. *Clinical psychology: Science and practice, 8*, 275–298.

Cassidy, J., & Shaver, P. R. (Eds.). (1999). *Handbook of attachment: Theory, research, and clinical applications.* New York: Guilford.

Cohn, J. F., & Tronick, E. (1987). Mother–infant face-to-face interaction: The sequence of dyadic states at 3, 6, and 9 months. *Developmental Psychology, 23*, 68–77.

Cohn, J. F., & Tronick, E. (1989). Specificity of infants' responses to mothers' affective behavior. *Journal of the American Academy of Child and Adolescent Psychiatry, 28*, 242–248.

Cowan, P. A. (1978). *Piaget with feeling: Cognitive, social, and emotional dimensions.* New York: Holt, Rinehart, and Winston.

DeCasper, A. J., & Fifer, W. P. (1980). Of human bonding: Newborns prefer their mothers' voices. *Science, 208*, 1174–1176.

Fraiberg, S., Adelson, E., & Shapiro, V. (1975). Ghosts in the nursery: A psychoanalytic approach to the problems of impaired mother–infant relationships. *Journal of the American Academy of Child Psychiatry, 14*, 387–421.

Gopnik, A., Meltzoff, A. N., & Kuhl, P. K. (1999). *The scientist in the crib: Minds, brains, and how children learn.* New York: Morrow.

Hoffman, M. L. (1982). Development of prosocial motivation: Empathy and guilt. In N. Eisenberg (Ed.), *The development of prosocial behavior* (pp. 281–313). New York: Academic Press.

Hoffman, M. L. (1998). Varieties of empathy-related guilt. In J. Bybee (Ed.), *Guilt and children* (pp. 91–112). San Diego, CA: Academic Press.

Hoffman, M. L. (2000). *Empathy and moral development: Implications for caring and justice.* Cambridge, UK: Cambridge University Press.

Karen, R. (1998). *Becoming attached.* New York: Oxford.

Kochanska, G., Gross, J. N., & Lin, M. H. (2002). Guilt in young children: Development, determinants, and relations with a broader system of standards. *Child Development, 73*, 461–482.

MacFarlane, J. (1975). Olfaction in the development of social preferences in the human neonate. In M. Hofer (Ed.), *Parent–infant interaction.* Amsterdam, The Netherlands: Elsevier.

Main, M. (1995). Discourse, prediction, and recent studies in attachment: Implications for psychoanalysis. In T. Shapiro and R. N. Emde (Eds.), *Research in psychoanalysis: Process, development, outcome* (pp. 209–244). Madison, CT: International Universities Press.
Piaget, J. (1951). *The child's conception of the world.* Totowa, NJ: Rowman & Littlefield.
Piaget, J. (1955). *The language and thought of the child.* Cleveland, OH: World.
Solomon, J., & George, C. (Eds.). (1999). *Attachment disorganization.* New York: Guilford.
Stone, L. J., Smith, H., & Murphy, L. (Eds.). (1973). *The competent infant.* New York: Basic Books.
Thompson, R. A. (1998). Early sociopersonality development. In N. Eisenberg (Volume Ed.), *Handbook of child psychology: Social, emotional, and personality development* (Vol. 3, 5th ed.). New York: John Wiley & Sons.
Tronick, E. Z. (1986). Interactive mismatch and repair: Challenges to the coping infant. *Zero to Three: Bulletin of the National Center for Clinical Infant Programs, 6,* 1–6.
Tronick, E. Z. (1989). Emotions and emotional communication in infants. *American Psychologist, 44,* 112–119.
Weiss, J., Sampson, H., & The Mount Zion Psychotherapy Research Group. (1986). *The psychoanalytic process: Theory, clinical observation, and research.* New York: Guilford.
Werner, H. (1961). *Comparative psychology of mental development.* New York: Science Editions.
Werner, H., & Kaplan, B. (1963). *Symbol formation.* New York: John Wiley.
Zahn-Waxler, C., & Kochanska, G. (1990). The origins of guilt. In R. A. Thompson (Ed.), *Nebraska symposium on motivation, 1988: Socioemotional development* (pp. 182–258). Lincoln, NE: University of Nebraska Press.
Zahn-Waxler, C., & Radke-Yarrow, M. (1982). The development of altruism: Alternative research strategies. In N. Eisenberg-Berg (Ed.), *The development of prosocial behavior* (pp. 109–137). New York: Academic Press.
Zahn-Waxler, C., Radke-Yarrow, M., Wagner, E., & Chapman, M. (1992). Development of concern for others. *Developmental Psychology, 28,* 126–136.

11

AN OVERVIEW OF RESEARCH ON CONTROL-MASTERY THEORY

George Silberschatz

One of the most distinctive features of control-mastery theory is the strong interconnection between clinical observation, theory development, and empirical research. Clinical observations lead to the development of the theory, which gave rise to a large program of research. The results of the research studies in turn shaped subsequent clinical discoveries and theoretical elaboration. The research has consistently followed general principles of the scientific method. First, theoretical concepts are articulated precisely and clearly so that the links between the concepts and observation may be specified. Second, the research verifies that (clinical) observations can be made reliably (i.e., judges or raters must be able to agree about the phenomenon being observed). Finally, results are evaluated based on a reasonable correspondence between theoretical predictions (hypotheses) and actual observations.

The purpose of this chapter is to provide a broad overview of research on control-mastery theory. I will not provide an exhaustive review of the research literature, nor will I provide extensive statistical details. My focus is on *psychotherapy research* and consequently the large program of control-mastery research outside the therapeutic setting is beyond the scope of this chapter (e.g., Meehan, O'Connor, Berry, Weiss, & Acampora, 1996; Morray & Shilkret, 2002; O'Connor, Berry, & Weiss, 1999; O'Connor, Berry, Weiss, & Gilbert, 2002; Shilkret & Nigrosh, 1997; Shilkret & Vecchiotti, 1997).

Empirical research has guided the development of control-mastery theory from its inception. When Weiss began to study process notes of therapy sessions, he relied on an empirical approach as his primary investigative tool. He investigated how patients change in psychotherapy by identifying instances of significant therapeutic progress and he then systematically examined what the therapist had done immediately preceding such instances. Similarly, when Weiss and Sampson began their collaboration in 1967, they did so with "the crucial conviction that therapeutic processes—although case-specific, subtle, and always dependent on subjective experiences within and between the participants—are ordinarily understandable and lawful" (Sampson, 1995, p. 4).

This conviction about the inherent lawfulness of therapeutic processes stimulated an extensive body of research on control-mastery theory. It is important to emphasize that most of this research focused on therapies that had been completed, tape-recorded, and transcribed. Moreover, the research is based on therapies in which both therapists and patients were unfamiliar with the control-mastery theory. In fact, the research paradigm has been to empirically investigate how psychotherapy works regardless of the therapist's (or the patient's) theory of how therapy works.

Before describing and summarizing some of this research, I would like to briefly address some of the salient issues in psychotherapy process research in order to provide a broader context for studies of control-mastery theory. Although most theories of psychotherapy assume that the therapist plays a significant role in the change process, surprisingly little research evidence exists demonstrating *how* the therapist contributes to the success or failure of psychotherapy (Goldfried & Wolfe, 1996, 1998; Lambert & Bergin, 1994; Parloff, Waskow, & Wolfe, 1978; Persons & Silberschatz, 1998; Seligman, 1996; Stiles, Shapiro, & Elliott, 1986). A major problem in most of the research literature is that investigators have typically attempted to assess therapist interventions without regard to a particular patient's specific problems and needs (Rice & Greenberg, 1984; Silberschatz, Curtis, Fretter, & Kelly, 1988; Silberschatz, Curtis, & Nathans, 1989; Silberschatz & Curtis, 1993; Stiles et al., 1986; Strupp, 1986). The prevailing assumption has been that a given therapist's behavior "is either 'good' or 'bad' without regard to the context in which it appears. This fits poorly with the observation of experienced clinicians that a given therapist response or client performance seems to be crucial at one point and irrelevant or even detrimental at another" (Rice & Greenberg, 1984, p. 10). Kiesler (1966) referred to this assumption as the "homogeneity myth" because it erroneously assumes that there is little variability between or within patients, therapists, and treatments.

One strategy, called the "events paradigm" (Stiles et al., 1986), avoids the homogeneity assumption by identifying clinically significant incidents or key events within therapy sessions (e.g., the patient's describing a particularly salient problem or interpersonal conflict). Sampson and Weiss used this method in their studies of process notes (Sampson, Weiss, Mlodnosky, & Hause, 1972), as did Brenman, Gill, and Knight (1952) in their research on hypnosis. Luborsky also used the events paradigm in his research on "momentary forgetting" during psychotherapy (Luborsky, 1967) and in his "symptom-context" studies (Luborsky, Singer, Hartke, Crits-Christoph, & Cohen, 1984). Investigators who have studied the process and outcome of psychotherapy have also used this strategy (e.g., Crits-Chrisoph, Cooper, & Luborsky, 1988; Elliott, 1983, 1984; Fretter, 1984; Gassner, Sampson, Weiss, & Brumer, 1982; Greenberg, 1982, 1986; Horowitz, Sampson, Siegelman, Wolfson, & Weiss, 1975; Mahrer, 1985; Norville, Sampson, & Weiss, 1996; Pole, 1999; Silberschatz, 1978, 1986; Silberschatz, Fretter, & Curtis, 1986; Silberschatz & Curtis, 1993). In the events paradigm, the investigator identifies significant episodes within the therapy session and evaluates the extent to which the therapist's intervention is helpful to the patient.

The focus on significant events in therapy is a clear advance over previous homogenized approaches to psychotherapy research. However, the events approach does not address another methodological problem evident in most studies of how the therapist's behavior influences the process and outcome of psychotherapy—namely, an evaluation of the quality or suitability of the therapist's behavior. The events paradigm can lead investigators to identify critical incidents in therapy, but it does not provide a framework or method for determining whether the therapist's interventions in response to these critical incidents are well suited to the patient's particular needs. Consider, for example, a patient who consistently failed to respond to transference interpretations; it would be impossible for the researcher to ascertain whether transference interpretation as a technique is ineffective or whether the particular transference interpretation or line of interpretation is ill suited to that patient.

How have psychotherapy researchers addressed the assessment of suitability? Some investigators have proposed measures such as therapist "skillfulness" (Schafer, 1982) or "generic helpfulness" (Elliott, 1984). Others have developed treatment manuals and assessed the therapist's level of adherence or fidelity to the treatment manual (Elkin et al., 1989), assuming that therapists who adhere closely to the interventions prescribed in the treatment manual provide more skillful (and therefore optimal) treatment. However, such broad approaches ignore the lessons of the events paradigm. They fail to recognize that interventions that are helpful to one patient may not be helpful to another, even when patients share identical diagnostic and demographic profiles. The helpfulness, skillfulness, or suitability of any given therapeutic intervention cannot be meaningfully determined without first knowing the specific problems and needs of the individual patient.

THE FORMULATION AND ASSESSMENT OF PATHOGENIC BELIEFS: RESEARCH ON THE PLAN FORMULATION METHOD

In clinical practice, therapists typically develop some type of case formulation, which directs the therapist's attention to what the patient's problems and goals are. It also informs the therapist on how best to intervene to help the patient, how to evaluate the effectiveness of interventions, and finally how to assess overall therapeutic progress (Eells, 1997; McWilliams, 1999; Perry, Cooper, & Michels, 1987; Persons, 1989; Silberschatz et al., 1989). As such, it constitutes an informal paradigm for the evaluation of psychotherapy. Most of the control-mastery research has relied on case formulations as a research tool to study psychotherapy. Because one of the cardinal requirements for scientific research is the objective specification and measurement of phenomena, the first broad topic I will discuss is how researchers were able to achieve reliable formulations of patients' problems.

The initial effort to study whether appropriately trained judges could arrive at reliable control-mastery case formulations was carried out by Caston (1986). He devised a three-step procedure for assessing the interjudge reliability of control-mastery case formulations. First, he divided the formulation into relevant component parts: goals, obstructions (pathogenic beliefs), tests, and interventions. Next, he had a team of formulating judges develop a narrative formulation, which was then broken down into a series of statements or items for each of the formulation components (goals, obstructions, etc.). To these actual statements, the team added "alternative" items that were clinically plausible but less relevant to the particular case. Finally, he asked a new team of judges to rate each of the items ("actual" and "alternative") for its degree of relevance to the particular case.

Caston applied this procedure to the process notes of the first five sessions of a completed psychoanalytic case and found excellent interjudge reliability (reliability coefficients ranging from .72 to .92). He replicated his method on a second psychoanalytic case and found comparable results. This method was subsequently applied to studies of brief therapies with very similar results: interjudge reliabilities for five brief psychotherapy cases were typically in the .8 to .9 range (Rosenberg, Silberschatz, Curtis, Sampson, & Weiss, 1986; Curtis, Silberschatz, Sampson, Weiss, & Rosenberg, 1988).

Curtis and Silberschatz (1991) modified Caston's original approach and called their new procedure the Plan Formulation Method. Instead of developing a consensus narrative formulation, which is then broken down into statements, each of the formulation judges independently reviews the clinical material and generates lists of items (this procedure allows each judge to independently formulate the case). Judges are instructed to use a standard format in preparing their items, and they are asked to include items they believe are relevant to the case, as well as items that are plausible but of lesser relevance. After the formulation judges have created their lists of items, the lists are compiled into a master list, which is then returned to the judges who independently rate all the items for their relevance to the case. The rating scale ranges from 0, not relevant, to 4, highly relevant.

The Plan Formulation Method includes five components: the patient's *goals* for therapy, the *obstructions* (*pathogenic beliefs*) that have impeded the patient from pursuing these goals, the life *traumas* that led to the development of pathogenic beliefs, the *tests* that the patient will enact in therapy in order to disconfirm pathogenic beliefs, and the *insights* that will help the patient understand the pathogenic beliefs and achieve therapy goals. Examples of items for each of the formulation components are provided in Table 11.1 (a detailed illustration and application of the method to a particular case can be found in Curtis & Silberschatz, 1997). Excellent interjudge reliabilities (typically in the .8 to .9 range) have been reported (Curtis, Silberschatz, Sampson, & Weiss, 1994), and the Plan Formulation Method has been successfully applied to a wide variety of cases treated under diverse theoretical models—psychodynamic, interpersonal, and cognitive–behavioral (Curtis & Silberschatz, 1997). Foreman and his colleagues (Foreman, Gibbins, Grienenberger, & Berry, 2000) also showed that the Plan Formulation Method could be reliably applied to a child psychotherapy case. The method has also been used to study family therapy (Bigalke, 2004) and psychobiography (Conrad, 1995, 1997).

Table 11.1 Plan Formulation Items for 5 Components

Examples of Plan Formulation Items

Goals

- To pursue her interests without modifying or subjugating them to the interests of others.
- To overcome her fear of sex.
- To become less involved with her family.
- To be more emotionally accessible to his family.
- To feel entitled to the help and interest of others.

Obstruction (Pathogenic Beliefs)

- She believes that she is capable of seriously harming others if she does not carefully tend to them.
- She believes that she has failed in her responsibility to make her parents happy and thus does not deserve to feel happy.
- He believes that his wife would be hurt if he were to assert himself and so holds himself back and permits her to make all the decisions.
- She believes that her assertiveness, intellect, and high energy level overwhelmed her mother and drove her mother away.
- She believes that if she asks for more from people, she will feel guilty for draining them.
- He believes that it would be disloyal to his father if he were to be a better father with his own children and consequently, he remains under-involved with his children.

Tests

- She will take control of the session to see if the therapist is bothered by her strength and direction.
- She will exaggerate her needs and wishes as a way of testing whether the therapist feels that her true needs and wishes are legitimate.
- He will ignore the therapist's comments and interpretations to see if the therapist, unlike the patient in childhood, can fight back rather than withdraw.
- He will question the therapist to see if the therapist—unlike father—can acknowledge mistakes or uncertainty.

Insights

- To become aware that her intense worry about losing her boyfriend is a defense against feeling guilty about wanting to leave him (i.e., she is the victim, rather than the victimizer).
- To become aware that he does not feel entitled to the interest, help, and concern of others because of compliance with parental neglect.
- To become aware that his inability to get along with others is based on an unconscious identification with his parents' inability to get along with people.

(continued)

Table 11.1 (continued)	Plan Formulation Items for 5 Components
	Examples of Plan Formulation Items

Traumas

- Father was easily wounded by the patient's knowing more than he did or surpassing him (e.g., they stopped playing chess once the patient could beat his father).
- Mother and father's frequent fights (often over him and for which he felt responsible) made him become isolated and withdrawn.
- His excessively controlling, critical, disapproving father never allowed him to enjoy his intellect and accomplishments.
- Mother always confided in the patient and told him that she remained in an unhappy marriage for his sake; consequently, he has felt overly responsible for and worried about her.

In short, empirical research has consistently shown that appropriately trained clinicians can achieve a high degree of interjudge reliability in formulating basic control-mastery concepts (e.g., pathogenic beliefs, traumas, tests) and case formulations based on these concepts.

THE PATIENT'S TESTS OF THE THERAPIST

One of the primary ways a patient may disconfirm pathogenic beliefs is by testing them in the therapeutic relationship. According to control-mastery theory, the therapist's response to the patient's tests plays a decisive role in the process and outcome of therapy. If the patient perceives the therapist's response as disconfirming the pathogenic belief—passing the test—it is predicted that the patient will feel relieved and less anxious, and will be more productive, in therapy. On the other hand, if the therapist's response confirms the pathogenic belief—failing the test—the patient is likely to feel distressed and show signs of therapeutic retreat.

A research study designed to test this hypothesis was carried out on the verbatim transcripts of the first 100 hours of an audio tape-recorded psychoanalysis (Silberschatz, 1978, 1986). The patient, Mrs. C., was a 28-year-old married professional woman who sought treatment because she was unable to feel close to and enjoy sex with her husband. The analysis, carried out by an experienced psychoanalyst, was completed long before this study was planned. The method for this study involved four steps:

1. Isolating all putative tests
2. Identifying key tests, that is, those tests that are particularly relevant to the patient's specific pathogenic beliefs
3. Rating the degree to which the therapist passed or failed each test
4. Assessing the patient's behavior immediately before and immediately after each test to determine whether the patient changed in the predicted direction (see Table 11.2)

To carry out Step 1, nine judges read the verbatim transcripts of the first 100 sessions and selected all the instances in which the patient attempted to elicit a response from the therapist (it was assumed that this would provide a large pool of potentially relevant test sequences). In all, 87 such instances were identified. Typescripts of the patient's attempts to elicit a response, as well as the therapist's interventions (which included silence), were then prepared. To carry out Step 2, three control-mastery judges (who were familiar with the concept of testing) read a plan formulation of the case (which had been reliably developed as part of a separate study) and identified which of the incidents represented key tests. The judges selected 46 episodes as key tests of the patient's pathogenic beliefs.

Step 3 used four experienced control-mastery judges. They read the case formulation and then independently rated the extent to which the therapist passed or failed each key test. In Step 4, the researchers assessed the immediate effects on the patient of the therapist passing or failing a test. Several different patient measures were used, including

Table 11.2 Diagram of a Test Sequence

Patient Speech Pre-segment
(3–5 minutes)
Rated on a variety of patient scales
(e.g., experiencing, relaxation, insight, voice stress)

Test Sequence
Patient Test
Rated for the degree to which it is a key test
Therapist Response
Rated for the degree to which the test is passed or failed

Patient Speech Post-segment
(3–5 minutes)
Rated on a variety of patient scales
(e.g., experiencing, relaxation, insight, voice stress)

rating the patient's level of experiencing, boldness, relaxation, and affect. A segment of speech preceding the test sequence (pre-segment) and a segment of speech immediately following the test sequence (post-segment) were rated on each of the measures by different groups of judges. The segments (approximately 4 to 6 minutes of patient speech) were presented in random order without any context and with the judges unaware whether it was was a pre- or post-segment.

The following are two examples of key tests from the case of Mrs. C. The first is a passed test and the second a failed one.[1] In the *passed test*, the patient attempted to disconfirm her pathogenic belief that she had to diminish herself to make the analyst (and others) feel superior to her. The analyst's response implied that she did not have to diminish herself and conveyed that she did not need to belittle her ideas for him to maintain his sense of authority. In the *failed test*, Mrs. C. attempted to find out whether the analyst could tolerate her being in control in the sessions. The analyst's response—as she experienced it (given her particular pathogenic beliefs)—conveyed a demand that she submit to his authority.

Passed Test

Patient: (Silence.) It's funny. I just, when I finished saying what I said about, um, the way I'm emphasizing what, what the trouble is or what's important, last night when I was thinking about it, it just seemed such an important thing to have realized. And now today when I think about it, it, I just sort of feel, well, of course, there's no point in even saying it. Or perhaps I'm feeling; that's what you're thinking.

Analyst: Ah. (Patient laughs.) I was going to just say that here you are again sort of taking it away from yourself, degrading it immediately. It can't be worth much if you thought it, that kind of feeling.

Failed Test

Patient: (Silence.) Is it better to force yourself to say something that you feel sort of not ready to say?

Analyst: Well, what was the rule I told you? Or what did I say was your job?

This research study produced several interesting results. First, complex clinical judgements about what constitutes an important test and whether the therapist was passing the test were made with impressive reliability. In other words, appropriately trained judges show a high degree of agreement about where and when the patient is testing in any given session, and they agree about which therapist responses pass the test and which fail. Second, the extent to which the therapist passes or fails the test has immediate consequences for the patient's subsequent behavior. Statistically significant correlations were found between the ratings of the therapist passing/failing tests and changes (from the pre- and post-test segments) in the patient's level of experiencing, boldness, relaxation, and expression of loving feelings, anxiety, and fear. These results indicate that the patient became significantly more productive, relaxed, and expressive of positive emotion when the therapist disconfirmed pathogenic beliefs, that is, when the therapist passed the tests. Third, correlations between the therapist's behavior and the patient's immediate responses were *not* statistically significant for the larger sample of 87 instances (i.e., those episodes broadly defined as the patient's attempts to elicit a response). The correlations were significant *only* for the subsample of episodes that were most pertinent to the patient's pathogenic beliefs, that is, the sample of 46 key tests. This pattern of results provided further validation for the concept of testing.

Impressive as these results were, they clearly needed to be replicated to address the obvious question of generalizability. Because the results were based on a single case, it was essential to determine whether a similar pattern of results could be found in other cases and in other treatment modalities. Investigators from the control-mastery research group (Horowitz et al., 1975) had reported pilot data earlier, suggesting that previously warded-off mental contents were more likely to emerge following passed tests, but further replication of research on testing was needed. Because the meaning of any given test or therapist response can only be evaluated in a case-specific way (i.e., in relation to a patient's particular pathogenic beliefs), researchers continued to employ intensive single-case designs (Kazdin, 1982) in subsequent studies of testing.

We carried out the next series of studies on brief (typically 16 weekly sessions) psychodynamic therapies. The therapists were experienced clinicians (a minimum of 3 years in private practice) who had received specialized training in brief dynamic therapy. Patients presented with a range of problems, though none suffered from psychotic disorders, serious substance abuse, or presented a suicide risk (Silberschatz & Curtis, 1993). All therapy sessions were audio tape-recorded and transcribed; verbatim transcripts comprised the primary data. The method developed in the original testing study (Silberschatz, 1978, 1986) was used (see Table 11.2). Tests were identified in the transcripts, the degree to which the therapist passed or failed the test was rated, the patient's behavior immediately before and after each test was assessed, and changes in the patient's behavior (from pre- to post-test) were correlated with the therapist's test-passing scale.

Before reviewing some of the results of this research, I will provide clinical examples of a passed and a failed test, as well as the patient material (post-segments) that immediately followed each test (excerpted from Silberschatz & Curtis, 1993). The patient, Diane, was a 34-year-old attorney who sought treatment because she could not motivate herself to find employment as a lawyer. She lacked self-confidence and frequently felt terrified that other attorneys would dominate or humiliate her. Her primary pathogenic belief was that her needs, wishes, or concerns would hurt others. She unconsciously believed that if she was strong or assertive she risked hurting others by intimidating them (this belief stemmed from childhood experiences). Consequently, she felt compelled to control and inhibit herself, which she did by either identifying with or complying with those whom she feared she might hurt by her actions. The first example is of a strongly passed test and the second, of a mildly failed test. Each example includes the test segment, the therapist's intervention(s), and Diane's immediate response. The therapist's interventions are denoted in slash marks.

Example 1 (Passed Test)

Test Segment

(Silence) ... I was just thinking about how I would cope with all my problems ... that, of course, are going to come up as soon as therapy ends and ... you know, they've all been hiding, right, for 4 months. And they'll all spring out, but I mean, I'll just do it the same way I've been doing it. It's not a catastrophe; it's not the end of the world. How shall I sort this out, whatever it is? (pause)

/The problems that come up in the last couple of weeks, you seem quite comfortable in solving on your own./

Post-Segment

Yeah. And I did. Yes, when I keep working something up to stand in front of me, that will be the real test, which of course I'll fail ... like going in, observing in court, or going to the clinic last Thursday night and I ... it seems to me I could put up another one in front of that, you know, having a trial, but I mean they're all just steps now I think. They're not road blocks. (pause) So even if I hadn't gone to the clinic on Thursday night, I could still go next month, for example. If I hadn't ... I mean, it would not have meant the failure of my whole life, if I'd lost my nerve or thrown up or something like that. You know, it wouldn't have been the end of everything. I mean, actually I had a choice Thursday. I mean, I could have gone or stayed home, or done something else.

Comment

The plan formulation for this case indicated that Diane suffered from the pathogenic belief that her strength and success were hurtful or intimidating to others, especially her parents. In the example just presented, Diane was testing this belief by acting needy and fragile. The therapist was rated as passing this test (test passing score, 5.6 on a scale of 0 to 6) because he clearly acknowledged the patient's competence, thereby disconfirming her pathogenic belief that he would be bothered by her strength. After this test, the patient's levels of boldness, relaxation, and experiencing all increased relative to her baseline (pretest) ratings.

Example 2 (Mildly Failed Test)

Test Segment

I thought I would be more, uh, frightened when this happened, or more lonely. I think we talked about that some, you know, that I would feel deserted and alone and everything. But I don't. I don't. And I thought that I would hate my mother, end up in some huge confrontation with her. And instead it just seems as though something has adjusted definitely. But easily, you know? She, her remarks are, and her feelings ... which she's still expressing, 'cause I'm noticing some of them ... but they just sort of are sliding off my back. I mean, I feel, "Oh, really?" Or she feels differently or something, but I don't feel that I have to do anything about it, or that even that I will. I feel embarrassed to think this is a mother problem, but it is.

/Why would you feel embarrassed about that?/

It just seems so, so childish, and then she's just had such a great influence on me, or I've let her, or whatever. But I mean, just really, really large influence. That I'm embarrassed about that. (sighs)

/How do you see that influence now? What's your kind of current kind of thinking and understanding about it?/

About?

/About the large influence she *did* have on you./

Post-Segment

(Sigh, pause) I'm still not sure why that happened, or why it was so. (sigh) But it seems to me now that the reason it was ... one reason it was so large was because it was crippling for me, the way I was using it, or the way I was (pause) being influenced. I would, I was always looking towards her reaction for something. And she's not consistent in her reactions in the first place, but even that aside. So there was just this constant me looking towards her reaction, and so then I would never know what I was doing. It was like a little girl I read about in a book who never learned the multiplication tables. She used to just look at her teacher's face and try to guess. So she never really learned anything; she didn't even have a place to start, with 2 by 2, you know. It was all looking at somebody else. And then you lose confidence and you ... I lose confidence, and then I would screw something up, and I mean it just ... just kept on and on. And I look back and I think that I was never *there*, really, as a personality. I was just there as a, in a way as a sort of a, I don't know what, a watcher, an observer, or something like that.

Comment

In this example, the patient again tested the therapist to see if he would recognize her accomplishment (that she was less vulnerable to her mother's remarks). The therapist focused on the influence Diane's mother did have and overlooked the patient's feelings of accomplishment; hence, his intervention was rated as mildly failing her test (test passing score, 2.9). As predicted, the patient was less productive after this test; there was an immediate drop on two of the three process measures.

In both of these clinical examples, it was important for the therapist to acknowledge Diane's competence and strength. When he did so in Example 1, she showed signs of immediate improvement. However, it must be emphasized that this focus is specific to this particular case. For another patient with different issues, the therapist's focusing on the patient's strengths might be experienced as an unwillingness or an inability to tolerate the patient's problems and thus fail important tests.

What did the research data show in the case of Diane? As in the first testing study, judges were able to reliably identify test sequences, and they reliably rated the extent to which tests were passed or failed. When tests were passed, Diane tended to immediately become more productive, bolder, and more relaxed; that is, correlations between ratings on the therapist test passing scale and changes in Diane's level of experiencing, boldness, and relaxation were all statistically significant (Silberschatz & Curtis, 1993). In addition to assessing the immediate impact of the therapist passing or failing tests, we investigated the cumulative impact of the therapist's behavior over the course of the entire therapy. To do so, we computed, for each session, an average score on the therapist's test-passing scale and for the change in the patient's experiencing level. A graph of the mean-per-hour therapist score and the averaged experiencing score showed that when the therapist passed tests Diane's experiencing level was high, and when the therapist failed them her experiencing levels were low (the correlation was .67; see Figure 11.1).

A similar pattern of results was reported in a second brief therapy case on a patient named Gary (Silberschatz & Curtis, 1993). Unlike Diane, who tested primarily by presenting transference tests, Gary tested the therapist primarily by passive-into-active tests. Nonetheless, the results were very similar. Figure 11.2 shows the impressive regularity in the rise and fall of the patient's level of experiencing as a function of the degree to which the therapist passed or failed Gary's tests.

In another brief therapy case with predominantly passive-into-active testing, Mr. M. (refer to chapter 1), there was a significant correlation between the therapist's test-passing scale and Mr. M.'s level of relaxation (Silberschatz, 2000). In other words, when the therapist

An Overview of Research on Control-Mastery Theory • 203

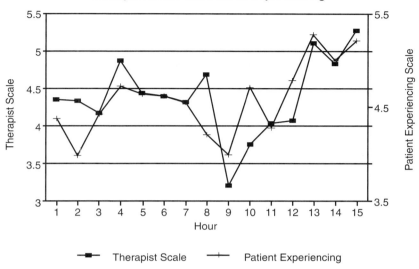

Figure 11.1

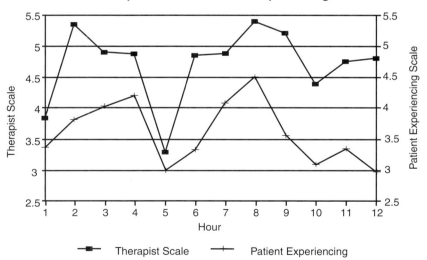

Figure 11.2

passed a test the patient tended to become more relaxed. In a fourth brief therapy case, researchers found significant correlations among therapist test-passing and insights (Linsner, 1987), adaptive regression (Bugas, 1986), and anxiety as manifested in a voice stress measure (Kelly, 1986).

THE EFFECTS OF THERAPIST'S INTERPRETATIONS

According to control-mastery theory, the therapist's attitude, passing tests, and/or the therapist's interpretations can help the patient disconfirm pathogenic beliefs. Interpretations (or other therapist interventions) that the patient experiences as disconfirming a pathogenic belief are considered plan-compatible, whereas interventions that confirm a pathogenic belief are termed plan-incompatible. A central postulate or hypothesis of control-mastery theory is that patients tend to show therapeutic progress following plan-compatible interventions and therapeutic retreat following plan-incompatible interventions. Considerable research supports this hypothesis (e.g., Bush & Gassner, 1986; Broitman, 1985; Caston, Goldman, & McClure, 1986; Davilla, 1992; Foreman et al., 2000; Fretter, 1984; Fretter, Bucci, Broitman, Silberschatz, & Curtis, 1994; Holtz, 2003; Norville et al., 1996; Pole, 1999; Sammet & Spitzer, 1998; Silberschatz et al., 1986).

The methodology developed in the testing studies (Silberschatz, 1978, 1986; Silberschatz & Curtis, 1993) was used to study how therapist interpretations affect the patient's therapeutic progress (Fretter, 1984; Silberschatz et al., 1986). The research design involved three steps: (1.) locating all therapist interpretations, (2.) rating the plan compatibility of interpretations, and (3.) measuring the patient's behavior immediately before and immediately after interpretations (see Table 11.3). Verbatim transcripts of three brief psychotherapies (16 weekly sessions) served as the primary data for this study. A team of four judges classified all verbal interventions (i.e., any therapist comment). A total of 66 interpretations were reliably identified in two of the cases and 76 were identified in the third case.

Next, a group of experienced control-mastery judges rated each interpretation using the Plan Compatibility of Intervention Scale (PCIS). The PCIS is a seven-point scale, ranging from +3 (strongly proplan—the intervention clearly disconfirms a pathogenic belief) to −3 (strongly antiplan—the intervention clearly confirms a pathogenic belief). All interpretations were isolated from the transcripts and presented to the judges in random order. The judges were blind to the patient's response

Table 11.3 Diagram of an interpretation sequence

Patient Speech Pre-segment
Rated on a variety of patient scales
(e.g., experiencing, insight)

Therapist Interpretation
Rated on the Plan Compatibility of Interpretation Scale (PCIS)

Patient Speech Post-segment
Rated on a variety of patient scales
(e.g., experiencing, insight)

---

to interpretations, and thus the only criterion for making their ratings was the plan compatibility of the intervention. The patient's behavior immediately preceding and following the interpretations was assessed using the experiencing scale. Six judges independently rated the pre- and postinterpretation segments (approximately 3 minutes of patient speech). The segments were isolated from the transcript and presented to judges again in random order. Thus, the judges didn't know when the segment occurred in therapy or what interpretation was associated with it. The judges showed impressive levels of agreement in rating the plan compatibility of interpretations (the intraclass correlations were .89 for case 1, .88 for case 2, and .85 for case 3).

Did plan-compatible interpretations lead to more productive patient responses? The results of this study showed that they did. In each of the three cases, there was a statistically significant correlation existed between plan-compatibility ratings and changes in the patient's level of experiencing. In other words, when the therapist made an interpretation that disconfirmed a patient's pathogenic belief, the patient tended to show immediate improvement.

This study represents an important contribution to the psychotherapy literature in two ways. First, it provides strong empirical support for a central hypothesis of the control-mastery theory. Second, it provides a useful research model for how to study the quality or suitability of therapist interventions. It has thus become "a seminal work in the field of research on process and outcome of psychodynamic therapy" (Caspar et al., 2000, p. 310).

Professor Isa Sammet and her colleagues at the University of Goettingen in Germany carried out an independent replication (Sammet & Spitzer, 1998) of some of the control-mastery research. Unlike previous control-mastery studies that focused on outpatient therapies, Sammet and Spitzer studied a 25-session inpatient therapy of a patient suffering from a major depressive episode. Based on a videotaped diagnostic interview, four trained raters reliably assessed the patient's plan. One team of raters identified all the major tests and rated the degree to which the therapist passed or failed each test. Another team of judges rated all the therapist's statements for the degree of plan compatibility (i.e., the degree to which the statement disconfirmed the patient's pathogenic beliefs).

Sammet and Spitzer found a significant correlation between the plan compatibility of the therapist's statements and the patient's level of insight. They also examined how well the degree to which the therapist passed or failed major tests predicted the patient's own assessments of self-efficacy and ratings of the therapeutic relationship (these weekly ratings were made by the patient on the evening after the therapy session). They found very substantial correlations: Ratings of the therapist's test passing/failing correlated .69 with the patient's rating of the therapeutic relationship and .66 with the patient's self-efficacy ratings. These results lend strong empirical support for the control-mastery theory, particularly because this was an independent replication carried out on inpatient (as opposed to outpatient) treatment, and because the research included the patient's own ratings (self-efficacy and therapeutic relationship) in addition to the clinical judges' ratings.

Caspar and his colleagues (2000) designed a study to more closely examine the concept of plan compatibility. They hypothesized that in addition to the content aspects of plan compatibility, there is also a process component of plan compatibility. The content of a plan-compatible intervention concerns the degree to which the therapist's words disconfirms the patient's pathogenic belief. The process component refers to the extent to which the interpersonal or relational aspects of the intervention disconfirm the pathogenic beliefs. An interpretation could thus be plan-compatible in terms of content but incompatible in terms of process (e.g., an interpretation regarding a patient's fear of acting independently could be delivered in a very controlling manner).

The goals of Caspar's study were (a) to determine whether the content and process components of plan compatibility could be reliably distinguished, and (b) to assess whether the process and content components differentially predict patients' in-session progress. Caspar and his colleagues used the data from the Silberschatz et al. (1986) study to carry out their research, and two judges read the plan formulations used in the previous study. Working on one case at a time, they independently rated the plan compatibility of each interpretation with respect to its content (CPC) and process (PPC). High correlations were found between the ratings in the Caspar study and those reported in Silberschatz et al. Thus, even though the two rates in the Caspar study lacked extensive training in control-mastery theory, they were able to understand the plan-compatibility concept and used their understanding to rate therapist interpretations. The content and process ratings of plan compatibility differed in about 40% of the interventions. In one case, the content of the interpretation carried more of the therapeutic effects; in another, the process carried more of the effects. Overall, the results of the Caspar et al. study suggested that the concepts and methods (plan compatibility) used by control-mastery researchers are exportable and can be successfully used by other investigators. They also suggested that the differentiation of the process and content aspects of plan compatibility may improve predictions of the therapeutic impact of interpretations and may thus "help further our understanding of how individual patients listen to and utilize therapist interventions" (Caspar et al., p. 309).

Foreman and his colleagues (Foreman et al., 2000) investigated the role of plan compatibility in child psychotherapy. They used the PCIS in their study of psychotherapy with a 10-year-old child and reported excellent interjudge reliability (intraclass correlation of .85). They found highly significant correlations between the plan compatibility of the therapist's interventions and immediate changes in the child's behavior (the overall level of therapeutic alliance).

In an ingeniously designed study, Pole (1999) hypothesized that plan-compatible interventions would be associated with greater safety emotions and a better therapeutic alliance, as well as increased in-session progress. He tested these hypotheses using three 16-session psychotherapies. The therapies were video-recorded and carried out in a psychophysiology laboratory so that continuous psychophysiological recordings could be obtained. Feelings of safety were assessed using (a) the pre- to postintervention change in the physiological measures, (b) the patients' facial expression during each intervention, and (c) the patients' subjective report of emotion. The therapeutic alliance was measured by applying the Working Alliance Inventory to videotaped excerpts of therapist–patient interaction. In-session progress was measured by applying the experiencing scale to brief passages of patient speech before and after each intervention.

The results were complex but may be summarized as follows. Higher plan compatibility of interventions ratings were associated with positive changes in experiencing, better therapeutic alliance, and greater safety emotions. This was evidenced by significant reductions in general somatic activity, longer cardiac interbeat intervals, decreases in skin conductance level, longer finger pulse transmission times, greater finger pulse amplitudes, greater pleasantness on the face, greater signs of safety on the face, and more subjective feelings of acceptance. Unexpectedly, a few associations were also discovered to exist between plan compatibility and the indices of danger emotions (e.g., greater physiological arousal and arousal on the face), suggesting the possibility that plan-compatible interventions may have made it safer for these patients to begin exploring more painful and emotionally threatening feelings.

These findings are directly parallel to the results obtained in the testing studies (see previous section). Taken together, this research suggests that the disconfirmation of pathogenic beliefs plays a major role in understanding the psychotherapeutic process. When a therapist disconfirms a patient's pathogenic belief—either by passing a test or by making an intervention that the patient experiences as disconfirming a central pathogenic belief—the patient tends to show signs of immediate therapeutic progress.

Is there any research evidence addressing the relationship between the disconfirmation of pathogenic beliefs and treatment outcome (i.e., a change from pre- to post-therapy)? It is certainly logical to assume that what happens during the process of therapy contributes to the ultimate treatment outcome and that a positive therapeutic process should result in a positive outcome. Consider, for example, the case of Kathy described in chapter 7. The therapist usually passed Kathy's tests, and her interventions typically helped Kathy disconfirm her primary pathogenic beliefs. Because this treatment was part of a research project (Jones, Ghannam, Nigg, & Dyer, 1993) in which patients were evaluated before, during, and after therapy ended, we can see what Kathy's outcome data showed.

Figure 11.3 provides a graph of three different outcome measures (the Beck Depression Inventory, the Automatic Thoughts Questionnaire, and the GSI—a symptom severity index). They are plotted across time from pre-therapy to termination, and at 6-month and 1-year followup interviews. This graph closely resembles what one would predict for therapy when the therapist consistently helps to disconfirm pathogenic beliefs. Kathy made steady progress, occasionally showed signs of heightened conflict or stress, mastered the conflicts, continued to make progress, and held on to therapeutic gains long after treatment had ended (in this case, 1 year after the therapy ended).

Patient Change Measures

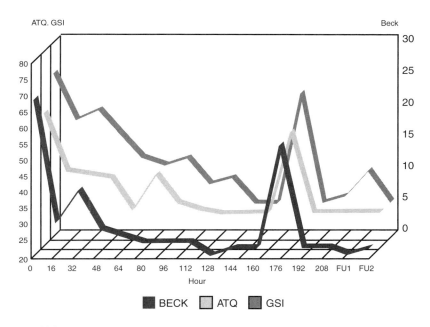

Figure 11.3

Outcome data were also collected for the three brief therapy cases reported in Silberschatz, Fretter, & Curtis (1986). The three cases represented a range of outcomes: Case 1 had an excellent result, Case 2 was moderately good, and Case 3 had a poor outcome. When interpretations were classified as pro-plan (interpretations rated between +1 and +3 on the PCIS, i.e., interventions that disconfirm pathogenic beliefs), antiplan (−1 to −3), and ambiguous (−1 to +1), the percentages of pro-plan interpretations in the good outcome cases were high (89% for Case 1 and 80% for Case 2), and the percentages of antiplan interpretations were very low. By contrast, the percentage of pro-plan interpretations in the poor outcome case was low (50%), and the percentages of antiplan (6%) and ambiguous (44%) interpretations were comparatively high. In a subsequent study of seven cases, Norville et al. (1996) found significant correlations between plan compatibility ratings and therapy outcome. Although these findings need to be replicated on larger samples, these results strongly suggest that patients who receive a high proportion of plan-compatible interventions tend to have better treatment outcomes than patients who receive a low proportion of such interventions.

RESEARCH ON THE PATIENT'S SENSE OF SAFETY

The studies of testing and plan compatibility of interventions showed that a change in the therapeutic relationship helps to increase (or decrease) the patient's sense of safety. This section briefly describes research on how changes in a person's defenses or internal regulatory control mechanisms may increase feelings of safety.

A person who has little control over a defense is likely to feel endangered by the emotions, ideas, experiences, or memories the defense is warding off. Once the person develops more reliable control over his defenses (e.g., through successful therapeutic work), then he or she can use the defense to regulate the emergence of unconscious contents. As Sampson et al. (1972) put it,

> The patient's capacity to regulate the warded-off mental content makes it safe for him to experience it, because he can control the experience, turning away from it at will if it becomes too painful or threatening. In this way, the patient can dose the new experience (warded-off content), and can reassess the danger associated with it. (p. 525)

Sampson and his colleagues carried out a research study to investigate whether a patient's increased control over his or her defenses led to enhanced feelings of safety. They hypothesized that as a patient developed greater control over his or her defenses (in their study, the defense of undoing), previously warded-off mental contents would be more likely to emerge. A strong, statistically significant relationship was found between the patient's developing control over undoing and his capacity to tolerate previously repressed emotions (Sampson et al., 1972). The results of this study support the hypothesis that the patient's increased capacity to control defenses made it possible to regulate previously warded-off emotion, thus making it safe to experience the emotion.[2]

In subsequent research, Horowitz, Sampson, Siegelman, Weiss, and Goodfriend (1978) studied how developing greater control over defenses makes it safer to experience previously warded-off feelings. They investigated the relationship between a particular patient's ability to *distance* herself from others (referred to as Type D behaviors and feelings) and her ability to express loving feelings and be *close* to others (Type C feelings). The patient sought treatment because of a chronic inability to feel close to her husband and enjoy sexual relations with him. Horowitz et al. suggested that the patient's difficulty feeling close to others was related to her inability to distance herself from others. They reasoned that if the patient lacked the capacity to distance herself, then intimacy could be experienced as dangerous because she would not be able to disengage from closeness when she wanted to and would thus run the risk of feeling stuck or entrapped. Once the patient gained the capacity to distance herself, she would have more confidence in her ability to regulate intimacy, and consequently feelings of closeness would not be as threatening. Indeed, the investigators found that progress in Type C feelings followed progress in expressing Type D feelings (see Figure 11.4). A "significant improvement" in Type D was consistently followed by a significant improvement in Type C, and setbacks in Type D were consistently followed by setbacks in Type C. These data suggest that as the patient became more comfortable

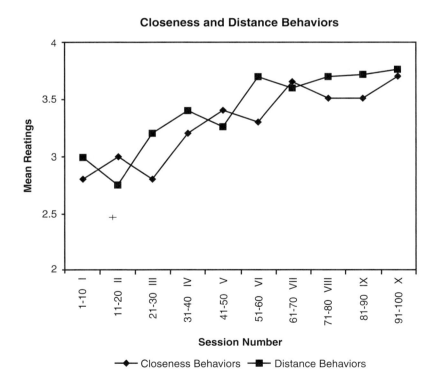

Figure 11.4

disagreeing with others and expressing critical feelings, she progressively felt less vulnerable. As a result, she could allow herself to experience feelings of closeness, affection, and intimacy.

Gassner, Sampson, Brumer, & Weiss (1986) carried out additional research on this same case (Horowitz et al., 1978), and their results shed further light on the role of safety in psychotherapy. They designed a study to determine how previously warded-off mental contents (memories, feelings, thoughts, and attitudes) become conscious during psychotherapy. Their results showed that (a) previously warded-off contents could be reliably identified, (b) they emerged without interpretation by the therapist, (c) the patient did not become anxious when discussing warded-off material, and (d) the patient showed a high degree of emotional involvement (as reflected in the experiencing scale) when warded-off contents emerged. These results support the control-mastery hypothesis that the patient has the capacity to bring forth previously warded-off mental contents when he or she perceives (consciously or unconsciously) they can be experienced safely. According to Gassner et al. (1986),

> The contents emerged without arousing anxiety because [the patient] kept them warded off until she unconsciously had overcome her anxieties about them, and only then did she make them conscious. She was able to experience the contents fully, think about them, and use them therapeutically because they no longer endangered her. (p. 185)

EMPIRICALLY SUPPORTED TREATMENTS AND CONTROL-MASTERY THEORY

In the past decade, there has been a growing movement for "evidence-based practice" in general health care (Institute of Medicine, 2001) and for "empirically-validated" (American Psychological Association Division of Clinical Psychology, 1995) or "empirically supported treatments" in psychotherapy (e.g., Chambless & Hollon, 1998; Kendall, 1998). In this concluding section, I argue that the research evidence summarized in this chapter provides empirical support for the major postulates and hypotheses of control-mastery theory.

Many proponents of empirically validated treatments tend to equate empirical validation with randomized controlled trials (Levant, 2003; Persons & Silberschatz, 1998). In such experimental trials, a very narrowly defined group of patients is randomly assigned to two or more narrowly defined treatments (typically manualized) in order to evaluate which treatment is most efficacious. However, as I and many others have argued elsewhere (see Persons & Silberschatz, 1998, pp. 128–130), the randomized control trial is simply the wrong method for studying psychotherapy as practiced by experienced clinicians.

Howard, Moras, Brill, Martinovich, and Lutz (1996) pointed out that three different questions can be asked about any given treatment and that the answers to these questions require fundamentally different research approaches: Does a treatment work under controlled experimental conditions? Does it work in clinical practice? And does it work for this particular patient? Although the randomized controlled trial is the standard method for addressing the first (efficacy) question, it cannot answer the other two. To assess how therapy works in practice or whether it works for a given patient requires quasi-experimental methods and a case-specific research approach (Howard et al.). This is precisely the kind of approach that has been successfully used in the research summarized previously. Many control-mastery researchers have used this approach to test and rule out alternative hypotheses about how psychotherapy works (e.g., Horowitz et al., 1975; Fretter, 1984; Gassner et al., 1986; Silberschatz, 1978; Silberschatz, Fretter, & Curtis, 1986; Silberschatz, Sampson, & Weiss, 1986). The results of this research are both conceptually and clinically meaningful.

In response to the numerous critiques of the empirically validated treatments movement, Norcross (2001) formed a task force to examine and "disseminate evidence-based means of improving the therapy relationship and effective means of customizing that relationship to the individual patient" (p. 350). Norcross pointed out that although little empirical support favors one therapy technique over another, considerable research data shows that the *quality* of the therapy relationship is a strong predictor of the treatment outcome. Thus, psychotherapy researchers should focus on data showing how the relationship can be improved and optimized for particular patients. The research on control-mastery theory provides an empirically supported approach for explaining how therapeutic relationships work and how they can be optimally tailored to patients' specific problems and needs. The identification of pathogenic beliefs (plan formulation), the concept of testing and plan compatibility of interventions, and the patient's efforts to create safety in the therapeutic relationship are examples of evidence-based means of improving therapy relationships.

ENDNOTES

1. For the sake of clarity and exposition, I present fairly brief, concise examples of tests. Many tests are more complex and subtle as illustrated in chapters 1, 6, and 8.
2. A series of studies by Stiles and his colleagues (Honos-Web, Lani, & Stiles, 1999; Knobloch, Endres, Stiles, & Silberschatz, 2001; Stiles, 2001; Stiles et al., 1990), although based on a different theoretical framework, lends strong support to the control-mastery hypothesis regarding the integration of defenses. In these studies, problematic experiences are defined as painful feelings, memories, or interpersonal behaviors. Stiles identified eight levels or stages of assimilation of problematic experiences, and the process of assimilation he describes closely resembles the integration of defenses studied by control-mastery investigators.

REFERENCES

American Psychological Association Division of Clinical Psychology (1995). Training in and dissemination of empirically-validated psychological treatments: Report and recommendations. *The Clinical Psychologist, 48*, 3–27.

Bigalke, T. (2004). *The theoretical implications of applying the control-mastery concept of testing to family therapy.* Unpublished doctoral dissertation, California School of Professional Psychology, Alameda, CA.

Brenman, M., Gill, M. M., & Knight, R. P. (1952). Spontaneous fluctuations in the depth of hypnosis and their implications for ego-function. *International Journal of Psychoanalysis, 33*, 22–33.

Broitman, J. (1985). Insight, the mind's eye: An exploration of three patients' processes of becoming insightful. *Dissertation Abstracts International, 46*(8). (University Microfilms No. 85-20425).

Bugas, J. S. (1986). Adaptive regression and the therapeutic change process. *Dissertation Abstracts International*, 47 (7b). (University Microfilms No. 86-22826).

Bush, M., & Gassner, S. (1986). The immediate effect of the analyst's termination interventions on the patient's resistance to termination. In J. Weiss, H. Sampson, & The Mount Zion Psychotherapy Research Group (Eds.), *The psychoanalytic process: Theory, clinical observation, and empirical research* (pp. 299–322). New York: Guilford.

Caspar, F., Pessier, J., Stuart, J., Safran, J. D., Wallner Samstag, L., & Guirguis, M. (2000). One step further in assessing how interpretations influence the process of psychotherapy. *Psychotherapy Research, 10*, 309–320.

Caston, J. (1986). The reliability of the diagnosis of the patient's unconscious plan. In J. Weiss, H. Sampson, & The Mount Zion Psychotherapy Research Group (Eds.), *The psychoanalytic process: Theory, clinical observation, and empirical research* (pp. 241–255). New York: Guilford.

Caston, J., Goldman, R. K., & McClure, M. M. (1986). The immediate effects of psychoanalytic interventions. In J. Weiss, H. Sampson, & The Mount Zion Psychotherapy Research Group (Eds.), *The psychoanalytic process: Theory, clinical observation, and empirical research* (pp. 277–298). New York: Guilford.

Chambless, D. L., & Hollon, S. D. (1998). Defining empirically supported therapies. *Journal of Consulting and Clinical Psychology, 64*, 497–504.

Conrad, B. (1995). *Personality and psychopathology reconsidered: A quantitative/qualitative control-mastery psychobiography on Henri de Toulouse-Lautrec (1864–1901).* Unpublished doctoral dissertation, The Wright Institute, Berkeley, CA.

Conrad, B. (1997). *Henri de Toulouse-Lautrec (1864–1901): Mastering trauma through creativity.* Paper presented at the annual convention of the American Psychological Association, Chicago, IL.

Crits-Christoph, P., Cooper, A., & Luborsky, L. (1988). The accuracy of therapist's interpretations and the outcome of dynamic psychotherapy. *Journal of Consulting and Clinical Psychology, 56,* 490–495.

Curtis, J. T., & Silberschatz, G. (1991). *The plan formulation method: A reliable procedure for case formulation,* UCSF. Unpublished manuscript.

Curtis, J. T., & Silberschatz, G. (1997). Plan formulation method. In T. D. Eells (Ed.), *Handbook of psychotherapy case formulation* (pp. 116–136). New York: Guilford.

Curtis, J. T., Silberschatz, G., Sampson, H., & Weiss, J. (1994). The plan formulation method. *Psychotherapy Research, 4,* 197–207.

Curtis, J. T., Silberschatz, G., Sampson, H., Weiss, J., & Rosenberg, S. E. (1988). Developing reliable psychodynamic case formulations: An illustration of the plan diagnosis method. *Psychotherapy, 25,* 256–265.

Davilla, L. (1992). *The immediate effects of therapists' interpretations on patients' plan progressiveness.* Unpublished doctoral dissertation, California School of Professional Psychology, Berkeley, CA.

Eells, T. D. (1997). Psychotherapy case formulation: History and current status. In T. D. Eells (Ed.), *Handbook of psychotherapy case formulation* (pp. 1–25). New York: Guilford.

Elkin, I., Shea, M. T., Watkins, J. T., Imber, S. D., Sotsky, S. M., Collins, J. F., et al. (1989). NIMH Treatment of Depression Collaborative Research Program: General effectiveness of treatments. *Archives of General Psychiatry, 46,* 971–982.

Elliott, R. (1983). Fitting process research to the practicing psychotherapist. *Psychotherapy: Theory, Research, and Practice, 20,* 47–55.

Elliott, R. (1984). A discovery-oriented approach to significant change events in psychotherapy: Interpersonal process recall and comprehensive process analysis. In L. Rice & L. S. Greenberg (Eds.), *Patterns of change* (pp. 249–286). New York: Guilford Press.

Fretter, P. B. (1984). The immediate effects of transference interpretations on patients' progress in brief, psychodynamic psychotherapy. *Dissertation Abstracts International, 46*(6). (University Microfilms No. 85–12, 112).

Fretter, P. B., Bucci, W., Broitman, J., Silberschatz, G., & Curtis, J. T. (1994). How the patient's plan relates to the concept of transference. *Psychotherapy Research, 4,* 58–72.

Foreman, S. A., Gibbins, J., Grienenberger, J., & Berry, J. W. (2000). Developing methods to study child psychotherapy using new scales of therapeutic alliance and progressiveness. *Psychotherapy Research, 10,* 450–461.

Gassner, S., Sampson, H., Brumer, S., & Weiss, J. (1986). The emergence of warded-off contents. In J. Weiss, H. Sampson, & The Mount Zion Psychotherapy Research Group (Eds.), *The psychoanalytic process: Theory, clinical observation, and empirical research* (pp. 187–205). New York: Guilford Press.

Gassner, S., Sampson, H., Weiss, J., & Brumer, S. (1982). The emergence of warded-off contents. *Psychoanalysis and Contemporary Thought, 5,* 55–75.

Goldfried, M. R., & Wolfe, B. (1996). Psychotherapy practice and research: Repairing a strained alliance. *American Psychologist, 51,* 1007–1016.

Goldfried, M. R., & Wolfe, B. (1998). Toward a more clinically valid approach to therapy research. *Journal of Consulting and Clinical Psychology, 66,* 143–150.

Greenberg, L. S. (1982). Psychotherapy process research, IL. E. Walker (Ed.), *Handbook of Clinical Psychology* (pp. 164–204). Dorsey Press, Homewood, IL.

Greenberg, L. S. (1986). Change process research. *Journal of Consulting and Clinical Psychology, 54,* 4–9.

Holtz, P. J. (2003). *The self and interactive regulation and coordination of vocal rhythms, interpretive accuracy, and progress in brief psychodynamic psychotherapy.* Unpublished doctoral dissertation, The Fielding Graduate Institute, Santa Barbara, CA.

Honos-Webb, L., Lani, J. A., & Stiles, W. B. (1999). Discovering markers of assimilation stages: The fear of losing control marker. *Journal of Clinical Psychology, 55,* 1441–1452.

Horowitz, L. M., Sampson, H., Siegelman, E. Y., Weiss, J., & Goodfriend, S. (1978). Cohesive and dispersal behaviors: Two classes of concomitant change in psychotherapy. *Journal of Consulting and Clinical Psychology, 46,* 556–564.

Horowitz, L. M., Sampson, H., Siegelman, E. Y., Wolfson, A. W., & Weiss, J. (1975). On the identification of warded-off mental contents. *Journal of Abnormal Psycholoqy, 84,* 545–558.

Howard, K. I., Moras, K., Brill, P. L., Martinovich, Z., & Lutz, W. (1996). Evaluation of psychotherapy: Efficacy, effectiveness, and patient progress. *American Psychologist, 51,* 1059–1064.

Institute of Medicine (2001). *Crossing the quality chasm: A new health system for the 21st century.* Washington, DC: Author.

Jones, E. E., Ghannam, J., Nigg, J. T., & Dyer, J. F. P. (1993). A paradigm for single-case research: The time series study of a long-term psychotherapy for depression. *Journal of Consulting and Clinical Psychology, 61,* 381–394.

Kazdin, A. E. (1982). *Single-case research designs: Methods for clinical and applied settings.* New York: Oxford University Press.

Kelly, T. J. (1986). *The immediate effect of therapist interventions on patient stress as measured by lonq-term voice spectrum.* Paper presented at the 17th Annual Meeting of the Society for Psychotherapy Research, Wellesley, MA.

Kendall, P. C. (1998). Empirically supported psychological therapies. *Journal of Consulting and Clinical Psychology, 66,* 3–6.

Kiesler, D. J. (1966). Some myths of psychotherapy research and the search for a paradigm. *Psychological Bulletin, 65,* 110–136.

Knobloch, L. M., Endres, L. M., Stiles, W. B., & Silberschatz, G. (2001). Convergence and divergence of themes in successful psychotherapy: An assimilation analysis. *Psychotherapy, 38,* 31–39.

Lambert, M. J., & Bergin, A. E. (1994). The effectiveness of psychotherapy. In A. E. Bergin & S. L. Garfield (Eds.), *Handbook of psychotherapy and behavior change* (4th ed., pp. 143–189). New York: Wiley.

Levant, R. F. (2003). The empirically-validated treatments movement: A practitioner perspective. *Psychotherapy Bulletin, 38,* 36–39.

Linsner, J. P. (1987). Therapeutically effective and ineffective insight: The immediate effects of therapist behavior on a patient' insight during short-term dynamic therapy. *Dissertation Abstracts International, 1988, 48*(12b). (University Microfilms 88-07131).

Luborsky, L. (1967). Momentary forgetting during psychotherapy and psychoanalysis: A theory and research method. In R. R. Holt (Ed.), *Motives and thought: Psychoanalytic essays in honor of David Rapaport* (pp. 177–217). New York: International Universities Press.

Luborsky, L., Singer, B., Hartke, J., Crits–Christoph, P., & Cohen, M. (1984). Shifts in depressive state during psychotherapy: Which concepts of depression fit the context of Mr. Q's shifts? In L. Rice & L. S. Greenberg (Eds.), *Patterns of change* (pp. 157–193). New York: Guilford Press.

Mahrer, A. (1985). *Psychotherapeutic change: An alternative approach to meaning and measurement.* New York: Norton.

McWilliams, N. (1999). *Psychoanalytic case formulations.* New York: Guilford.

Meehan, W., O'Connor, L. E., Berry, J. W., Weiss, J., & Acampora, A. (1996). Guilt, shame and depression in men and women recovering from drug addiction. *Journal of Psychoactive Drugs, 28,* 125–134.

Morray, M. G., & Shilkret, R. (2002, April). *"Mother, please! I'd rather do it myself!" Maternal intrusiveness, daughters' guilt and separation as related to college adjustment.* Poster presented at the Biennial Meeting of the Society for Research on Adolescence, New Orleans, LA.

Norcross, J. C. (2001). Purposes, processes, and products of the task force on empirically supported therapy relationships. *Psychotherapy: Theory, Research, Practice, Training, 38,* 345–356.

Norville, R., Sampson, H., & Weiss, J. (1996). Accurate interpretations and brief psychotherapy outcome. *Psychotherapy Research, 6,* 16–29.

O'Connor, L. E., Berry, J. W., & Weiss, J. (1999). Interpersonal guilt, shame and psychological problems. *Journal of Social and Clinical Psychology, 18,* 181–203.

O'Connor, L. E., Berry, J. W., Weiss, J., & Gilbert, P. (2002). Guilt, fear, submission, and empathy in depression. *Journal of Affective Disorders, 71,* 19–27.

Parloff, M. B., Waskow, I. E., & Wolfe, B. E. (1978). Research on therapist variables in relation to process and outcome. In S. L. Garfield & A. E. Bergin (Eds.), *Handbook of psychotherapy and behavior change: An empirical analysis* (2nd ed., pp. 233–282). New York: Wiley.

Perry, S., Cooper, A. M., & Michels, R. (1987). The psychodynamic formulation: Its purpose, structure, and clinical application. *American Journal of Psychiatry, 144,* 543–550.

Persons, J. B. (1989). *Cognitive therapy in practice: A case formulation approach.* New York: Norton.

Persons, J. B., & Silberschatz, G. (1998). Are results of randomized controlled trials useful to psychotherapists? *Journal of Consulting and Clinical Psychology, 66,* 126–135.

Pole, N. (1999). *Client appraisals of danger and safety in psychotherapy and its physiological, facial, and subjective correlates.* Unpublished doctoral dissertation, University of California, Berkeley.

Rice, L. N., & Greenberg, L. S. (1984). *Patterns of change.* New York: Guilford Press.

Rosenberg, S. E., Silberschatz, G., Curtis, J. T., Sampson, H., & Weiss, J. (1986). A method for establishing reliability of statements from psychodynamic case formulations. *American Journal of Psychiatry, 143,* 1454–1456.

Sammet, I., & Spitzer, K. (1998). *Changes in the patient's speech and insight after therapeutic interventions: A study based on control-mastery theory.* Paper presented at the Annual Meeting of the Society for Psychotherapy Research, Snowbird, UT.

Sampson, H. (1995). Psychoanalysis: the second century. Invited address, American Psychological Association, Division 39, Los Angeles, CA, April 26.

Sampson, H., Weiss, J., Mlodnosky, L., & Hause, E. (1972). Defense analysis and the emergence of warded-off mental contents: An empirical study. *Archives of General Psychiatry, 26,* 524–532.

Schafer, N. D. (1982). Multidimensional measures of therapist behavior as predictors of outcome. *Psychological Bulletin, 92,* 670–681.

Seligman, M. E. P. (1996). Science as an ally of practice. *American Psychologist, 51,* 1072–1079.

Shilkret, R., & Nigrosh, E. (1997). Assessing students' plans for college. *Journal of Counseling Psychology, 44,* 222–231.

Shilkret, R., & Vecchiotti, S. (1997). *Parenting styles, college adjustment, and guilt.* Poster presented at biennial meeting of the Society for Research in Child Development (SRCD), Washington, DC.

Silberschatz, G. (1978). Effects of the analyst's neutrality on the patient's feelings and behavior in the psychoanalytic situation. *Dissertation Abstracts International, 39,* 3007-B. (University Microfilms No. 78-24,277).

Silberschatz, G. (1986). Testing pathogenic beliefs. In J. Weiss, H. Sampson, & The Mount Zion Psychotherapy Research Group (Eds.), *The psychoanalytic process: Theory, clinical observation, and empirical research* (pp. 256–266). New York: Guilford Press.

Silberschatz, G. (2000, December). *The process of change in psychoanalysis and psychotherapy.* Paper presented at the George S. Klein Forum, American Psychoanalytic Association Mid-winter Meeting, New York, NY.

Silberschatz, G., & Curtis, J. T. (1993). Measuring the therapist's impact on the patient's therapeutic progress. *Journal of Consulting and Clinical Psychology, 61,* 403–411.

Silberschatz, G., Curtis, J. T., Fretter, P. B., & Kelly, T. J. (1988). Testing hypotheses of psychotherapeutic change processes. In H. Dahl, H. Kachele, & H. Thoma (Eds.), *Psychoanalytic process research strategies* (pp. 129–145). Springer-Verlag: Berlin.

Silberschatz, G., Curtis, J. T., & Nathans, S. (1989). Using the patient's plan to assess progress in psychotherapy. *Psychotherapy: Theory, Research, Practice, Training, 26,* 40–46.

Silberschatz, G., Fretter, P. B., & Curtis, J. T. (1986). How do interpretations influence the process of psychotherapy? *Journal of Consulting and Clinical Psychology, 54,* 646–652.

Silberschatz, G., Sampson, H., & Weiss, J. (1986). Testing pathogenic beliefs versus seeking transference gratifications. In J. Weiss, H. Sampson, & The Mount Zion Psychotherapy Research Group (Eds.), *The psychoanalytic process: Theory, clinical observation, and empirical research* (pp. 267–276). New York: Guilford.

Stiles, W. B. (2001). Assimilation of problematic experiences. *Psychotherapy: Theory, Research, Practice, Training, 38,* 462–465.

Stiles, W. B., Elliott, R., Llewelyn, S. P., Firth-Cozens, J. A., Margison, F. R., Shapiro, D. A., et al. (1990). Assimilation of problematic experiences by clients in psychotherapy. *Psychotherapy: Theory, Research, Practice, Training, 27,* 411–420.

Stiles, W. B., Shapiro, D. A., & Elliott, R. (1986). "Are all psychotherapies equivalent?" *American Psychologist, 41,* 165–180.

Strupp, H. H. (1986). Psychotherapy: Research, practice, and public policy (How to avoid dead ends). *American Psychologist, 41,* 120–130.

12

THE CONTROL-MASTERY THEORY
An Integrated Cognitive–Psychodynamic–Relational Theory

George Silberschatz

Control-mastery theory is not a new school of therapy, nor is it a new set of therapeutic techniques. Rather, it is a theory of how the mind operates, how psychopathology develops, and how psychotherapy works. The theory provides a powerful set of concepts that can help a clinician understand and formulate a particular patient's problems, goals for therapy, and a broad sense of how the therapist can help the patient achieve therapeutic goals.

So what kind of theory is this? In the course of presenting and teaching it to a wide variety of professional audiences, I have heard people say, "This is straight interpersonal theory" (i.e., based on the work of Sullivan, 1953), "This is cognitive therapy," or "This is just a repackaged version of contemporary Freudian theory." In fact, it is none of these, even though it shares some similarity with all of them. The control-mastery theory integrates cognitive, psychodynamic, and relational[1] perspectives at the conceptual level. It is an integration of theories and concepts, rather than a synthesis of interventions and techniques.

The theory was originally developed within a psychoanalytic framework, but it is currently best described as an integrated cognitive–psychodynamic–relational theory. Unlike other integrative approaches, the theory did not evolve by gradually assimilating

(Messer, 1992, 2001) concepts or techniques from cognitive, psychodynamic, or relational theory. Weiss developed the theory by carefully studying psychotherapy sessions and developing hypotheses about how psychotherapy worked or failed to work. These hypotheses were subsequently refined and empirically tested on other cases and ultimately on a wide variety of treatment modalities (e.g., time-limited therapies, psychoanalyses, cognitive therapies, and inpatient treatment).

PSYCHOTHERAPY INTEGRATION

Historically, different therapeutic approaches have typically evolved on the basis of intuitions, observations, and insights of experienced clinicians. There are currently hundreds of schools or brands of therapy, the vast majority of which have never been systematically studied or examined (Norcross & Newman, 1992). But the research that has been done clearly shows that no one school of therapy or any particular set of therapeutic techniques is more effective than another (Lambert, 1992; Lambert & Bergin, 1994; Lipsey & Wilson, 1993; Norcross & Newman, 1992; Stiles, Shapiro, & Elliott, 1986; Wampold, Mondin, Moody, Stich, Benson, & Ahn, 1997; Weinberger, 1993). The relationship between the patient and the therapist is one variable that obviously cuts across all schools of therapy. The therapeutic relationship has long been regarded as an important change agent among psychodynamic therapists (e.g., Alexander & French, 1946; Sullivan, 1953) and has more recently become a topic of considerable interest among behavioral, experiential, and cognitive therapists (e.g., Hayes, Follette, & Follette, 1995; Kohlenberg & Tsai, 1991; Gaston et al., 1990).

Integrative theorists (Arkowitz, 1992; Norcross & Newman, 1992) have outlined three primary ways in which different psychotherapy models may be integrated. The *common factors approach* is based on the assumption that all psychotherapies share certain common curative factors and that, regardless of the therapist's theoretical framework, it is these common factors that account for an efficacious treatment. The therapy relationship, patient qualities, and therapist variables such as warmth, genuineness, accurate empathy, and unconditional positive regard (Rogers, 1961) are well-known examples of common factors. The second primary method, *technical eclecticism,* utilizes interventions and techniques from various schools of therapy without subscribing to the theories on which the techniques are based. Specific techniques are selected by the therapist based on his or her clinical experience, research findings, or an effort to respond to the patient's particular preferences or needs. Finally, *theoretical integration* involves synthesizing theories or clinical concepts of two or more psychotherapeutic models, as exemplified in the innovative contributions of Wachtel (1977, 1987, 1997). The theoretical integration approach is the focus of this chapter.

KEY CONCEPTS IN CONTROL-MASTERY THEORY

A complete presentation of control-mastery theory is presented in chapter 1. I will briefly review the theory's main concepts here in order to provide the necessary context for discussing the theory as an integrated theory of psychotherapy.

A fundamental premise of the theory is that from birth onward humans are geared toward adaptation to the environment. For the first few years of life, the family unit comprises the child's environment, and consequently the child's most powerful motivation is to preserve his or her attachments to family members. The child forms theories or beliefs about self and others as part of this adaptive process. Traumatic experiences lead to the formation of dysfunctional or pathogenic beliefs, which are typically not conscious. Pathogenic beliefs develop as a result of a parent's consistently adverse reactions to the child's normal developmental strivings (a "stress" trauma) or the child experiencing a severely traumatic event (a "shock" trauma).

For instance, a child who grew up with a depressed mother developed the belief that going to school was dangerous because his mother would feel more lonely and depressed. He also developed a distorted view about his ability to affect his mother's emotional states. By staying at home with his mother, he felt he could cheer her up and prevent her depressive feelings. His occasional success at staving off his mother's depression led him to feel excessively responsible for her moods. Thus, when she was sad or depressed (a very frequent occurrence), he came to believe it was his fault and that he should have been able to prevent her unhappiness. What began as an adaptive effort soon became maladaptive—indeed, pathogenic—because it forced him to renounce crucial developmental goals (e.g., appropriate separation, attending school, developing friendships), led to exaggerated feelings of responsibility and self-blame, and ultimately resulted in severe psychopathology.

The control-mastery theory assumes that people are motivated to disconfirm or relinquish pathogenic beliefs and that this represents a patient's most powerful motivation in psychotherapy. This primary motivation toward mastering conflict and solving problems is embedded in the concept of the *patient's plan*. The theory posits that patients come to therapy to get better and that they have a plan for doing so; the plan is to test and ultimately disconfirm pathogenic beliefs. Saying that a patient has a plan to disconfirm pathogenic beliefs is not to say that it is easy or straightforward to do so. Altering any theory or attitude is difficult and requires considerable work; the plan concept simply states that the patient is powerfully motivated to take on this work. Strong evidence supports the fact that people make and carry out plans consciously as well as unconsciously. In psychotherapy, as in everyday life, a person's plans organize behavior and influence how the person is likely to filter and process information.

Psychopathology stems from pathogenic beliefs originating from traumatic experiences. In psychotherapy, patients and therapists work together to disconfirm the patient's pathogenic beliefs in three primary ways: Patients may (a) use the therapeutic relationship per se to disconfirm beliefs, (b) use the knowledge or insight conveyed by the therapist's interpretations to disconfirm beliefs, and (c) test the pathogenic belief directly with the therapist. A test is a trial action initiated by the patient that is intended to provide information about and to assess the validity of a pathogenic belief. Patients initiate tests in order to disconfirm pathogenic beliefs and are usually not conscious that they are testing. These three ways of working are by no means mutually exclusive; indeed, most patients rely on a combination of these three.

CONTROL-MASTERY THEORY AS AN INTEGRATED MODEL OF PSYCHOTHERAPY

Developed within a psychoanalytic framework, the control-mastery theory was originally presented as an extension of psychoanalytic ego psychology (Weiss, 1967, 1971; Sampson, Weiss, Mlodnosky, & Hause, 1972) or what Weiss described as Freud's "higher mental functioning paradigm" (Weiss, 1986; see also Eagle, 1984; Gassner, 2001; Sampson, 1976). I believe that the control-mastery theory has moved beyond its psychoanalytic roots and I view it as an integrated cognitive–psychodynamic–relational theory. The overlap between control-mastery and cognitive theories is readily apparent and is most evident in the concepts of pathogenic beliefs and patient plans. Concepts such as "schemas," "tacit assumptions," outmoded "rules for living," "dysfunctional attitudes," and "core operating principles" (Meichenbaum & Gilmore, 1984) are similar to the control-mastery concepts of plans and pathogenic beliefs. The cornerstones of psychodynamic theory are the concepts of the unconscious and unconscious intrapsychic conflict (Horowitz, 1988, 1998). These essential psychodynamic elements are also central to control-mastery theory in that pathogenic beliefs are typically unconscious and are a source of considerable internal conflict. Finally, the relational aspects of control-mastery theory are evident in several of its key postulates: Pathogenic beliefs typically develop in early childhood relationships, pathogenic beliefs are usually activated in significant relationships (or internalized representations of relationships), and patients disconfirm pathogenic beliefs through new relational experiences with the therapist and with other significant people.

Cognitive Therapy

In articulating his conception of cognitive therapy, A. T. Beck (1967, 1976) proposed that a person's perceptions, beliefs, and interpretations of his or her experiences play a pivotal role in behavioral and emotional responses. The cognitive therapy model proposes that a patient's distorted patterns of thinking lead to dysphoric emotions and dysfunctional behavior. If the patient can find ways to change the distorted beliefs, then his or her behaviors and emotional reactions will change accordingly. In other words, a person's distorted thoughts, beliefs, and expectations bear primary responsibility for the development of psychopathology.

The concept of schemas is central to the cognitive therapy model. Schemas are "organized elements of past reactions and experience that form a relatively cohesive and persistent body of knowledge capable of guiding subsequent perception and appraisals" (Segal, 1988, p. 147). Beliefs are conceptualized by Beck (1967) as cognitive schemas that represent how a person views him- or herself and others. J. S. Beck (1996) pointed out that schemas develop early in life so that children can make sense of themselves and their world.

> They develop schemas, or cognitive structures, to organize the massive amount of data they are constantly receiving. Schemas are the means by which they understand what they are experiencing and decide how to proceed. ... A schema can be relatively narrow or broad, rigid or modifiable, prominent or relatively quiescent. (p. 167)

A particularly active or highly significant schema may override other more adaptive schemas (Beck, 1967).

Building on A. T. Beck's work, Young (1990) described "early maladaptive schemas" as stable cognitive–affective structures that develop during childhood and that typically become "templates for the processing of later experience" (p. 9). These early maladaptive schemas originate in painful problematic experiences with parents or family members, and they shape the person's subsequent beliefs, feelings, and interpersonal relationships. For example, children who are raised by neglectful, unprotective parents frequently develop the "Emotional Deprivation" schema. As adults, they are likely to be hypersensitive to neglect or rejection, may overlook evidence that disconfirms or contradicts the schema, and frequently distort information in order to maintain the schema. These early maladaptive schemas tend to be self-perpetuating and consequently are very resistant to change. The control-mastery concept of pathogenic beliefs is very similar to this formulation of early maladaptive schemas.

Psychodynamic Principles

In contrast to the cognitive therapy model, which focuses largely on conscious beliefs, psychodynamic theorists (e.g., Horowitz, 1988; Luborsky, 1984; Strupp & Binder, 1984) focus on the role of unconscious beliefs, motives, and expectations in the development of psychopathology. Psychodynamic theories also emphasize the role of unconscious, intrapsychic conflict (e.g., Brenner, 1976, 1982; Menninger & Holzman, 1973), transference (Gill, 1982; Luborsky & Crits-Christoph, 1990), and resistance (Gray, 1995; Gill, 1982; Waelder, 1960) in psychopathology and treatment.

To illustrate the difference between cognitive therapy and psychodynamic approaches, consider Beck's (1976) example of a successful novelist who cried uncontrollably whenever he received compliments for his literary work. The novelist consistently and irrationally concluded that the compliments were neither honest nor authentic. Indeed, he maintained the irrational belief that people felt he was a mediocre writer and they were simply protecting him with their effusive compliments. Following the cognitive therapy model, the therapist focused on showing the writer the distorted and irrational aspects of his thought process. By contrast, a psychodynamically trained clinician would have tried to understand the motivation, context, history, and unconscious meanings of the writer's consciously articulated beliefs—that is, why and how the writer came to develop these distorted, false beliefs. For instance, underlying his conscious belief that he is a mediocre writer could be an unconscious pathogenic belief that warns him against the danger of feeling proud, accomplished, and successful. Such unconscious beliefs frequently stem from early, persistently adverse reactions by family members to the child's success or accomplishments.

Relational Theory

Traditional psychodynamic theorists emphasize that insight, interpretation, and analysis of transference and resistances are the primary effective ingredients of psychotherapeutic change. Relational theorists (e.g., Aron, 1996; Frank, 1999; Kohut, 1984; Lichtenberg, 1989; Mitchell, 1988; Shane, Shane, & Gales, 1997; Sullivan, 1953) argued against the primacy of interpretation and insight as the sole or even primary mutative factors in psychotherapy. They proposed that new *relational experiences*, described as corrective emotional experiences by Alexander and French (1946), were in many instances far more important than insights in helping to bring about therapeutic change. These theorists also drew attention to the powerful impact of interpersonal experiences in the development and maintenance of psychopathology and maladaptive behavior (Benjamin, 1993; Bowlby, 1988; Gold & Stricker, 1993; Stricker & Gold, 1996; Strupp & Binder, 1984; Sullivan, 1953; Wachtel, 1997). Indeed, early relational theorists such as Fairbairn, Guntrip, Winnicott, and Sullivan (discussed later) fundamentally altered the accepted psychodynamic theory of motivation and psychopathology. Rather than giving primacy to sexual and aggressive impulses as Freud had done, these theorists proposed that humans are motivated primarily by relational adaptation and attachment needs (Bowlby, 1958).

Bowlby (1988) posited two powerful motives (drives) in the human infant: attachment seeking and exploration. Satisfaction of the child's attachment needs results in a "secure base," thereby allowing the child to feel safe enough to explore his or her environment. After a period of exploration, the child returns to the attachment figure to refuel his or her sense of security and then resumes exploratory behavior. Bowlby proposed that, in healthy infants, attachment seeking and exploration alternate in this way. This relational view has been substantially bolstered by infant and developmental research (e.g., Ainsworth, Blehar, Waters, & Wall, 1978; Beebe & Lachmann, 2002; Lichtenberg, 1989; Main, Kaplan, & Cassidy, 1985; Stern, 1985; refer to chapter 10). It is also consistent with the emphasis in control-mastery theory on the role of safety (refer to chapters 2 and 3) and has been supported by some of the control-mastery research (e.g., Gassner, Sampson, Weiss, &

Brumer, 1982; Horowitz, Sampson, Siegelman, Weiss, & Goodfriend, 1978; Sampson et al., 1972; Silberschatz, 1986; Silberschatz, Sampson, & Weiss, 1986; refer to chapter 10).

The conceptual basis for relational theory can be found in Sullivan's interpersonal theory (Sullivan, 1953). Although developed over 60 years ago, Sullivan's basic concepts anticipated and serve as a theoretical foundation for contemporary work in social cognition (Andersen & Chen, 2002; Andersen, Reznik, & Glassman, in press; Carson, 1982; Glassman & Andersen, 1999; Kiesler, 1982; Markus, 1977) as well as psychotherapy (e.g., Benjamin, 1993; Greenberg & Mitchell, 1983; Safran & Segal, 1990; Strupp & Binder, 1984; Stricker & Gold, 1996). A central concept in Sullivan's interpersonal theory is "personification." Personifications are internal structures (schemas) that organize the perception and acquisition of new interpersonal knowledge. He described the personification of self and the personification of others, noting that both types develop on the basis of actual interpersonal experiences. Sullivan pointed out that self-personifications are based on "reflected appraisals." On this topic, Mullahy (1940/1953) contributed the following:

> The child appraises himself as he is appraised by the significant adults. He lacks the experience and equipment necessary for a careful and dispassionate evaluation of himself. He has no guide except what he has learned from the significant adults. His evaluation of himself is, therefore, based on the appraisals of the significant adults. There may be no, or very little, conflicting data about his performances which would cause him to question the appraisals of those who take care of him. And in any case, he is far too helpless to question or revolt, because he depends on them for life itself. Therefore, he is not in a position to risk his security by doubting, challenging, questioning the treatment of others, even if he could doubt or question. (p. 265–266)

This view has much in common with the development of pathogenic beliefs (see chapter 1, pp. 4–8).

The personified self, according to Sullivan, is essentially a set of assumptions, expectations, and beliefs that a person holds about him- or herself. Personifications of the self can be thought of as self-schemas (Markus, 1977; see also Andersen & Chen, 2002; Glassman & Andersen, 1999) that organize and guide the acquisition and processing of information. Sullivan described the self as "the custodian of awareness" (Sullivan,

1953, p. 21). Information that is consistent with the self-personification is more likely to be incorporated into awareness than information that is inconsistent.

Sullivan further proposed that information that is inconsistent with the personified self provokes anxiety. He termed the mechanism used to reduce or control anxiety *security operations*—persistent, recurring patterns of relating that serve to keep anxiety out of awareness. Selective inattention, a central security operation, helps a person reduce anxiety by keeping him- or herself unaware of information that would arouse anxiety because it is inconsistent with the self-system. Selective inattention makes it difficult to learn from new experiences, thereby preserving reflected appraisals. Moreover, selective inattention leads a person to organize information about new relationships on the basis of experiences and expectations from old relationships, which often leads to self-perpetuating or cyclical maladaptive patterns and relationships. Wachtel (1977, 1997; Gold & Wachtel, 1993) referred to these as cyclical psychodynamics, and in control-mastery theory this maladaptive pattern has much in common with the concept of pathogenic beliefs (see chapter 1, pp. 4–8).

Sullivan pointed out that patients repeat their maladaptive relational cycles in the therapeutic relationship. In order for the therapist to be helpful to the patient, he must place himself in the role of "participant-observer" (Sullivan, 1953)—a view that is very similar to the control-mastery concept of testing (see chapter 1, pp. 10–17). According to Sullivan, the therapist must allow himself to experience the patient's interpersonal pull while simultaneously observing the interaction in which he is the participant. Only by experiencing and participating in the patient's characteristic interpersonal cycles can the therapist begin to understand and help the patient understand the nature and origins of these maladaptive cycles.

Sullivan's formulation of introjection is another important concept in his understanding of the psychotherapeutic process. As noted earlier, a person's self-representation is based on how the person was treated by parental and other important figures during childhood (a reflected appraisal). Sullivan described this process as introjection. Henry, Schacht, & Strupp (1990) suggested that introjection plays a central role in shaping distorted interpersonal expectancies that result in cyclical maladaptive patterns and relationships. They argued that therapist/patient interactions are introjected by the patient in a way that either perpetuates earlier pathogenic experiences or ameliorates them. The control-mastery concept of pathogenic beliefs and the patient's efforts to disconfirm these beliefs, particularly through passive-into-active tests, is very similar to introjection. When a therapist repeatedly disconfirms a patient's pathogenic beliefs, the therapist's new actions may be introjected, leading to new patterns of interpersonal behavior in the patient (refer to chapters 1 and 7, and for detailed clinical examples, refer to chapter 8).

Safran and Segal's (1990) cognitive–interpersonal model, which integrates cognitive therapy with Sullivan's interpersonal theory, bears a substantial similarity to control-mastery theory. They presented the concept of an interpersonal schema, which is a generalized representation of self–other relations. Safran and Segal argued that the fundamental change mechanism in therapy is the disconfirmation of the client's pathogenic interpersonal schema and the modification of maladaptive strategies for maintaining relatedness. They suggested three change processes, or mechanisms, whereby clients can begin to alter their pathogenic schemata and their consequent maladaptive interpersonal cycles: (a) *decentering*—the therapist helps the client understand how his or her beliefs, expectations, and appraisals contribute to the client's construction of reality and to problematic interactions; (b) *experiential disconfirmation*—the therapist provides new relational experiences that disconfirm pathogenic expectations about self, others, and relationships; (c) *accessing new information (insights)*—"discovering aspects of one's own inner experience that have previously been out of awareness" (p. 6). The process of experiential disconfirmation is essentially synonymous with the control-mastery concept of testing.

Other Presentations of Control-Mastery Theory as an Integrated Theory

In addition to my presentation of control-mastery theory as an integrated cognitive–psychodynamic–relational theory, I will briefly describe two recent discussions of how control-mastery theory synthesizes concepts from other conceptual models.

Lieb and Kanofsky (2003) presented control-mastery theory as a constructivist–narrative therapy, integrating (among others) the work of Bruner (1986), Schafer (1992), Spence (1982), Mahoney (1991), Neimeyer (1995), and White & Epston (1990). Lieb and Kanofsky argued that the theory "can be effectively reformulated as a constructivist approach to psychotherapy by virtue of the fact that its tenets are inherently consistent with the core constructivist principle that individuals do not simply observe the world. Instead, individuals actively participate in creating meaning" (p. 189). The constructivist–narrative and the control-mastery models both agree that parents' empathic or attunement failures lead to later psychopathology:

> We believe that pathogenic narratives are commonly created from parents' failure to attune their "storying" of the child to the child's felt experience. When these empathic failures are persistently egregious, the child will accept these imposed stories through compliance and identification in order to preserve the essential ties with his or her caretakers. While it was adaptive in the early family environment to subscribe to these dominant stories, they inevitably become pathogenic later in life. These flawed and incomplete narratives limit individuals' capacity to interpret adult experience, but it is the narratives' "alien" quality that compels them to seek help because, as we argue, people are inherently motivated to assume greater authorship of their lives or, in control mastery language, to master their pathogenic beliefs. (p. 194)

The constructivist–narrative and the control-mastery models share a fundamental humanistic outlook in which the client is viewed as the final "arbiter" of his or her own experience and reality (Rogers, 1961). Both approaches also share a strong emphasis on adaptive and mastery motives.

Migone and Liotti (1998) proposed an unusually ambitious, far-reaching, and fascinating integrative effort. They suggested that control-mastery theory is an excellent candidate for a theory that integrates evolutionary epistemology, neurobiology, ethology, cognitive science, infant research, psychoanalytic theory, and psychotherapy research. I will briefly summarize some of their argument, though this abbreviated synopsis cannot do justice to their richly detailed model.

Beginning with Bowlby's attachment theory, Migone and Liotti (1998) noted that "the basic, innate universal 'plan' of attachment develops in different individuals, according to the interpersonal influences to which they are subjugated" (p. 1076). They went on to point out that Lichtenberg's (1989) five motivational systems (the psychological regulation of physical needs, attachment/affiliation, exploration/assertion, aversion, and sensual/sexual gratification) are based on "innate plans for the processing of interpersonal information" (Migone & Liotti, 1998, p. 1076). Geared toward adaptation, these innate plans are shaped by evolution and natural selection, as well as by the beliefs that we build from experience.

Migone and Liotti (1998) emphasized that we do not inherit innate knowledge (plans). Evolution provides the genetic codes that guide the developmental process so that the infant can adapt to the environment and develop a cognitive orientation that fosters further adaptation. "The tacit nature of innate 'knowledge' and its relationship to the pursuing of inborn values of adaptation and survival is in keeping with the control-mastery theory, which assumes that the patient's plan, guiding his or her strivings towards self-righting and healing, is usually unconscious"(p. 1077).

INTEGRATING THE PATIENT'S PROBLEM, TREATMENT PROCESS, AND OUTCOME

One factor that has substantially contributed to the interest in psychotherapy integration is the failure of theoretical models to integrate and successfully account for the development of psychopathology, the therapist's role in ameliorating it, and treatment outcome and behavior change (Norcross & Newman, 1992). Strupp, Schacht, & Henry (1988) referred to a lack of congruence between the patient's *problems*, the *treatment* process, and the therapy *outcome* (or PTO). They pointed out that it is essential for the field of psychotherapy to have a way of linking how patients' problems, change processes, and treatment outcomes are linked. Control-mastery theory achieves this integration in two ways. First, the model of pathology and change mechanisms is described in a language that is shared by the cognitive, interpersonal, and psychodynamic frameworks. Second, control-mastery theory describes the nature of psychopathology and its origins (pathogenic beliefs), links the patient's presenting problems and goals to the model of pathology (the patient's plan), connects the interventions and treatment processes to the model of pathology (the disconfirmation of pathogenic beliefs), and provides a meaningful way of evaluating outcome (to what degree the patient's pathogenic beliefs have been disconfirmed).

When integrating theories of psychotherapy, it is essential to take into account the patient's preferences, needs, goals, and personality (Frank, 1999; Gold, 1994; Messer, 1992; Ramsay, 2001). Gold suggested that clients frequently guide their therapists in accord with their own "integrative" needs. Ramsay argued that clinicians must "effectively orchestrate a good fit between the process of psychotherapy and the client's prevailing goals for personal growth." He also noted that "tailoring interventions to fit the needs of clients at specific points in therapy facilitates their progression through treatment" (p. 21). Duncan, Hubble, & Miller (1997) studied a group of "impossible cases," patients who had repeated, unsuccessful experiences in psychotherapy. They emphasized that in such cases it is essential for the therapist to pay careful attention to the patient's frame of reference, and they reconceptualized "resistance" as a mismatch between the patient's needs or frame of reference and those of the therapist. This view is consistent with the basic premise of control-mastery theory that the patient is motivated to disconfirm pathogenic beliefs (the patient's plan), and the therapist's primary role is to help the patient disconfirm his or her maladaptive beliefs.

One important way in which control-mastery theory differs from the cognitive, psychodynamic, or relational models is that it does not advocate or prescribe a particular set of techniques. The theory provides a clinically useful model of how psychopathology develops (traumatic experiences lead to pathogenic beliefs) and how psychotherapy works (the disconfirmation of pathogenic beliefs). If a therapist correctly formulates the nature of the patient's traumas and pathogenic beliefs, he or she uses the formulation, rather than a particular technique, to help the patient disconfirm his or her pathogenic beliefs. With such a correct formulation in mind, thee are a myriad number of ways (techniques) that a therapist could employ to help the patient. The most effective approaches or techniques will be those that match the patient's problems, needs, and personality.

ENDNOTE

1. In this chapter, I use the terms "relational" and "interpersonal" synonymously. In the psychoanalytic literature (e.g., Mitchell, 1988), these terms are not typically used interchangeably because "interpersonal" is associated with Sullivan's work.

REFERENCES

Ainsworth, M. D. S., Blehar, M. C., Waters, E., & Wall, S. (1978). *Patterns of attachment: A psychological study of the strange situation.* Hillsdale, NJ: Erlbaum.

Alexander, F., & French, T. M. (1946). *Psychoanalytic therapy: Principles and applications.* New York: Ronald Press.

Andersen, S. M., & Chen, S. (2002). The relational self: An interpersonal social–cognitive theory. *Psychological Review, 109,* 619–645.

Andersen, S. M., Reznik, I., & Glassman, N. S. (in press). The unconscious relational self. In R. Hassin, J. S. Uleman, & J. A. Bargh (Eds.), *The new unconscious.* New York: Oxford University Press.

Arkowitz, H. (1992). Integrative theories of therapy. In D. K. Freedheim (Ed.), *History of psychotherapy: A century of change* (pp. 261–303). Washington, DC: American Psychological Association.

Aron, L. (1996). *A meeting of minds: Mutuality in psychoanalysis*. Hillsdale, NJ: Analytic Press.

Beck, A. T. (1967). *Depression: Clinical, experimental, and theoretical aspects*. New York: Harper & Row.

Beck, A. T. (1976). *Cognitive therapy and the emotional disorders*. New York: International Universities Press.

Beck, J. S. (1996). Cognitive therapy of personality disorders. In P. M. Salkovskis (Ed.), *Frontiers of cognitive therapy* (pp. 165–181). New York: Guilford Press.

Beebe, B., & Lachmann, F. M. (2002). *Infant research and adult treatment: Co-constructing interactions*. Hillsdale, NJ: Analytic Press.

Benjamin, L. S. (1993). *Interpersonal diagnosis and treatment of personality disorders*. New York: Guilford Press.

Bowlby, J. (1958). The nature of the child's tie to his mother. *International Journal of Psychoanalysis, 39*, 350–373.

Bowlby, J. (1988). *A secure base: Parent–child attachment and healthy human development*. London: Routledge.

Brenner, C. (1976). *Psychoanalytic technique and psychic conflict*. New York: International Universities Press.

Brenner, C. (1982). *The mind in conflict*. New York: International Universities Press.

Bruner, J. S. (1986). *Actual minds, possible worlds*. Cambridge, MA: Harvard University Press.

Carson, R. C. (1982). Self-fulfilling prophecy, maladaptive behavior, and psychotherapy. In J. C. Anchin & D. J. Kiesler (Eds.), *Handbook of interpersonal psychotherapy* (pp. 64–77). New York: Pergamon Press.

Duncan, B. L., Hubble, M. A., & Miller, S. D. (1997). *Psychotherapy with "impossible" cases: Time efficient treatment of therapy veterans*. New York: Norton.

Frank, K. A. (1999). *Psychoanalytic participation: Action, interaction, and integration*. Hillsdale, NJ: The Analytic Press.

Eagle, M. N. (1984). *Recent developments in psychoanalysis: A critical evaluation*. New York: McGraw-Hill.

Gassner, S. (2001). The central role of pathogenic expectations and beliefs in a case of intense genital damage anxiety. *Psychoanalytic Psychology, 18*, 92–119.

Gaston, L., Goldfried, M. R., Greenberg, L. S., Hovarth, A. O., Raue, P. L., & Watson, J. (1995). The therapeutic alliance in psychodynamic, cognitive–behavioral and experiential therapies. *Journal of Psychotherapy Integration, 5*, 1–26.

Gassner, S., Sampson, H., Weiss, J., & Brumer, S. (1982). The emergence of warded-off contents. *Psychoanalysis and Contemporary Thought, 5*, 55–75.

Gill, M. (1982). *The analysis of transference: Vol. 1*. New York: International Universities Press.

Glassman, N. S., & Andersen, S. M. (1999). Transference in social cognition: Persistence and exacerbation of significant–other based inferences over time. *Cognitive Therapy and Research, 23*, 75–91.

Gold, J. R. (1994). When the patient does the integrating: Lessons for theory and practice. *Journal of Psychotherapy Integration, 4*, 133–158.

Gold, J., & Stricker, G. (1993). Psychotherapy integration with personality disorders. In G. Stricker & J. R. Gold (Eds.), *Comprehensive handbook of psychotherapy integration* (pp. 323–336). New York: Plenum Press.

Gold, J. R., & Wachtel, P. L. (1993). Cyclical psychodynamics. In G. Stricker & J. R. Gold (Eds.), *Comprehensive handbook of psychotherapy integration* (pp. 59–72). New York: Plenum Press.

Gray, P. (1995). *The ego and the analysis of defense.* New York: Jason Aronson.

Greenberg, J. R., & Mitchell, S. A. (1983). *Object relations in psychoanalytic theory.* Cambridge, MA: Harvard University Press.

Hayes, S. C., Follette, W. C., & Follette, V. M. (1995). Behavior therapy: A contextual approach. In A. S. Gurman & S. B. Messer (Eds.), *Essential psychotherapies: Theory and practice* (pp. 128–181). New York: Guilford Press.

Henry, W. P., Schacht, T. E., & Strupp, H. H. (1990). Patient and therapist introject, interpersonal process and differential psychotherapy outcome. *Journal of Consulting and Clinical Psychology, 58,* 768–774.

Horowitz, L. M., Sampson, H., Siegelman, E. Y., Weiss, J., & Goodfriend, S. (1978). Cohesive and dispersal behaviors: Two classes of concomitant change in psychotherapy. *Journal of Consulting and Clinical Psychology, 46,* 556–564.

Horowitz, M. J. (1988). *Introduction to psychodynamics: A new synthesis.* New York: Basic Books.

Horowitz, M. J. (1998). *Cognitive psychodynamics: From conflict to character.* New York: Wiley.

Kiesler, D. J. (1982). Confronting the client–therapist relationship in psychotherapy. In J. C. Anchin & D. J. Kiesler (Eds.), *Handbook of interpersonal psychotherapy.* New York: Pergamon Press.

Kohlenberg, R. J., & Tsai, M. (1991). *Functional analytic psychotherapy: Creating intense and curative therapeutic relationships.* New York: Plenum.

Kohut, H. (1984). *How does analysis cure?* Chicago, IL: University of Chicago Press.

Lambert, M. J. (1992). Psychotherapy outcome research: Implications for integrative and eclectic therapists. In J. C. Norcross & M. R. Goldfried (Eds.), *Handbook of psychotherapy integration* (pp. 94–129). New York: Basic Books.

Lambert, M. J., & Bergin, A. E. (1994). The effectiveness of psychotherapy. In A. E. Bergin & S. L. Garfield (Eds.), *Handbook of psychotherapy and behavior change* (4th ed., pp. 143–189). New York: Wiley.

Lichtenberg, J. D. (1989). *Psychoanalysis and motivation.* Hillsdale, NJ: Analytic Press.

Lieb, R. J., & Kanofsky, S. (2003). Toward a constructivist control mastery theory: An integration with narrative therapy. *Psychotherapy: Theory, Research, Practice, Training, 40,* 187–202.

Lipsey, M. W., & Wilson, D. B. (1993). The efficacy of psychological, educational, and behavioral treatment: Confirmation from meta-analyses. *American Psychologist, 48,* 1181–1209.

Luborsky, L. (1984). *Principles of psychoanalytic psychotherapy: A manual for supportive–expressive treatment.* New York: Basic Books.

Luborsky, L., & Crits–Christoph, P. (1990). *Understanding transference: The Core Conflictual Relationship Theme method.* New York: Basic Books.

Mahoney, M. J. (1991). *Human change processes.* New York: Basic Books.

Main, M., Kaplan, K., & Cassidy, J. (1985). Security in infancy, childhood and adulthood: A move to the level of representation. In I. Bretherton & E. Waters (Eds.), Growing points of attachment theory and research. *Monographs of the Society for Research in Child Development, 50* (1–2, Serial No. 209), 66–104.

Markus, H. (1977). Self-schemata and processing information about the self. *Journal of Personality and Social Psychology, 35,* 63–78.

Meichenbaum, D. H., & Gilmore, B. (1984). The nature of unconscious processes: A cognitive–behavioral perspective. In K. S. Bowers & D. H. Meichenbaum (Eds.), *The unconscious reconsidered* (pp. 273–298). New York: Wiley.

Menninger, K. A., & Holzman, P. S. (1973). *Theory of psychoanalytic technique*. New York: Basic Books.

Messer, S. B. (1992). A critical examination of belief structures in integrative and eclectic psychotherapy. In J. C. Norcross & M. R. Goldfried (Eds.), *Handbook of psychotherapy integration* (pp. 130–165). New York: Basic Books.

Messer, S. B. (2001). Introduction to the Special Issue on assimilative integration. *Journal of Psychotherapy Integration, 11,* 1–4.

Migone, P., & Liotti, G. (1998). Psychoanalysis and cognitive–evolutionary psychology: An attempt at integration. *International Journal of Psychoanalysis, 79,* 1071–1095.

Mitchell, S. A. (1988). *Relational concepts in psychoanalysis: An integration*. Cambridge, MA: Harvard University Press.

Mullahy, P. (1940/1953). A theory of interpersonal relations and the evolution of personality. In H. S. Sullivan, *Conceptions of modern psychiatry* (pp. 239–294). New York: W. W. Norton.

Neimeyer, R. A. (1995). Constructivist psychotherapies: Features, foundations, and future directions. In R. A. Neimeyer & M. J. Mahoney (Eds.), *Constructivism in psychotherapy* (pp. 11–38). Washington, DC: American Psychological Association.

Norcross, J. C., & Newman, C. F. (1992). Psychotherapy integration: Setting the context. In J. C. Norcross & M. R. Goldfried (Eds.), *Handbook of psychotherapy integration* (pp. 3–46). New York: Basic Books.

Ramsay, J. R. (2001). The clinical challenges of assimilative integration. *Journal of Psychotherapy Integration, 11,* 21–42.

Rogers, C. R. (1961). *On becoming a person*. Boston: Houghton Mifflin.

Safran, J. D., & Segal, Z. V. (1990). *Interpersonal process in cognitive therapy*. New York: Basic Books.

Sampson, H. (1976). A critique of certain traditional concepts in the psychoanalytic theory of therapy. *Bulletin of the Menninger Clinic, 40,* 255–262.

Sampson, H., Weiss, J., Mlodnosky, L., & Hause, E. (1972). Defense analysis and the emergence of warded-off mental contents: An empirical study. *Archives of General Psychiatry, 26,* 524–532.

Schafer, R. (1992). *Retelling a life: Narration and dialogue in psychoanalysis*. New York: Basic Books.

Segal, Z. V. (1988). Appraisal of the self-schema construct in cognitive models of depression. *Psychological Bulletin, 103,* 147–162.

Shane, M., Shane, E., & Gales, M. (1997). *Intimate attachments: Toward a new self psychology*. New York: Guilford Press.

Silberschatz, G. (1986). Testing pathogenic beliefs. In J. Weiss, H. Sampson, & The Mount Zion Psychotherapy Research Group (Eds.), *The psychoanalytic process: Theory, clinical observation, and empirical research* (pp. 256–266). New York: Guilford Press.

Silberschatz, G., Sampson, H., & Weiss, J. (1986). Testing pathogenic beliefs versus seeking transference gratifications. In J. Weiss, H. Sampson, & The Mount Zion Psychotherapy Research Group (Eds.), *The psychoanalytic process: Theory, clinical observation, and empirical research* (pp. 267–276). New York: Guilford.

Spence, D. P. (1982). *Narrative truth and historical truth: Meaning and interpretation in psychoanalysis*. New York: Norton.

Stern, D. N. (1985). *The interpersonal world of the infant: A view from psychoanalysis and developmental psychology*. New York: Basic Books.

Stiles, W. B., Shapiro, D. A., & Elliott, R. (1986). "Are all psychotherapies equivalent?" *American Psychologist, 41,* 165–180.

Stricker, G., & Gold, J. (1996). An assimilative model for psychodynamically oriented integrative psychotherapy. *Clinical Psychology: Science and Practice, 3,* 47–58.

Strupp, H. H., & Binder, J. L. (1984). *Psychotherapy in a new key: A guide to time-limited dynamic psychotherapy.* New York: Basic Books.

Strupp, H. H., Schacht, T. E., & Henry, W. P. (1988). Problem–treatment–outcome congruence: A principle whose time has come. In H. Dahl, H. Kachele, & H. Thoma (Eds.), *Psychoanalytic process research strategies* (pp. 1–14). Berlin: Springer-Verlag.

Sullivan, H. S. (1953). *The interpersonal theory of psychiatry.* New York: W. W. Norton.

Wachtel, P. L. (1977). *Psychoanalysis and behavior therapy: Toward an integration.* New York: Basic Books.

Wachtel, P. L. (1987). *Action and insight.* New York: Guilford.

Wachtel, P. L. (1997). *Psychoanalysis, behavior therapy, and the representational world.* Washington, DC: American Psychological Association.

Waelder, R. (1960). *Basic theory of psychoanalysis.* New York: International Universities Press.

Wampold, B. E., Mondin, G. W., Moody, M., Stich, F., Benson, K., & Ahn, H. (1997). A meta-analysis of outcome studies comparing bona fide psychotherapies: Empirically, "all must have prizes." *Psychological Bulletin, 122,* 203–215.

Weinberger, J. (1993). Common factors in psychotherapy. In G. Stricker & J. R. Gold (Eds.), *Comprehensive handbook of psychotherapy integration* (pp. 43–56). New York: Plenum Press.

Weiss, J. (1967). The integration of defenses. *International Journal of Psychoanalysis, 48,* 520–524.

Weiss, J. (1971). The emergence of new themes: A contribution to the psychoanalytic theory of therapy. *International Journal of Psychoanalysis, 52,* 459–467.

Weiss, J. (1986). Theory and clinical observations. In J. Weiss, H. Sampson, & The Mount Zion Psychotherapy Research Group (Eds.), *The psychoanalytic process: Theory, clinical observation, and empirical research* (pp. 3–138). New York: Guilford

White, M., & Epston, D. (1990). *Narrative means to therapeutic ends.* New York: Norton.

Young, J. (1990). *Cognitive therapy for personality disorders: A schema-focused approach.* Sarasota, FL: Professional Resource Exchange.

INDEX

A

Assessment of pathogenic beliefs
   basic assumptions and, 77
   childhood trauma and, 77–80
   counter-transference and, 74–76
   examples of, 72–74
Attachment, guilt and, 47
Attachment needs, 225
Attachment style
   clinical example of pathogenic beliefs and, 176–177
   pathogenic beliefs and, 174–178
Attachment theory
   compliance and, 177
   control-mastery theory and, 174–178, 225

B

Beliefs; *see* Pathogenic beliefs

C

Childhood trauma
   assessment of pathogenic beliefs and, 77–80
   clinical example of major depressive disorder and, 100–104
   development of guilt and, 53–56
Cognitive therapy, control-mastery theory and, 222–224
Cognitive-evolutionary theory, control-mastery theory and, 229–230
Cognitive-interpersonal model, 228
Common factors in psychotherapy, 220
Constructivist-narrative therapy, control-mastery theory and, 228–229
Control-mastery theory
   attachment theory and, 174–178, 225
   cognitive therapy and, 222–224
   cognitive-evolutionary theory and, 229–230
   constructivist-narrative therapy and, 228–229
   empirically supported relationships and, 213
   empirically supported treatments and, 212–213
   problem-treatment-outcome congruence and, 230
   psychodynamic theory and, 223, 224–225
   relational theory and, 223, 225–228
Corrective emotional experiences, 20–21, 117–118, 225
   therapist attitude and, 117–118
Counter-transference, clinical example of testing pathogenic beliefs and, 111–115, 132–134
Crying at the happy ending, 25–26, 32–33
   detailed example, 33–34
Cyclical maladaptive relationships, 227

D

Depression; *see* Major depressive disorder

Developmental goals, 5
    safety and, 31
Disconfirmation of pathogenic beliefs
    example of therapeutic relationship
        and, 104–108
    therapist attitude and, 113–115,
        118–119
    treatment outcome and, 208–210
Dreams, safety and, 41

E

Early cognition, pathogenic beliefs and,
    178–181
Eating disorder, clinical example of
        control-mastery theory and,
        123–151
Empathy, development of in early
    childhood, 181–183
Empirically supported relationships,
        control-mastery theory and,
        213
Empirically supported treatments, 19–20
    control-mastery theory and, 212–213

F

Fantasized relationships, safety and, 31,
    39–41
Fear of hurting loved ones, 46–47

G

Guilt
    anxiety and, 48
    as an adaptive interpersonal emotion,
        44
    attachment and, 47
    defenses against, 45
    development of, 46–50
        in early childhood, 181–183
    fear of hurting loved ones and, 46–47
    feeling of responsibility and, 47–48
    identification with impaired siblings
        and, 55–56
    interpretation of, 60–62
    negative therapeutic reaction and,
        58–59
    parental illness and development of,
        53–56
    passive into active test and, 59–60
    pathogenic beliefs and, 46
    prosocial aspects of, 44
    resistance and, 58–59
    safety and danger and, 48
    self-blame and, 49
    separation, 50, 53–56
        clinical example, 53–56
        example of in child therapy, 50
    shame and, 46
    signal, 48
    survivor, 51–56
        clinical example, 53–56
    testing and, 59–60
    therapeutic attitude and, 60–62
    therapeutic technique and
        interpretation of, 60–62
    transference and, 57–58
    transference test and, 59–60
    trauma and, 48, 50–53
    trauma and development of, 53–56
    unconscious and conscious, 44–45

I

Identification with impaired siblings,
    55–56
Infant regulation of interactions,
    172–174
Internal Working Model, pathogenic
    beliefs and, 176
Introjection, 227–228

M

Major depressive disorder
    clinical example of childhood trauma
        and, 100–104
    clinical example of control-mastery
        theory and, 94–109
    clinical example of therapeutic
        relationship and, 104–108
    clinical example of unconscious guilt
        and, 100–104
    control-mastery case formulation
        and, 100–104
Motivation to master trauma, 33–34

N

Negative therapeutic reaction, guilt and, 58–59

P

Panic disorder, clinical example of control-mastery theory and, 123–151
Passing tests, clinical example of therapist attitude and, 141–142
Passive-into-active test
 clinical example, 142, 145–146
 guilt and, 59–60
Pathogenic beliefs, 4
 assessment of, 72–80
 development of, 6–7
 disconfirming in therapy, 10–17
 disconfirming therapeutic technique and, 20
 disconfirming, corrective emotional experiences and, 20–21
 early cognition and, 178–181
 example of, 5
 guilt and, 46
 in child abuse, 5–7, 51
 interpretation of, 11–12
 patient's therapy goals and, 80–83
 presenting complaints and, 83–86
 symbolic representation and, 180
 testing, 12–17
 theory of mind and, 178–179
 therapeutic relationship and, 10–11, 86–87
 why they persist, 8, 71, 177–178
Pathogenic compliance, 70
 examples of, 70–71
Pathogenic identification, 70
 examples of, 70–71
Patient coaching
 beginning of therapy and, 157–159
 definition, 153
 helping therapists pass tests and, 159–164
 self-healing and, 153–154
 therapeutic relationship and, 164–165
Patient plan, coaching and, 157
Patient testing, research on in psychoanalysis, 195–198

Patient tests
 empirical research, 195–204
 examples of, 197, 199–202
 research on in brief psychotherapy, 198–204
Patient's therapy goals, pathogenic beliefs and, 80–83
Personality disorder, clinical example of control-mastery theory and, 121–151
Personification, 226–227
Plan (patient's), 8–10, 221–222
Plan compatibility
 effects on physiological measures, 207–208
 research in child psychotherapy, 207
 research on process and content dimensions of, 206–207
 research on safety emotions and, 207–208
Plan compatibility of interventions, treatment outcome and, 208–210
Plan compatibility of therapist interventions, 204–210
 Inpatient therapy and, 205–206
Plan formulation method, 87–91
 development of, 192–195
 goals, 89
 insights, 90–91
 obstructions, 88–89
 research on, 192–195
 tests, 89–90
 traumas, 88
Presenting complaints, pathogenic beliefs and, 83–86
Problem-treatment-outcome congruence, control-mastery theory and, 230
Psychodynamic theory, control-mastery theory and, 223, 224–225
Psychotherapy integration, 220–221
Psychotherapy process research, 190–192

R

Relational theory, control-mastery theory and, 223, 225–228
Resistance, 18–19, 58–59, 231
 guilt and, 58–59
 survivor guilt and, 58–59

testing and, 18
    example of, 18–19
Responsibility, feelings of, 47–48

S

Safety
    clinical example of therapeutic relationship and, 146
    clinical example of therapeutic technique and, 125, 136–140
    developmental goals and, 31
    dreams and, 41
    regulation of defenses and, 32
    research on control over defenses and, 210–212
    sexual fantasies and, 39–41
    testing and, 35–36
    therapeutic attitude and, 35, 37
    therapist attitude and, 113–115
Safety and danger, 4, 25–28, 31–32, 34–37, 39–41, 113–115, 125, 136–140, 207–208, 210–212
    control over defenses and, 25, 26, 27
        regulation of interpersonal closeness and distance, 27
    disconfirmation of pathogenic beliefs, 28
    external circumstances, 25, 26
        example of, 26
    guilt and, 48
    therapeutic relationship and, 25, 27–28, 34–36
    therapeutic relationship and testing, example of, 28
    unconscious decisions, 25–26
Safety and fantasized relationships, 31, 39–41
Safety and relationships, 31
Safety and therapeutic relationship, 31
Safety and therapeutic technique, 31–32
Safety emotions, research on plan compatibility and, 207–208
Schemas, 223–224
Security operations, 227
Self-blame, guilt and, 49
Separation and survivor guilt, clinical example, 53–56
Separation guilt, 50, 53–56, 70
    clinical example, 53–56
    example of in child therapy, 50

Shame, 46
Signal guilt, 48
Social interactions in infancy, 172–174
Survivor guilt, 51–52, 70
    clinical example, 53–56
    resistance and, 58–59
Symbolic representation, pathogenic beliefs and, 180

T

Testing, 12–16, 59–60, 111–115, 132–134, 154–155
    guilt and, 59–60
    passive-into-active test, 14–16
    passive-into-active test, example of, 15–16
    pathogenic beliefs, detailed clinical example of countertransference and, 111–115, 132–134
    therapist confrontation and, 13–14
    transference test, 12–13
    transference test, example of, 13, 16
Theory of mind, pathogenic beliefs and, 178–179
Therapeutic alliance, 17
Therapeutic relationship, clinical example of safety and, 146
    detailed clinical example of disconfirmation of pathogenic beliefs and, 104–108
    example of therapist attitudes and, 115–117
    pathogenic beliefs and, 86–87
    patient coaching and, 164–165
    safety and, 31
    safety and danger, 25
    therapist attitudes and, 115
Therapeutic technique, case-specific, 16–17
    confrontation, 13–14
    detailed clinical example of safety and, 125, 136–140
    example treatment by attitudes and, 111–117
    interpretation of guilt and, 60–62
    safety and, 31–32, 37–38
    testing and, 16
    treatment by attitudes and, 119

Therapist attitude, clinical example of
    passing tests and, 141–142
  corrective emotional experiences
    and, 117–118
  disconfirmation of pathogenic beliefs
    and, 113–115, 118–119
  example of therapeutic relationship
    and, 115–117
  guilt and, 60–62
  safety and, 37, 113–115
  therapeutic relationship and, 115
Therapist interpretations
  research on the effects of, 204–210
  research on the effects of in inpatient
    therapy, 205–206
Transference, 12–13, 19
Transference, guilt and, 57–58
Transference test, guilt and, 59–60
Trauma
  definition, 4, 50–51
  guilt and, 48, 50–56
  motivation to master, 33–34
  patient's interpretation of, 69–70
  shock, 6
  stress, 6
Traumatic experiences, 4
Treatment by attitudes
  example of therapeutic technique
    and, 111–117
  therapeutic technique and, 119
Treatment outcome
  disconfirmation of pathogenic beliefs
    and, 208–210
  plan compatibility of interventions
    and, 208–210

U

Unconscious decisions, 25–26
Unconscious guilt, detailed clinical
    example of major depressive
    disorder and, 100–104
Unconscious identification, 5
Unconscious plan, 8–10
  research in psychology, 9